John Webster

MERMAID CRITICAL COMMENTARIES

MERMAID CRITICAL COMMENTARIES

John Webster

Edited by

BRIAN MORRIS

ERNEST BENN LIMITED

LONDON

First published 1970 by Ernest Benn Limited
Bouverie House, Fleet Street, London, EC4

© *Brian Morris 1970*

Distributed in Canada by
The General Publishing Company Limited, Toronto

Printed in Great Britain

Library 510-34331-7

Paperback 510-34332-5

Introduction

AFTER THE PUBLICATION of the first of the *Mermaid Critical Commentaries* in the autumn of 1968 it was decided to hold the Second York Symposium on the Plays of John Webster, another playwright whose work was well represented in the *New Mermaid* series of Jacobean dramatic texts. The symposium occupied the weekend of 11 to 13 April 1969, and took place once again at Langwith College, in the University of York. Numbers were deliberately restricted, as a matter of policy, to allow all those taking part to meet one another, or to renew acquaintance, informally and in a civilised atmosphere untainted by lapel labels and all the other impedimenta of a large 'Conference'. Eighteen scholars, critics, and men of the theatre accepted invitations either to read papers or to contribute to the critical debate (though for different reasons two of them were unable to be present) and the quality of public discourse was matched by the vigour and the edge of more aleatory discussion.

Although all the members were professional academics, attached to one university department or another, we were not all specifically literary critics. Peter Thomson is a member of the Drama Department at Manchester University, and Roger Warren is Leverhulme Fellow attached to the Nuffield Theatre at the University of Southampton, and their contributions were directly concerned with the production and staging of Webster's plays, and the problems and opportunities which his dramatic language offers to actor and director. This set up a sustained dialogue with the scholars and critics, among whom we were able to hear both from those already acknowledged as experts on Webster, like Elizabeth M. Brennan, Inga-Stina Ewbank, and J. R. Mulryne, and those who were writing on the plays for the first time. We were especially pleased to welcome that doyen of Webster scholars, Gunnar Boklund, whose work on the plays over many years has established him as an authority of international standing.

There were three ghosts. Professor John Russell Brown was unable

v

to accept our invitation because of other commitments, but his name and his work were so frequently invoked that his non-corporeal presence might have been assumed. D. C. Gunby could not travel from New Zealand with his paper, but sent it to be read by Michael Hattaway, who delivered it with an assurance and aplomb which could not have been greater if he had written every word of it himself. And J. R. Mulryne was, at the last moment, overwhelmed with work and unable to complete his paper in time. In this last case it was decided to include the paper in the published record, despite the fact that it had not been read at the symposium, since it was possible to allow all the other contributors to see a copy of it before publication, and this might be taken as a substitute for the normal discussion. Two other features distinguish this present volume from the first of the *Critical Commentaries*: the illustrations and the dust-jacket. The essays by Roger Warren, Inga-Stina Ewbank, and Dominic Baker-Smith needed pictures to enforce their major points, and the authors have added summer-long research to their paschal labours in order to provide appropriate illustrations and to document them thoroughly. It was part of the initial policy for this series to use on each dust-jacket a portrait of the dramatist whose work formed the subject of the volume, and, in the case of the *Marlowe* volume we were fortunately allowed to reproduce the alleged portrait of him at Corpus Christi College, Cambridge. But there is no portrait of Webster. Not only is there no contemporary likeness, but we have been unable to trace even an imaginary portrait by a nineteenth- or a twentieth-century artist. Yet if we lack the playwright himself, we have one of his most striking characters. The cover to this volume shows Alessandro Allori's portrait of the White Devil herself, Vittoria Accoramboni, whose features and mien form a minatory preface to any consideration of Webster's plays.

The fact that no portrait of Webster has survived (if any ever existed) epitomises neatly one of the strongest and most widely diversified feelings of the symposium: the sense that we were in the presence of the most enigmatic of the Jacobean dramatists. The complex, cryptic, hidden character of Webster preoccupied us, and one speaker after another demonstrated ways in which the dramatist will never let his audience rest in easy assumptions about character or shallow judgements of motive. Elizabeth M. Brennan struck this note in the first paper:

An audience which is uncomfortable at the prospect of responding to the need to assess the characters in the play is able to vent some of its unease in discussion of the problems which those characters have to face.

And in the last paper to be delivered Dominic Baker-Smith used Bosola's words in *The Duchess of Malfi* to remind us of the same point:

Security some men call the suburbs of hell.

In his close analysis of one of the scenes in *The White Devil* A. J. Smith described the 'curious impact of randomness, momentary force', and concluded that 'we have to reckon with the force of a calculated randomness'. A similar insight informs much of Mulryne's essay, while the same sense of obliquity and strange patterning caused Inga-Stina Ewbank to investigate how far a knowledge of Renaissance perspective can help us towards an understanding of Webster's art. In our discussions Webster emerged as an imperiously modern dramatist, giving a form and a language to many of the most urgent obsessions of the twentieth century, a playwright whose art was governed by and deeply concerned with the nature, limits, and control of the sceptical, undeceived human intelligence.

This general recognition of the realism and immediacy of Webster's dramaturgy was exemplified in the kind of analogies his plays suggested. Comparison was more frequently made with Pinter, or Beckett, or Weiss, than with any of Webster's fellow dramatists: Webster was our contemporary, not theirs. But apart from a shared general sense of the quality of his art, the symposium asserted its own particular emphases and explored some areas in preference to others. We began in the auditorium, moved on to the stage, and ended in the heavens. Between the theatrical and theological poles stood three close studies of individual plays and two more spacious, synthesising accounts of Webster's art. The theatrical concern is perhaps not surprising, since plays of the Jacobean period are becoming increasingly popular on the professional stage, but both Thomson and Warren made it very clear that Webster poses special problems of interpretation, tone, and articulation for the director, and that no style of acting currently available can adequately express all that the roles require. The interest in Webster's theology was less predictable. Few, if any, of his previous critics have looked at him in this light, and it might, at first sight, have seemed unpromising to attempt an explication of *The Duchess of Malfi* as 'essentially a work of theodicy', as D. C. Gunby did. But both he and Dominic Baker-Smith demonstrated how deeply Webster was enmeshed with the leading theological issues of his time—with free will, grace, security, despair, and the pessimism generated by a Calvinistic view of the human predicament. For many of us the plays began to lookquite different when set in this perspective of Jacobean Anglicanism, and the now commonplace observation that 'Webster was much possessed by death' achieved fresh resonance.

As might have been expected methods of argument differed from paper to paper. Some contributors offered closely reasoned academic cases, supported by a wealth of documentation and reference; others preferred to expatiate more freely and to convince us as much by eloquence as evidence. Indeed, the second method is the only method when one is dealing with such intangibles as the possible effects of a suggested interpretation for a scene or a character on the stage. Some of the essays direct our attention outwards, with footnotes which invite exploration of related fields of study; others do not. A. J. Smith, for example, argues a complete, self-contained case, and his pages are designedly unsullied by the presence of a single footnote. I have encouraged this diversity of method and approach, and not attempted to impose any editorial uniformity on contributors. Each quotes, for example, from whatever edition of Webster's plays best suits his purpose, and although a few notes were added to some essays after the symposium, as cross-references or second thoughts, I have intervened only to regularise their presentation. The papers are printed as they were delivered, and no concessions are offered in the way of plot-summaries or guides to further reading. This is not a book for the beginner seeking a painless introduction to plays he has not yet read. It is the record of an attempt by a group of professional scholars, critics, and producers to deepen their understanding of one of the darkest and most richly powerful of English dramatists.

BRIAN MORRIS

Langwith College
York

Members of the Symposium

Nigel Alexander, University of Glasgow

Dominic Baker-Smith, Fitzwilliam College, Cambridge

Dr N. W. Bawcutt, University of Liverpool

Professor Gunnar Boklund, University of Denver, Colorado

Dr Elizabeth M. Brennan, Westfield College, University of London

Professor Nicholas Brooke, University of East Anglia

Mrs Inga-Stina Ewbank, University of Liverpool

Dr Brian Gibbons, University of York

Dr D. C. Gunby, University of Canterbury, New Zealand

Dr Michael Hattaway, University of Kent at Canterbury

Dr Ernst Honigman, University of Newcastle-upon-Tyne

Dr J. D. Hunt, University of York

J. C. Lingard, English Library, Cambridge

Dr Brian Morris, University of York

Dr J. R. Mulryne, University of Edinburgh

A. J. Smith, University College of Swansea

Peter Thomson, University of Manchester

Roger Warren, University of Southampton

Contents

xi

Illustrations

(All are inserted between pages 112 and 113)

Acknowledgements

ACKNOWLEDGEMENT is made to the following for permission to reproduce illustrations:

Graphische Sammlung Albertina, Vienna: 5*a*, 5*b*, 6
The Trustees of the British Museum: 4*a*, 4*b*
Avvocato Fabio Caracciolo del Leone: 1
Angus McBean: 2
The Tate Gallery: 7

'An Understanding Auditory': an Audience for *John Webster*

ELIZABETH M. BRENNAN

'An Understanding Auditory': an Audience for John Webster

N O T   M A N Y   D R A M A T I S T S can afford to present their works before a fit audience, though few. John Webster's account of the initial failure of *The White Devil* on the stage, that the English winter when the play was performed, and the construction of the theatre in which it was performed, caused it to want '(that which is the only grace and setting out of a tragedy) a full and understanding auditory'[1] is one which we receive with sympathy. This quality should also temper our response to his following remarks, in the address to the reader of the play, on the kind of theatre-goers who frequented the Red Bull, in Clerkenwell:

> most of the people who come to that playhouse, resemble those ignorant asses (who visiting stationers' shops, their use is not to inquire for good books, but new books) . . .

Against the possible objection that his tragedy was 'no true dramatic poem' Webster defended himself by further attacking the audience:

> If it be objected this is no true dramatic poem, I shall easily confess it,—*non potes in nugas dicere plura meas: ipse ego quam dixi,*—willingly, and not ignorantly, in this kind have I faulted: for should a man present to such an auditory, the most sententious tragedy that ever was written, observing all the critical laws, as height of style, and gravity of person; enrich it with the sententious *Chorus*, and as it were lifen death, in the passionate and weighty *Nuntius*: yet after all this divine rapture, *O dura messorum ilia*, the breath that comes from the uncapable multitude is able to poison it, and ere it be acted, let the author resolve to fix to every scene, this of Horace,
> – – – – *Haec hodie porcis comedenda relinques.*

As a dramatist Webster so obviously wrote with his well-stocked

[1] Quotations from 'To the Reader' of *The White Devil* are taken from the New Mermaid edition (second impression, 1969).

3

commonplace-book beside him that one cannot judge whether the classical ammunition in this attack proceeded from his natural disposition to annex for his own purposes other men's good ideas and expressions, or from the genuinely outraged dignity of a careful, studious dramatist whose work has been rejected by the ignorant. As R. G. Howarth has recently pointed out:

There is no evidence of Webster's having attended the Merchant Taylors' School, as he was entitled to do. Since at the outset of his literary career he had little or no acquaintance with Latin, he probably did not receive a grammar-school education.[2]

Though the frequency of trial scenes and legal allusions in his work have given credence to the identification of the dramatist with the John Webster who was admitted to the Middle Temple in 1598, we have, in fact, no external evidence for supposing him to have been a scholar. Such a work as R. W. Dent's *John Webster's Borrowing* testifies to the range of Webster's reading. We also know that when he transformed the ancient history of Appius and Virginia and the true modern story of Vittoria Accoramboni into dramatic tragedies, he did not rely on a single source for either play.[3]

Turning again to the address to the reader of *The White Devil* we find that Webster balanced his scorn for the audience with praise for his fellow dramatists:

... For mine own part I have ever truly cherish'd my good opinion of other men's worthy labours, especially of that full and height'ned style of Master Chapman, the labour'd and understanding works of Master Jonson: the no less worthy composures of the both worthily excellent Master Beaumont, and Master Fletcher: and lastly (without wrong last to be named) the right happy and copious industry of Master Shakespeare, Master Dekker, and Master Heywood, wishing what I write may be read by their light: ...

It is, I think, significant that Chapman and Jonson head the list, for they had much in common with each other and with Webster. Both Chapman and Jonson were renowned classical scholars, though there is no evidence that either of them attended a university. Their involve-

[2] R. G. Howarth, 'Two Notes on John Webster', *Modern Language Review*, LXIII (1968), 785.
[3] See Gunnar Boklund, *The Sources of 'The White Devil'* (Uppsala, 1957); F. L. Lucas, *The Complete Works of John Webster* (1927), iii, 131–3.

ment with the world of the theatre, like Webster's, would seem to date from the time of their connection with Philip Henslowe. Why George Chapman, a middle-aged man of scholarly inclinations, should have worked for Henslowe at all is no less a mystery than how, at the age of thirty-six or thereabouts, he should have composed that smash-hit of a farce *The Blind Beggar of Alexandria*. Chapman's later tragedies, especially *Bussy D'Ambois*,[4] were successful, though the classical tragedy *Caesar and Pompey* may not have been acted. Ben Jonson is first referred to by Philip Henslowe, in an entry in his Diary for 28 July 1597, as a player. When writing to Edward Alleyn about the duel in which Jonson killed a fellow actor, Gabriel Spencer, Henslowe snobbishly wrote of Jonson as a bricklayer, thus calling attention to the period in Jonson's life when he worked for his stepfather. Yet very shortly before the duel with Spencer, in September 1598, Jonson's success as a comic dramatist had been established with the production of *Every Man in His Humour*. Moreover, Jonson, like Chapman, was listed by Francis Meres in *Palladis Tamia*, published in 1598, among the English dramatists who were then 'our best for Tragedie', and within four years Henslowe was paying Jonson as much for writing additions to *The Spanish Tragedy* as he usually paid for a new play. Jonson's early tragedies, like Chapman's, have been lost. His surviving tragedies, *Sejanus His Fall* (1603) and *Catiline His Conspiracy* (1611), were both failures when they were first performed.

In writing tragedies based on classical history Jonson was consciously acting as an historian as well as a dramatist. In his address to the readers of *Sejanus* he claimed that he had discharged the offices of a tragic writer in his play in 'truth of argument, dignity of persons, gravity and height of elocution, fulness and frequence of sentence'. Where Jonson's contemporaries would have accepted as a true fable that which could be seen to be true on the stage, for Jonson himself 'truth of argument' meant accurate, historical truth.[5] Moreover, to

---

[4] See Nicholas Brooke, ed., *Bussy D'Ambois*, The Revels Plays (1964), pp. liv–lv.

[5] See Joseph Allen Bryant, Jnr, 'The Significance of Ben Jonson's First Requirement for Tragedy: "Truth of Argument" ', *Studies in Philology*, XLIX (1952), 195–213. In *Jonson's Romish Plot: A Study of 'Catiline' and its Historical Context* (Oxford, 1967) B. N. De Luna has argued persuasively that 'Jonson's *Catiline* of 1611 was both intended and in some circles understood as a classical parallelograph of the Gunpowder Plot of 1605' (p. 360), but this argument does not necessarily invalidate all earlier studies of Jonson's treatment of historical sources in order to produce an accurate classical tragedy.

substantiate his claim to this truth, when Jonson published *Sejanus* he provided his readers with marginal references to his sources, of which he declared:

> ... I have only done it to show my integrity in the story, and save myself in [i.e. from] those common torturers that bring all wit to the rack; whose noses are ever like swine, spoiling and rotting up the Muses' gardens; and their whole bodies like moles, as blindly working under earth, to cast any, the least hills upon virtue.

The attitude to the ignorant that is expressed here is echoed by Webster in his address to the reader of *The White Devil*, written seven years later, though Webster referred to their swinishness in Latin, not in English. The parallels between these addresses to their readers have been noticed and discussed by editors.[6] R. W. Dent speaks of Webster's answer to the objection that *The White Devil* is 'no dramatic poem' as 'Apparently an imitation of Jonson's second paragraph in the "To the Readers" of *Sejanus*' and goes on to make the point that Webster's practice accorded with the theory of his friend Chapman, expressed in the latter's dedication to *The Revenge of Bussy D'Ambois* (1613). Professor Dent also draws attention to the fact that

> Dekker's *Lectori* to *The Whore of Babylon* (1607) and Marston's to *Sophonisba* (1606) take the same position, and Dekker, although ignoring most of the 'rules', defends calling his work a 'Dramaticall Poem'.[7]

George Chapman also scorned the ignorant, and was on occasion conscious, as were Webster, Jonson, Dekker, and Marston, of a desire or need to justify to his readers the aims of a particular method of writing.[8] Each of these dramatists was obviously on the defensive, knowing that his dramatic method had its critics.[9] Jonson and Webster, in particular, were anxious to defend plays which had been unsuccessful

---

[6] See F. L. Lucas, op. cit., i, 196; J. R. Brown, ed., *The White Devil*, The Revels Plays (1960), pp. 2–3.

[7] R. W. Dent, *John Webster's Borrowing* (Berkeley and Los Angeles, 1960), pp. 70–1.

[8] See, for example, Chapman's answer to the criticism of obscurity in the *Justification of Andromeda Liberata*. Of Chapman's obscurity Professor Brooke has remarked that it 'seems wilful in the notoriously irascible defensiveness of his outbursts against his contemporaries ...' (op. cit., p. xix).

[9] It should be noted that the aims of Marston in writing *Sophonisba* and of Dekker in writing *The Whore of Babylon* were precisely the opposite of Jonson's

when first produced in the theatre. Dekker, too, expressed some dissatisfaction with the performance of his play *The Whore of Babylon*, though it would appear to have been the actors who marred it. John Webster's echoing of Jonson in his attack on the auditory of *The White Devil* at the Red Bull may, I think, be seen as something more than just another example of his habit of borrowing: it is part of Webster's contribution to the vital dialogue between the Jacobean dramatist and his audience, an audience in which his fellow dramatists were included.

One might be tempted to relate Webster's account of the reception of 'the most sententious tragedy that ever was written' to the initial response to Jonson's *Sejanus*, but this play does not quite fit Webster's description. *Sejanus* did contain a Nuntius, though it lacked a Chorus. On the other hand, Webster's comments might well have been applied to the audience's reception of Jonson's second classical tragedy, *Catiline His Conspiracy*. This play did have a Chorus and at the end of the play, in recounting the death of Catiline, Petreius performed the function of a classical Nuntius. Webster's attitude may, therefore, be interpreted as one of exasperation at the audience's failure to appreciate plays written slowly and carefully—'labour'd' would, I think, be an insult if applied to Ben Jonson's comedies; a compliment if applied to his tragedies—either adhering to the 'rules' or waiving them for good reason: in either instance written with a desire to introduce the public to a new kind of dramatic experience.[10]

A desire to communicate successfully with his public must be a basic concern with any creative artist. We do not know if Webster was financially dependent on the success of his plays in the theatre. The apparent gaps in his career and his confessed slowness in the composition of *The White Devil* seem to suggest that he had other means of livelihood. From the few known facts of his career as a dramatist we may, perhaps, deduce that his desire was not so much to please a particular audience—the audience who went to see plays presented by the King's Men or the Queen's Men—as to find a suitable audience for the kind of plays he wanted to write. *The White Devil* was not at all the

---

in the composition of *Sejanus*: see 'To the General Reader' of *Sophonisba* in H. Harvey Wood, ed., *The Plays of John Marston*, ii (1938), 5; 'Lectori' of *The Whore of Babylon* in Fredson Bowers, ed., *The Dramatic Works of Thomas Dekker*, ii (Cambridge, 1955), 497.

[10] See John J. Enck, *Jonson and the Comic Truth* (Madison, Wisc., 1957), pp. 89–109. I would not go so far as to endorse Enck's conclusion that the English stage is unworthy of the pure tragedy of Jonson.

type of play which was usually presented at the Red Bull by the Queen's Men between 1609 and 1619.[11] Webster's plays were in many respects experimental, but he was not avant-garde. Some of his later plays, for example *Appius and Virginia*, are essays in modes no longer popular at the time of their composition, and with these I shall not be concerned in this paper.[12]

Of Webster's lost plays written in collaboration with other dramatists for Philip Henslowe in 1602—*Caesar's Fall, Lady Jane*, and *Christmas Comes But Once a Year*— we may guess with Professor J. R. Brown that 'they did not provide a very promising start for the new dramatist'.[13] Two of the collaborators, Dekker and Heywood, were to work with Webster again, and he was to link them with William Shakespeare as men distinguished by their 'right happy and copious industry'.

Webster's contributions to *Westward Ho!* (1604) and *Northward Ho!* (1605) were probably minor, compared to Dekker's,[14] yet he no doubt shared with the more experienced dramatist the desire to please the taste of the kind of spectator who frequented plays presented in the private theatres.[15] Unfortunately, as Dr Brian Gibbons has recently demonstrated in his book *Jacobean City Comedy*, when one reads these two plays of Dekker and Webster in the light of the plays of Jonson, Marston, and Middleton which established city comedy as a genre one becomes aware both of their authors' desire to imitate the more obvious features of the successful new plays and also of their inability to go beyond mere imitation to the creation of some contribution to the developing genre. It is clear that Dekker and Webster were, as Dr Gibbons states, 'heeding the demands of this imaginary City Comedy spectator'. Especially at the beginning of each play, they echoed the satiric prose style of Marston and emphasised the London setting and the fact that the characters were citizens. Both plays contain satiric set speeches, and the London types are presented as 'of course, scurrilous and prone to bawdy jesting, thieving, deception and adultery'.[16] Despite all this, Dr Gibbons concludes that:

[11] See J. R. Brown, op. cit., pp. xix–xx.

[12] In the discussion which followed the reading of this paper Gunnar Boklund called attention to the fact that the ideas of *The Duchess of Malfi* are, in fact, old-fashioned for the time of the play's production.

[13] op. cit., p. xviii.

[14] See F. L. Lucas, op. cit., iv, 239–44; Fredson Bowers, op. cit., 313–17; 407–9.

[15] See Brian Gibbons, *Jacobean City Comedy* (1968), pp. 134–5.

[16] ibid., p. 140

It is indicative that so little of the method of satiric comedy is understood by Dekker and Webster that their trickery episodes suggest derivation from Jest Books, the source of so many episodes in Coney-Catching pamphlets, rather than Jonson, because of their *exclusion* of moral and didactic considerations which are the primary impetus of satiric drama.[17]

Two masters of the new genre, Jonson and Marston, collaborated with George Chapman to produce a parody of the plays by Dekker and Webster which they called, appropriately, *Eastward Ho!* The fact that Webster was more concerned at this stage in his career to learn from his betters than to take offence, is indicated by his friendship with and admiration of all three of them. The performance of *Eastward Ho!* only a few months after that of *Northward Ho!* was followed in the same year—1605—by Webster's writing an Induction for the production of *The Malcontent*, which had perhaps originally been staged at the Blackfriars theatre,[18] by the King's Men, at the Globe. The King's Men enjoyed the prestige of being the best acting company of their day. The play's most recent editor, Professor Bernard Harris, has said of it: 'To some extent, *The Malcontent* is a play for an actors' theatre, of gratifying interest initially to such a company as the King's Men, practised in the diverse modes of *Every Man Out of His Humour* and *Hamlet*.' Moreover, *The Malcontent* was a theatrically ambitious play.[19] Described in the Stationers' Register entry of 5 July 1604 as 'An Enterlude called *the Male-content Tragiecomedia*' it was an experiment in a type of drama which, cultivated by Beaumont and Fletcher, was to become an important genre on the Jacobean stage. Since some scholars classify Marston's *Antonio and Mellida*, which may be dated 1599–1600, as a tragicomedy, he may be seen as one of the first major Jacobean dramatists to concern himself with this form. It may here be noticed, briefly, that *The Merchant of Venice*, *Much Ado About Nothing*, and *Measure for Measure* are as close to the pattern of tragicomedy outlined in the definition which Fletcher borrowed from Guarini to enlighten the

---

[17] ibid., p. 140. On the other hand, Dr Gibbons allows that 'the many references to satiric themes and the jests about sex have their effect in creating an atmosphere similar to that in a Marstonian City Comedy; and since this was perhaps the aim of the collaborators, it may be inappropriate to dwell long on the more serious weaknesses of the two plays' (p. 141).

[18] Bernard Harris, ed., *The Malcontent*, The New Mermaids (1967), pp. xiv–xv.

[19] ibid., pp. xv; xvi.

reader of *The Faithful Shepherdess* as are Shakespeare's so-called 'late romances' about whose relationship with Fletcherian tragicomedy commentators have been concerned. Marston's *The Malcontent* must have been a success, or the King's Men would not have wished to revive it. Nevertheless, the opening words of the Epilogus—

> Your modest silence, full of heedy stillness,
> Makes me thus speak:...

—suggest that the original audience did not immediately respond to it with applause. Perhaps they were uncertain how the play should be interpreted.

The tragic component of Marston's tragicomedy is one which relies heavily on the conventions of the revenge play, leading the audience to expect the exaction of revenge not once, but twice; and to be twice defeated of their expectation: upon Duke Pietro's discovery of his wife with her lover, Ferneze, in Act II, Scene v, and in the 'ambushing' of the villain Mendoza in Act V, Scene iv. A precedent for Duke Pietro's refusal to execute private revenge on his Duchess, Aurelia, may be found in the instructions of the Ghost of the Elder Hamlet to his son, concerning Gertrude. The survival of Ferneze, and his being hidden from Duke Pietro while the latter is allowed to think himself partly responsible for the young man's death provides the basis for the use of *peripetia* specifically for didactic ends which recurs in later Jacobean plays. It is found, for instance, in Heywood's *A Woman Killed with Kindness* (1603), and in Middleton's and Rowley's *A Fair Quarrel* (*c.* 1615–17). In *The Devil's Law-Case* (*c.* 1617) Webster stretches the possible effects of sudden reversals of fortune on all his main characters almost beyond the audience's credence.[20] A late example of the didactic use of *peripetia* is found in Philip Massinger's *The Guardian* (1633). In each of these plays a man is, like Duke Pietro, allowed to think himself responsible for another's death and is then spiritually regenerated by a combination of repentance and the happy discovery that his former enemy is still alive. This use of *peripetia* may, perhaps, be seen as a variation of that found in *Much Ado About Nothing* (1598–1600), *Cymbeline* (1608–11), and *The Winter's Tale* (1608–11) in which a man is allowed to think himself responsible for the death of a woman until he has learnt to appreciate her love, when he is reunited with her. What

---

[20] Cf. D. C. Gunby, '*The Devil's Law-Case*: an Interpretation', *Modern Language Review*, LXIII (1968), 543–58.

John Webster learnt from Marston, and also from Chapman, of the art of tragic satire has been amply demonstrated by Professor Travis Bogard.[21] From Marston I believe that Webster may have received a misleading impression of the usefulness of well-tried and favourite dramatic conventions as vehicles for conveying new ideas to an audience. Marston could employ the conventions of the revenge play to encourage expectations which he did not intend to fulfil in *The Malcontent* precisely because he was writing a tragicomedy, not a tragedy. Indeed, these very conventions were similarly used by later writers of Jacobean tragicomedy. Middleton's *The Witch* (*c.* 1609–16), for example, which has a quadruple plot structure, is entirely composed of typical revenge tragedy situations which are treated with various degrees of seriousness before each separate plot is brought to a hurried and unsatisfactory happy ending. More interesting to the students of Webster's plays is the fact that Fletcher's *The Chances* (1613–25) gains tension from its echoes of *The Duchess of Malfi*, though its structure collapses when the confrontation between the Duke of Ferrara, father of Constantia's illegitimate child, and her supposedly avenging brother, Petruchio, leads to the latter's anticlimactic declaration that he has no objections to his sister's marrying the Duke.

When John Webster embarked on the composition of *The White Devil*, using the framework and conventions of the Kydian revenge play, he could not avoid following their implications. It was not simply that he was writing a tragedy, not a tragicomedy. He was using a set of conventions which had ceased to be treated seriously by his fellow dramatists. Cyril Tourneur has been associated with Webster in his persistence in writing plays on the old Kydian model after Shakespeare had relegated revenge to a subordinate position, in his tragedies of *King Lear* and *Macbeth*, and had gone on in later plays to demonstrate the limitations of the revenge ethic.[22] Yet Tourneur's *The Atheist's Tragedy* is basically an anti-revenge tragedy, preaching Christian patience. In *The Revenger's Tragedy* conventions are treated sceptically: Vindice's disguise of the revenger, assumed at the beginning of the play, becomes his true nature as the action progresses; the revenge ethic is condemned in the Lord Antonio's refusal to view the actions of

[21] Travis Bogard, *The Tragic Satire of John Webster* (Berkeley and Los Angeles, 1955).

[22] See Richard Proudfoot, 'Shakespeare and the New Dramatists of the King's Men, 1603–1613', *Stratford-upon-Avon Studies 8: Later Shakespeare* (1966), pp. 236–7.

Vindice and Hippolito against the Duke's family as revenge for the
rape and suicide of his wife. In writing *The White Devil* Webster was
limited by the historical facts of the deaths of Vittoria and her brother.
It should also be remembered that this was probably his first independent play, and the whole mechanism of revenge tragedy, so popular
with audiences and dramatists from the late 1580s up to the closing of
the theatres in 1642—even if later plays deal with revenge in a sceptical
or perfunctory fashion—was stronger than Webster's confidence. As
Professor Harold Jenkins has put it:

> It is as though his sources, with the murder of Camillo as well as
> Isabella, and the revenge tradition, with its ghosts and poisonings
> and mad scenes, have supplied him with too much material, which
> his imagination cannot effectively control.[23]

On the other hand, though Webster appears to be critical of the conventional use of a ghost in the revenge play, in Francisco's attitude to
the ghost of Isabella, he makes no attempt at a realistic interpretation
of the appearance of Brachiano in response to Flamineo's conjuration.

Though I feel that the example of Marston's success with *The Malcontent* may have encouraged Webster to produce his mixed tragedy of
old conventions and new ideas, he did not ask his readers to consider
The White Devil in the light of Marston's work. I do not propose to
examine the possible relationships between Webster's aims and intentions and those of each of the seven dramatists whom he named. What
knowledge of Webster's art is to be gained from reading his plays in
the light of those of Shakespeare and Chapman is sufficiently established to need no further comment here. What he might have learnt
from Beaumont and Fletcher is chiefly to be discovered from a reading
of *The Devil's Law-Case*, about which we are to hear from Dr Boklund. The names of Dekker and Heywood were included on the list, I
suspect, to indicate personal rather than literary indebtedness: unless,
which appears unlikely, *Appius and Virginia*, to which Heywood seems
to have lent words and ideas, if not material, is an early rather than a
later play. The remaining name, that of Jonson, is interesting because

[23] Harold Jenkins, 'The Tragedy of Revenge in Shakespeare and Webster',
Shakespeare Survey, 14 (Cambridge, 1961), p. 51. A less favourable account of
Webster's handling of the revenge plot structure in the play is given by Roma
Gill in ' "Quaintly Done": a Reading of *The White Devil*', *Essays and Studies*,
N.S. XIX (1966), pp. 42–3; 45.

Jonson's tragedies occupy an undeservedly minor place in his canon and in general esteem.

I have already indicated some things which Jonson and Webster had in common, and have remarked that, in dramatising the stories of Vittoria Accoramboni and Appius and Virginia, Webster relied on no single source. In this aspect of the treatment of his material Webster's method is parallel to Jonson's in the writing of tragedies based on classical history. Jonson achieved historical truth through an interpretation of the material available to him, and it is in this way that we see him acting as an historian as well as a dramatist. The opening comments of Silius and Arruntius in *Sejanus*, for example, and the critical remarks of Cicero made throughout *Catiline* provided an audience with these characters' interpretation of history at the time of its happening. Though it is more usual to associate the critical comments of characters in Webster's plays with a satiric tradition, I believe that they may also be related to Ben Jonson's method of providing a comment on historical figures and acts. At the same time, by such comments Webster was able to remind his audience that the main figures in his major tragedies were real people who had excited as much gossip or slander in their lives as the rich, famous, or notorious still do.

Strictly speaking, the action of *Sejanus* is not continuous. Relying always on his audience's knowledge of Roman history, Jonson omitted minor incidents or developments in relationships to give a series of impressions of his characters in moments of crisis or climax. Webster could not rely on his audience's knowledge of the story of Vittoria Accoramboni—the false description of her on the title page of the first quarto as 'the famous Venetian Curtizan' would not seem to encourage a concern for accurate historical knowledge—but he did present her to his audience as history presented her to him, through the series of great moments in her career. At the centre of the play stands her great public appearance at her arraignment.

Yet if Webster observed some of Jonson's aims in tragedy, he followed them as guides, not commanders. Jonson's characterisation in his Roman tragedies was influenced by moral considerations, by Jonson's desire to make clear the distinction between good and evil. Thus, in *Sejanus*, the complex personality of Tiberius that appears in Tacitus is turned into that of a bad man who simply becomes worse; in *Catiline* the character of Julius Caesar is interpreted entirely in Jonson's own

way, which was not that of his main source, Sallust.[24] Webster's characterisation, on the other hand, is related to his dramatic aims as well
as to his view of life and its relationship to art. In part, the characterisation of *The White Devil* was influenced by the revenge-tragedy
framework of the play. Thus Lodovico was represented as having, in
secret, passionately doted upon Brachiano's Duchess, the saintly Isabella, so that there was some motivation for his involvement in the
murder of Vittoria. In part, Webster had an aim in characterisation no
less didactic than Jonson's. This opinion has recently been expressed
by D. C. Gunby: 'Basic to my view of Webster is a belief that he was
essentially a didacticist (albeit a didacticist of genius), and that his
career shows a steady progression from implicit to explicit methods of
conveying his message.'[25] Webster's didacticism was, however,
expressed in an entirely different way from Jonson's. Jonson simplified
his major characters, judging them, classifying them as good or evil, for
moral reasons. Webster deliberately made some of his characters—for
example, Isabella—and some of their situations—for example, the relationship between Brachiano and Vittoria—more complex than they
were in real life.[26] Webster refused to judge or classify his characters:
also for moral reasons. What I mean is that Webster challenged his
audience to judge for themselves where good and evil lie in the characters of his tragedy; and the act of attempting such judgment was not
made easy for them. This point is well made by Roma Gill: 'Of all the
major figures in *The White Devil* only one, Camillo, elicits a response
that is unfalteringly straightforward from first to last.'[27] Miss Gill also
indicated Webster's achievements in the play as 'a new naturalism in
the presentation of Vittoria and a skilled manipulation of the audience
into unaccustomed and uncomfortable moral positions'.[28]

Both these achievements were unappreciated, seemingly, by the
auditory at the Red Bull. They had a further reason for feeling discon-
certed and dissatisfied in that *The White Devil* was too realistic a
tragedy to conclude with an effective catharsis.[29] No doubt the
audience could have felt that they should have confidence in the rule of

---

[24] Joseph Allen Bryant, Jnr, '*Catiline* and the Nature of Jonson's Tragic
Fable', *PMLA*, LXIX (1954), 265–77, but see also B. N. De Luna, op. cit., p. 36.
[25] op. cit., p. 546; cf. Elizabeth M. Brennan, ed., *The White Devil*, The New
Mermaids (1966; second impression, 1969), pp. xix–xxiv.
[26] Cf. Elizabeth M. Brennan, op. cit., pp. xiii–xvi.
[27] op. cit., p. 46.   [28] ibid., p. 59.
[29] Cf. Bertolt Brecht, *Brecht on Theatre*, tr. John Willett (1964), pp. 77–81.

the young Duke Giovanni; that they were being asked to believe that, purged of evil, this young Duke's court and rule would be, if not perfect, at least free from moral corruption. Apart from the fact that it is not difficult to see Giovanni at the end of the play as something of a prig, a knowledge of English history, or even of Elizabethan history plays, would have been enough to indicate to them that the reigns of hopeful young princes were not usually either long or uncorrupted by the ideas and actions of their advisers.

Again, the effect is similar to that of Jonson's tragedies. The fall of Sejanus may have ended his wicked career but, as we know from Tacitus, it introduced to Imperial Rome a reign of terror unique in the history of that corrupt and dying state. The death of Catiline is presented by Jonson as balanced by the rise of the tyrant, Julius Caesar. If, as Arruntius says in *Sejanus*, men, not the times, are 'base, poor and degenerate', all men are responsible for the manifest evil which overwhelms good and bad alike. Thus Jonson showed in his classical tragedies a society in which the removal of one evil was deliberately overshadowed by the audience's knowledge that a greater was treading on its heels, following the same path to powerful destruction. There is little comfort for an audience in the thought that Jonson's tragedies, like John Webster's, are based on historical events; less in the thought that 'history repeats itself'.

In a note added to the text of *The White Devil* Webster gallantly praised the Queen's Men for their performance. They had obviously tried hard with this difficult play, before a sparse and unresponsive audience. Yet one is led to assume that they were not the right company for this kind of drama; it was too different from the other plays in their repertoire. Could the passage of two years and the production of his second tragedy, *The Duchess of Malfi*, by a different—indeed the best—acting company completely account for its success? How did that slow writer, sensitive to the audience's response to his work, find courage after his initial failure quickly to follow it up with a play which the King's Men were willing to stage? The failure of his first tragedy must have discouraged John Webster. One is tempted to believe that among the understanding friends who realised what he was trying to do and encouraged him to continue there must have been someone—perhaps Shakespeare?—who knew that the King's Men could do the second tragedy justice. It has already been noticed that *The Malcontent* was the kind of experimental play which suited the temperament and abilities of the King's Men in 1604. Since then they had acquired the Blackfriars theatre, and it has been suggested by G. E. Bentley that they may have experimented with 'a new kind of play for the new theatre and audience'.[30] Professor J. R. Brown has indicated how Webster utilised some of the physical properties of the Blackfriars theatre in *The Duchess of Malfi*.[31] However, by the time that the King's Men took over the Blackfriars, in 1609, and possibly before, the distinctions between the audiences of public and private theatres had ceased to be as marked as they had been in the heyday of the children's companies. In fact, *The Duchess of Malfi* was presented both in the Blackfriars and in the Globe. As the cast list printed with the first quarto (1623) provides two sets of names for some characters we deduce, as further evidence of the success of the play in the theatre, that it was revived before the date of publication.

It is obvious that Webster had developed as a dramatist in the interval between the composition of his two major tragedies: 1612–14. Nevertheless, the 'uncomfortable' elements of the earlier tragedy—from the audience's point of view—were still present. The very fact that the Duchess of Malfi is less obviously an immoral character than Vittoria makes it even more challenging for an audience to judge her. Antonio's encomium of the Duchess, spoken shortly after the opening of the play and deliberately contrasting her with her two brothers, leads the audience to sympathise with her as Ferdinand is seen hiring Bosola to spy on her and, shortly afterwards, Ferdinand and the Cardinal harry her on the subject of her remarriage. Certainly Webster did not present her as he found her in his main source, Painter's *Palace of Pleasure*, and in other accounts of her life, as a wanton widow. Yet he did allow his audience to see how swiftly she could turn from protesting to her brothers that she would never marry to plotting with her maid, Cariola, how she will marry Antonio. There is no pause in the action. The Duchess's expressed determination not to marry is immediately followed by her secret marriage to her major-domo within the same scene of the play; in time, within the same hour. Similarly, Ferdinand's employment of Bosola to spy on her, constituting a deception of the Duchess, is swiftly followed by her deception of both brothers. Again, against the reality and realism of the Duchess's happy domes-

[30] Quoted by J. R. Brown, op. cit., p. xxii.
[31] ibid., pp. xxii–xxiv.

* *

ticity Webster sets the opinion of the common rabble, reported by her husband, that she is a strumpet. The rabble's point of view challenges our own judgement, not only of the Duchess, but of that other much discussed heroine, Vittoria. The Duchess's preparations for death suggest that she is able, finally, to make a good Christian end, yet when Webster shows her reviving for an instant he lets her utter only her husband's name and the word 'Mercy'. Scholars are still undecided how best to interpret that one word. Indeed, Webster has been severely censured for what some critics have seen as his amoral or morally ambiguous view of life. Webster's own answer to this charge would be, I think, that, in the characterisation of his heroines, he had 'willingly, and not ignorantly' refused to represent them in a clear light.

The conclusion of the second tragedy is similar to that of the first. Was the audience expected to believe that Antonio's eldest child would be established in his mother's right? I think not; for history relates that the young Duke of Amalfi reigned successfully from the time of his mother's departure with Antonio and their children to Ancona. It is usually assumed that, in the end of the play, Webster had forgotten about this young Duke who has not appeared on the stage, though he is mentioned by Ferdinand; but this may not be so. Had Webster presented the young Duke of Amalfi as his mother's successor his arrival on stage might have created more problems than are raised by his absence. He would have had to pass judgement on his mother and uncles. His accession might have been interpreted as the establishment of a good rule after the purging of a corrupt court, and this, in turn, would have led to the kind of pointing of a way to a moral judgement for his audience which Webster wished to avoid. Moreover, in the leading-in of Antonio's eldest child to be established in his mother's right Webster presents us with a final irony: the reversal of Antonio's dying wish—

And let my son fly the courts of princes.[32]

Webster's sources for *The Duchess of Malfi* were not, strictly speaking, as historical as those for *The White Devil*. Since neither history nor fiction explained how or precisely why the Duchess met her death, he could successfully use the pattern of revenge tragedy—not the old,

[32] Elizabeth M. Brennan, ed., *The Duchess of Malfi*, The New Mermaids (1964), V.iv.71. It was in discussion following the reading of this paper that my attention was drawn to this irony.

Kydian pattern of revenge for murder, but the pattern of revenge for honour which was closer to the lives and interests of his audience—both to arouse their interest and to challenge their interpretation of the known facts.[33]

One notable way in which the later tragedy differs from *The White Devil* is in its presentation of ethical problems. Vittoria Corombona has a much more imposing and more complex personality than the Duchess. It is about Vittoria herself, rather than the problems which her conduct raises, that the audience is expected to make a judgement. Despite the centrality of the 'bedroom' scene in the structure of *The Duchess of Malfi*, the heroine is, in some ways, presented to the audience in a less intimate way than Vittoria is. Her famous assertion of personal identity, 'I am Duchess of Malfi still', reminds us that we know her by no other name. Much as we feel for her personal situation, a situation no less historically real than that of Vittoria, we are forced to see in the actions of the Duchess of Malfi a wider significance than there is in those of Brachiano's second Duchess. So the questions which the play raises are: should a duchess neglect her duchy, and the young son for whom she is acting as regent, in order to satisfy her personal need for love; should a duchess marry beneath her own rank? There are, also, questions which do not relate to the heroine's public position: should a woman allow her brothers to control her choice of husband; should a widow remarry; what is one's attitude to secret marriages contracted outside the Church; what does one do about the corruption of churchmen or statesmen? An audience which is uncomfortable at the prospect of responding to the need to assess the characters in the play is able to vent some of its unease in discussion of the problems which those characters have to face.

More than any other aspect of his two tragedies, Webster's characterisation has aroused the interest and comment of critics. Posterity has provided John Webster with an understanding auditory: that is, with an audience not necessarily sympathetic, but essentially prepared to be concerned with his tragic characters and their dilemmas. In a sense Webster was right to appeal to the reader, as he did when he published *The White Devil*. At the same time, he must have been afflicted, as his friend John Marston was

[33] Cf. Elizabeth M. Brennan, 'The Relationship between Brother and Sister in the Plays of John Webster', *Modern Language Review*, LVIII (1963), 488–94.

... to think that scenes invented merely to be spoken should be enforcively published to be read.

With *The White Devil*, however, we are soon to be given another chance to test our capacity for understanding, as the play joins the repertoire of the National Theatre Company in November 1969.

Webster and the Actor

PETER THOMSON

Webster and the Actor

JOHN RUSSELL BROWN concludes the section on theatre productions in the preface to his edition of *The White Devil* with this comment:

Clearly, the audience for Webster is growing once more; it may not be long before another professional production can be attempted.[1]

I am not sure that I understand the sentence. *Was* the audience for Webster growing in 1958 when Professor Brown wrote his introduction? Is it still? How can one tell? Did the audience for Ford grow when *The Broken Heart* was staged at the first Chichester Festival in 1962? Or was the play selected for production because the audience for Ford had grown? Is there an audience for Webster that is distinct from the audience for Ford or for Middleton? Or does 'the audience' see on the one hand Shakespeare, and on the other a kind of composite Webblemont and Forcheur figure? What, finally, is the relationship that Professor Brown seems to be proposing between the Drama's patrons and the laws of a subsidised theatre? I shall not try to answer these questions, but if you will add to them an uneasiness about the condition of the British theatre you will recognise the sources of some of my later waywardness.

There is, of course, every likelihood that Webster's two best-known plays will be seen several times on the professional stage in the remaining thirty years of this century. There is an access into the theatre from the advanced level and university syllabus that is both direct and indirect. A number of productions in the north of England of *She Stoops to Conquer* announces that the play is a Northern Board set book this year. Webster's case is not as simple as Goldsmith's. Most repertory companies will select for their big cast, Elizabethan costume piece from among the Shakespeare set plays. But Webster, if not 'there', is

---

[1] J. R. Brown, ed., *The White Devil*, The Revels Plays (1960), p. lxii. My own quotations are from Lucas's edition of Webster's works, 4 vols. (1927).

'thereabouts'. No director can confidently claim to have achieved the
'definitive production', and the challenge is a tempting one. *The
Duchess of Malfi* has surely caught the eye of Michael Elliott, one of the
most enterprising and ambitious of our younger directors, and one with
whom Vanessa Redgrave enjoys working. It is out of this kind of
relationship that the decision to stage revivals is born. Fine actors
could be found for and attracted by Bosola, Ferdinand, the Cardinal,
even Julia and Cariola, and you can make a living if not a reputation in
Antonio. For the rest the principles of the stock company still apply. I
am talking, I think, fact not theory. Michael Elliott, who is in a better
position to know what he means than I, is fond of the phrase 'the best
casting in the country', but he would not apply it to Delio nor, being a
courteous man, to Castruchio and the Old Lady. The method is time-
honoured. It accommodates much of what is best in theatre. It has
accommodated honest productions of Shakespeare and dishonest ones,
and will continue to do so. It is the spirit of accommodation in the
British theatre that most disturbs me. Artaud, who proposes nothing so
vehemently as the annihilation of the theatre as we know it, has been
interpreted by the theatre as we know it, and Dame Edith Evans, who
wouldn't be seen dead with a sword up her, probably even admires
Irene Worth, who was. There is much to be said for an accommodating
theatre, but the dangers should not be underrated. The British theatre
can afford to indulge the eccentricities of a Peter Brook because it is
ultimately concerned to interpret, not ideas, not even texts, but itself
to itself.

The relevance of all this to Webster will, perhaps, become clearer if
I refer you to a passage in Sir John Gielgud's *Stage Directions*:

> A really evil person must be without moral sense—and Iago (like
> Duke Ferdinand in *The Duchess of Malfi*, a part I once acted without
> much pleasure) is really a monster.[2]

I do Gielgud's argument no justice by quoting a comment which is
incidental to a discussion of the actor's problems in playing Angelo and
Leontes,[3] but I have only a local point to make. It seems implicit in
the comparison that in trying to find the part of Ferdinand Gielgud
used Iago, a part he had never played, as a guide. The result was

---

[2] Gielgud, *Stage Directions* (1963), p. 45.
[3] But a discussion that draws together Angelo, Leontes, Iago, Ferdinand, and
Cassius is already alarmingly eclectic.

widely praised, though the critic of the *Evening Standard*, aware of the 'perilously thin line between great acting and ham acting', felt that this Ferdinand 'would have frightened and embarrassed the Borgias';[4] but eighteen years later Gielgud remembers it as 'a part I once acted without much pleasure'. In the context one is forced to wonder whether Ferdinand's failure to be Iago was a contributory factor to the actor's disappointment. The players' problems in recognising the particularity of Webster are not simplified by the response of reviewers, whose influence over the development of the British theatre is infinitely greater than that of literary critics. James Agate's placing of Bosola as 'this mixture of Enobarbus and Thersites'[5] is only less dangerous than his reflections on the 1925 production of *The White Devil*:

> As we watch this play we cannot help thinking how differently Shakespeare would have treated the unhappy passion of Vittoria and her duke. He, we feel, would have made another *Macbeth* of this theme, and by working out tragedy to its remorseful end have revealed the essential goodness ordaining that such things shall not be.[6]

There are two obvious dangers: the first, that actors will look for Shakespeare in Webster to counter the menace of his luminous contemporaneity, and the second, that they will be playing towards an inevitably lukewarm reception from reviewers who prefer Shakespeare and who seem generally to complain of Elizabethan revivals, not that they are too scholarly, but that they are not scholarly enough. Either way, Webster will be accommodated without creating much stir, as he has been in the recent past.

It is astonishing that the Webster anathematised by William Archer has been so imperceptible in the theatre. Kenneth Tynan found the 1947 production of *The White Devil* 'infinitely terrifying',[7] but his (largely unshared?) response is not authenticated by a review which ends:

> Yet we do not leave the theatre disgusted or appalled. After so much refinement upon death and transfiguration, after such orgiastic mur-

---

[4] London *Evening Standard* (21 April 1945).
[5] Quoted in J. R. Brown, ed., *The Duchess of Malfi*, The Revels Plays (1964), p. lviii.
[6] Agate, *The Contemporary Theatre*, 1925 (1926), pp. 38–9.
[7] Tynan, *He That Plays the King* (1950), p. 69.

dering-parties, we feel that death himself must be sated, and so spare us. The thought is a happy one.[8]

It is surely impossible to mount a production of *The Duchess of Malfi* or *The White Devil* without intending deeply to disturb your audience. There is at least a hint in the '*O dura messorum ilia*' of Webster's address to the reader of *The White Devil* that the spirit of accommodation displayed by his first audience disappointed him. The disturbance of the audience in a Webster play is, as D. L. Frost among many others has pointed out, quite un-Shakespearean:

> The comparisons with a tragedy like *Lear* can be made; but there is no initial violation of 'order' on a parallel scale, nor do we have any sense of a universe throwing off corruption at terrible cost.[9]

But the theatre has evidently a limited confidence in Webster's power to disturb its habitués. In 1946, a year after directing a revival of *The Duchess of Malfi* in London, George Rylands directed an adaptation by W. H. Auden of the same play in New York. In this version the bodies displayed to the Duchess fell out of an armoire, Antonio's son accompanied his father to his death in place of a servant, the incest theme was openly stated, the Lyke Wake Dirge was chanted to the imprisoned Duchess and Bosola was played in white-face by the Negro actor Canada Lee, a white devil of a nursery bogeyman kind.[10] Webster may, perhaps, have approved some of these changes, the last of which links him with Genet, a dramatist who *has* succeeded in shocking contemporary audiences; but the fact that the theatre has felt it necessary to increase the exoticism for which Webster has been so often condemned is enough to make us wonder whether it is the fit place to accord him due recognition. I am far from preferring the theatre of the mind to the stage itself. I merely protest, as a devotee of the theatre, against the often over-simple confidence of Webster's friendly literary critics that his genius will be finally vindicated *in the theatre* where it belongs. The conditions under which the British theatre generally rehearses and stages its productions are better suited to discovering what Webster has in common with Shakespeare than what is uniquely his. The latter task is still predominantly the responsibility of scholars.

---

[8]Tynan, op. cit., p. 71.

[9] D. L. Frost, *The School of Shakespeare* (Cambridge, 1968), p. 149.

[10] My account of this production relies on Mary McCarthy, *Sights and Spectacles* (New York, 1956), pp. 93–4.

This is not to deny the usefulness to scholars of a detailed investigation of theatre records. John Russell Brown has illustrated this point splendidly in a short comment on *The White Devil*:

A review after the performance . . . in London on 6 March 1947, points to the importance of a one-line part in this play—which many have read, but few have been able to see. It describes the sense of embarrassment which Webster achieved by introducing a young, anonymous page to contradict Cornelia's attempt to shield her son from Bracciano's anger, with a simple 'This is not true, madam'; attention is thus drawn away, rapidly and without warning, from the centre of a very 'dramatic' situation, and a silence follows.[11]

Professor Brown goes on to point up the significance of the reviewer's perception. It 'illustrates Webster's power of using violent and crowded scenes for sudden, and therefore striking, manifestations of an individual's lies or hypocrisy'. One might instance from the same play Francisco's self-satisfied scheming (IV.iii.53–61) against a background of the papal election as a variation on the method. But the Page's line is also a succinct illustration of the dizzying shifts of focus that characterise Webster's scenic composition. The Webster scholar will neither expect the theatre to do his work for him nor ignore its findings.

The modern actor in Elizabethan and Jacobean drama

Webster had the great dramatist's ability to see and hear in the theatre what he wrote as he wrote it. The precise vision that makes such exquisite horror of Ferdinand's entry to the 'merry' Duchess of Malfi (III.ii) is thoughtfully retained in *Monuments of Honour*, where Webster requests that the chariot bearing the arms of the Merchant Taylors should be 'drawne with fower horses, (for Porters would have made it move tottering and Improperly)' (ll.164–5). I have not made the comparisons necessary for an authoritative statement, but I sense in *Monuments of Honour* an attractive consideration of the pageant-constructors' problems. If so it need not surprise us. The extravagant effects of Webster's plays are achieved without any stretching of theatrical resources. A few heavy props—the vaulting-horse is less familiar than the bed or the coffin—are needed, but all Webster's plays have the important quality of easy transportability. *The Duchess of Malfi* was

---

[11] J. R. Brown, *Shakespeare's Plays in Performance* (1966), p. 226. The review appeared in *The Sunday Times* (9 March 1947).

performed at theatres as different as the Globe, the Blackfriars, and, almost certainly, the newly constructed Cockpit-in-Court where, whatever the previous practice, it had no inner stage and probably no traps to aid its surprises.[12] Webster raises no unanswerable staging problems in the modern theatre.

For the actor, who is my main concern, the case is not so simple. Webster presents to him certain problems that are common in most Elizabethan and Jacobean drama, and certain that are more characteristic of him than of his contemporaries. I propose to deal with these in turn, without, of course, making any attempt to be exhaustive on either.

The size of the cast, which is a problem now to all but the wealthiest of British theatres, was not without its drawbacks in the companies Webster served. Pallant, Towley, Underwood, and, presumably, others had to double parts in the first performance of *The Duchess of Malfi*, though none quite so hectically as the Paul's boy who was required in *Antonio and Mellida* to act Alberto and Andrugio.[13] The actor of Camillo may well have doubled the role of the pedantic lawyer in *The White Devil*, thus failing twice to bring Vittoria to book. The practice of doubling is often unpopular in the contemporary theatre, where refinements of make-up and costume have increased its hardships.[14] There is no certain evidence of its unpopularity among Elizabethan actors. The versatility it encouraged in apprentice players is, perhaps, recognised in the frequency with which dramatists introduce role-playing and disguises into their plays. It is, after all, a theatrically logical promotion for Robert Pallant from doubling Cariola and the Doctor to playing Portia. In the Induction to *Antonio and Mellida* the boy-player of Antonio complains of having to impersonate an Amazon, and is reproved by Alberto/Andrugio:

> Not play two parts in one? away, away; 'tis common fashion. Nay, if you cannot bear two subtle fronts under one hood, idiot go by, go by, off this world's stage.[15]

[12] For a discussion of the design of the Cockpit-in-Court see G. Wickham, *Shakespeare's Dramatic Heritage* (1969), pp. 151–62.

[13] Induction to *Antonio and Mellida*, ll.21–7. (For references to and quotations from *Antonio and Mellida* and *Antonio's Revenge* I have used G. K. Hunter's editions in the Regents Renaissance Drama series.)

[14] Against this A. C. Sprague cites two examples of modern productions of *Henry V*. At the Marlowe Theatre, Canterbury in 1953 17 actors played 39 parts; and at the Library Theatre, Manchester in 1957 18 actors played 35 parts. Sprague, *Shakespeare's Histories* (1964), p. 104 and note.

[15] Induction to *Antonio and Mellida*, ll.73–6.

Webster is not alone in pressing home with relish the satire of the world's seeming, implicit in all role-playing, but in the modern 'psychological' theatre the assumption of a role has sometimes seemed disastrously to reduce the chance of acting truthfully the part of the deceived or the deceiver. The fact that the audience may accept such conventions as the credibility of slander and the impenetrability of disguise does not altogether simplify the actor's task. He will only really persuade an audience if he has persuaded himself.[16]

Gunnar Boklund illustrates the psychological discontinuity of Webster's characterisation in referring to the sentence on which Ferdinand dies:

> Whether we fall by ambition, blood, or lust,
> Like Diamonds, we are cut with our owne dust.
>
> (V.v.91–2)

It cannot, he suggests, be accepted as psychologically possible. But,

> At this stage of the play psychological considerations matter little. The characters behave according to parts assigned them by the author in his capacity of conductor of the concluding argument.[17]

This is of small comfort to the modern actor, who will have painstakingly composed a consistent portrait of Ferdinand. He might, at worst, share the alarm of a flautist who finds a *pizzicato* passage marked in his part. More probably he will attempt, by a vocal inflection perhaps, to make the final couplet consistent with the character he has created, thus falling into the danger of misrepresenting the play. The need for psychological consistency exerts an irresistible pressure on the modern actor. Webster's characteristic cross-reference between the ontological and the psychological is probably indiscernible to him, and even if he perceives it he is unlikely to be able to enact it. The problem, for which the effect of Stanislavsky's teaching on an exaggeratedly structured profession is, ironically, partly responsible, comes from the stress the theatre lays on acting *parts* instead of acting *plays*. Anyone who saw the television film of 'The Epic That Never Was' will have seen in Charles Laughton's behaviour the extremity of suffering that can burden an

---

[16] 'Persuasion [of the audience] is what matters in art, not conviction.' Michael Redgrave, *Mask or Face* (1958), p. 145.

[17] Boklund, *The Duchess of Malfi: Sources, Themes, Characters* (Cambridge, Mass., 1962), p. 139.

actor unable to find his character. If the text is insufficient the actor will look for a subtext, and it is in this increasingly popular notion that the old battle over Lady Macbeth's children is being fought again— and again. Stanislavsky, who coined the word that has been translated as 'subtext', used it to guide his trainee actors towards the creation of a role, defining it as,

> the manifest, the inwardly felt expression of a human being in a part, which flows uninterruptedly beneath the words of the text, giving them life and a basis for existing. . . . It is the subtext that makes us say the words we do in a play.[18]

The usefulness to critics of the idea of a subtext is already being debated. John Russell Brown defends its applicability to Shakespeare in a persuasive chapter of *Shakespeare's Plays in Performance*,[19] in which he is careful to point out that among actors the deed has a much longer history than the word. Certainly among modern actors it has all the popularity of platitude. In order to develop a character, she explained to her *Guardian* interviewer, Patience Collier 'must know all about it, what kind of child, what life she had, why the author was interested'.[20] It is precisely this kind of information that Webster withholds. The lack of information about the Duchess of Malfi's dead husband is astonishing. Was he, perhaps, impotent and she, therefore, frustrated? It is the kind of question the play doesn't invite us to ask, but the kind a modern actress almost certainly will. The actor of Antonio has the clearest bearing on my argument. I cannot believe with Professor Boklund that the character 'was most deliberately created by the dramatist'.[21] Most of Webster's characters contrive to present them-selves as acted on rather than active, and the hole in the play half filled by Antonio is the price Webster must pay for the technique; but the actor cannot willingly embody the dramatist's failure. His Antonio is likely to be in intermittent conflict with a text which builds for him the outward appearance of a hero, offers him so many opportunities for heroic gesture, and has him muff them all. The disparity between the Antonio of the play's language and the Antonio of its plot is a cruel one for the man who plays him. The temptation to search for a subtext must be extreme.

[18] Stanislavsky, *Building a Character*, tr. Elizabeth R. Hapgood (1950), p. 113.
[19] Brown, *Shakespeare's Plays in Performance*, pp. 50–66.
[20] *The Guardian* (28 March 1969).   [21] Boklund, op. cit., p. 95.

There is little for actors to learn from the stage directions in Webster's plays. Vittoria '*throwes her selfe upon a bed*' (IV.ii.129), curiously placed in the reception room of the House of Convertites, an indelicate reminder of departed glories or token of a happy relapse. That she throws herself face down is further indicated by Flamineo's bawdy advice to Brachiano:

> Women are caught as you take Tortoises,
> Shee must bee turn'd on her backe. (IV.ii.154–5)

This is a piece of business that might have been missed without the direction, but that may be omitted in modern productions anyway. Against Francisco's dismissal of the wordy Lawyer:

> Sir,
> Put up your papers in your fustian bag—
> Cry mercy Sir, tis buckeram—and accept
> My notion of your learn'd verbosity. (III.ii.48–51)

is printed, '*Francisco speakes this as in scorne*', but it would be a poor actor who failed to find this in the text. The directions for the dumb-shows are, of necessity, crucial. They confirm an impression gained from the text that Webster had an unusually sharp eye for the visual composition of a scene. Perhaps the most intriguing stage directions are those to the dying Brachiano and the mad Cornelia:

> *These speeches are severall kinds of distractions*
> *and in the action should apeare [so]*. (against V.iii.80–87)

and,

> *Cornelia doth this in severall formes of distraction.*
> (against V.iv.90–92)

The primary insistence is probably on vocal variation, but the direction to Cornelia in particular[22] suggests a possible formalised pattern of gesture associated with the imitation of madness. Such a pattern would be likely to grow up along with the plays that required the acting of madness, so that by the time Webster wrote it may have become a formalised 'inset' that gratified both actor and audience. A notated

[22] Brown argues for a different placing of the s.d. that would strengthen my argument. See his edition of *The White Devil*.

representation of distraction is certainly implied by the countless scenes of feigned madness in Jacobean drama. Ferdinand, when he falls victim to a 'strange distraction' (V.ii.87), may be repeating vocal and physical tricks that had been tested in Webster's earlier tragedy and elsewhere.

It is the verdict of Michael Redgrave that Shakespearean actors 'should be able to go to it like French falconers and act, quite simply, "jealousy" '.[23] The same is true, of course, in all Elizabethan and Jacobean drama. '*Give seeming passion*' is a stage direction in *Antonio's Revenge*, when Piero must feign distress at the report of Andrugio's death.[24] We cannot be certain whether the direction was an authorial instruction to the boy-actor—if so, the context makes it almost tautologous—nor whether the formal gestures of 'seeming passion' were distinct from those of true passion, but the words emphasise the kind of flat demand for emotional acting that is characteristic of Elizabethan plays. For Stanislavsky the ability simply to *give* an emotion is essential to any actor who wishes simultaneously to maintain his own sense of truth in a role and convey it to an audience:

> ... when you are called upon to experience a tragedy do not think about your emotions at all. Think about what you have to *do*.[25]

But recognition on the part of an actor of a *desideratum* is some way from the achievement of it, and we must expect the 'impure' confusion of realism and convention that T. S. Eliot observed in Webster to reach the point of crisis for anyone who tries to act in his plays.

Interpreting Webster on the stage

The theatre is double-edged in the scope it offers for startling reinterpretations. It was suggested by a student director in a Studio production of scenes from *The Duchess of Malfi* that the Cardinal's lines which open II.iv:

> Sit: thou art my best of wishes—pre-thee tell me
> What tricke didst thou invent to come to Rome,
> Without thy husband?

should be spoken post-coitally by a man who has pushed through the

[23] Redgrave, op. cit., p. 90.   [24] *Antonio's Revenge*, I.ii.241.
[25] Stanislavsky, *An Actor Prepares*, tr. Elizabeth R. Hapgood (1967), p. 142.

business of the meeting before getting down to the small-talk. The idea
is not without its justification. The Cardinal's condemnation of women
is tactless in a man about to seduce one, and Julia's tears a feminine
reaction to the abrupt dying away of masculine passion—'You have
prevailed with me/Beyond my strongest thoughts'. The psychological
explanation is improbably plausible. The further suggestion, deriving
from Brecht's *Leben des Galilei*, that the Cardinal should be shown
donning his scarlet robes as he speaks would surely have appealed to
Webster, even if it didn't occur to him. *Cucullus non facit monachum.*
The interpretation may outrage some. There is no doubt of its theatrical effectiveness.

The staging of any play creates problems that are not apparent to a
reader. At IV.iii.18 of *The White Devil*, Francisco, who was talking to
Lodovico eleven lines before, asks,

> Where's Count Lodowicke?

A director must either cut the line or find a way of 'losing' Lodovico on
a not very crowded stage. The example is trivial, but the next is not.
The brilliant *bizarrerie* of Brachiano's strangling threads a theatrical
tightrope. These are the crucial ten lines:

> *Enter Vittoria and the attend[ants].*
> *Gasparo*: Strangle him in private. What! will you call him againe
>   To live in treble torments? for charitie,
>   For Christian charitie, avoid the chamber. [*Exeunt.*]
> *Lodovico*: You would prate, Sir. This is a true-love knot
>   Sent from the Duke of Florence. *Brachiano is strangled.*
> *Gasparo*: What, is it done?
> *Lodovico*: The snuffe is out. No woman-keeper i'th world,
>   Though shee had practis'd seven yere at the Pest-house,
>   Could have done't quaintlyer. My Lordes hee's dead.
>   [*Enter Vittoria, Francisco, and Flamineo, with Attendants.*]
> *Omnes*: Rest to his soule.
> *Vittoria*: O mee! this place is hell.
>   *Exit Vittoria. [Gasparo and Attendants.]*
>   (V.iii.172–82)[26]

The speed, clarity, and sinister humour of the action are obvious at a

---

[26] Where the stage directions differ from Lucas, they are supplied from
Brown's edition of *The White Devil*.

reading, and the bustle of Vittoria's two entrances and two exits with her attendants is an essential part of it; but such a bustle on stage can easily become simply messy. The actual humour of her first exit could be too readily marred by the accidental humour of an actress's precipitate arrival on stage precipitately reversed. Granting Vittoria a minimum of two attendants, we have in these ten lines three people rushing on, the same three rushed off, six lines to cover the strangling, a hurried entry by five people, a divided line and the exit of four people. It is a scene in which the grotesque could step too near to farce. I am not sure how far it could be relied on to improve in performance.

No such doubts need surround the wooing scene in *The Duchess of Malfi*. Here the traditional symbolism of parting with a ring is a visual indication of the firmness of purpose towards which the words fumble.

'The tension between the visual meaning of the scene and the verbal riddles reflects the tension in the personalities caused because embarrassment prevents them from expressing their true feelings in words.[27]

One could, of course, compile *ad nauseam* from the plays of Webster and his contemporaries examples of scenes in which the read and staged values are interestingly disparate. The analysis of such scenes is intimately bound up with the whole idea of the separate study of Drama at university level. I had better move on.

In two respects at least Webster makes peculiar demands on the modern actor. He requires him to die as he has never died before, and he expects him to demand and to relinquish the audience's attention with unrivalled frequency and abruptness. The convention of the dying speech is a difficult one for actors to master in the wake of so many parodies. The problem is accentuated in Webster by the tendency of his characters to undergo a sententious change of heart *in extremis*. John Russell Brown has noted with interest the independent testimony of a number of reviewers to the impact on stage of Flamineo's lines following Cornelia's dirge:

I have a strange thing in mee, to th' which
I cannot give a name, without it bee
Compassion. (V.iv.107–9)

---

[27] R. J. Millington, 'Properties in Elizabethan Drama', unpublished M.A. thesis in the University of Manchester (1970), p. 28.

He compares it with Vittoria's equally uncharacteristic dying couplet:

O happy they that never saw the Court,
Nor ever knew great Man but by report. (V.vi.261–2)

Professor Brown's suggestion must provoke thought in anyone acting either part:

. . . perhaps Flamineo, witnessing the winding of his brother's corpse, and Vittoria facing death itself are both meant to 'come to themselves' (the phrase is Webster's), and speak their inmost, truest, thoughts and feelings.[28]

The idea has a theatrical appeal, and provides actors with a comfortingly reasonable pretext for speaking the author's words; but a reappraisal of Ferdinand in the light of his last words would be a suspect undertaking in or out of the theatre. Is there an essential difference in the case of Vittoria or Flamineo? I fear the need to reconsider the off-stage Thane of Cawdor! There is, I think, no help for Vittoria. She must die with Webster's words, not her own, on her lips. I know of no better actor's model for Senecal dying than Humphrey Bogart, who realised in countless films a new and unconditional serenity in the face of death.

The need to demand and relinquish the audience's attention is a result of Webster's fondness for a composite stage picture in which observers and observed are clearly divided from each other. If I give the method less attention than it deserves, it is because modern stage practice has made it the distinctive preserve of the director. But the rapid shifts of focus can bewilder any audience if they are not clearly defined by the actors, for whom the adjustment can be taxingly abrupt. Webster had a clear image of stage groupings as he wrote. His use of downstage and upstage areas, distance and proximity, stillness and movement, as a visible reinforcement of the action is ingenious and economical. For example, the carpet brought out by Zanche (*The White Devil*, I.ii.192) localises the lovers. They may be flanked, in performance, by Flamineo and Zanche, the licensed voyeurs, whilst Cornelia, standing upstage, completes the image of a devastated family triangle. Scenes like this are in essence *ensemble* pieces, and the visual

[28] Brown, *Shakespeare's Plays in Performance*, p. 234. B. J. Layman tends towards the same conclusion, but he confines himself, more satisfactorily, to suggesting that Flamineo comes to appreciate his sister for the first time when he hears her dying defiance (see note 30, below).

imagination that created them deserves an equal imaginativeness from those who interpret them. Webster's scenes are normally alive with movement. The stillness when it comes, as it does so memorably in *The Duchess of Malfi*, III.ii, must be a contrast. It is an irony that Antonio's trick of stealing off with Cariola should turn so quickly sour with Ferdinand's entry. Playing at spying in a world so full of intelligencers leads very quickly into spying in earnest.

The White Devil on the stage

I come finally to consider in more detail some aspects of the staging of *The White Devil*. Both Irving Ribner and B. J. Layman have particularised the play's most active polarity:

> Vittoria in her defiance stands for life, as her brother, Flamineo, stand for death.[29]

> . . . their consanguinity is as convincing as it is paradoxical. We begin to appreciate the feat when we recognise the extreme inwardness of the portrait of Flamineo as contrasted with the extreme objectivity of that of Vittoria.[30]

In Layman's words the difference begins to sound like a conflict of two acting styles, and something of the sort is, indeed, to be expected from the actors. Flamineo is the play's most constant observer, Vittoria the most consistently observed of its characters. The actor/observer is brought into direct relationship with the audience, which shares the object of his interest. Flamineo, who contrives to observe even the two murders he commits, is never under serious scrutiny until the play's last scene. Vittoria is singled out for scrutiny by Flamineo, by Camillo, by Cornelia, by Monticelso, by Francisco, and by Lodovico. Scrutinised by them, she is scrutinised also by her audience, to whom the actress consciously displays herself. It is Flamineo who does most to direct our attention towards Vittoria, and in doing so places himself at the opposite extreme of the actor/audience relationship.

A peculiar responsibility rests on the actress of a role as ambiguous as Vittoria's. She will not find it easy to reserve judgement, as the play does, on 'the superlative whore who locks in the widest possible extremes of appearance and reality'.[31] Most who play her will, I think, accept her own reading of her motives:

[29] Irving Ribner, *Jacobean Tragedy* (1962), p. 106.
[30] B. J. Layman, 'The Equilibrium of Opposites in *The White Devil*', *PMLA*, LXXIV (1959), 337.   [31] Layman, op. cit., 339.

> Summe up my faults I pray, and you shall finde,
> That beauty and gay clothes, a merry heart,
> And a good stomacke to [a] feast, are all,
> All the poore crimes that you can charge me with.
>
> (III.ii.215–18)

It may be sentimental of me to suppose it matters what the actress believes, but it seems to me unacceptable that anyone should act a Vittoria in whom the simple desire for happiness so predominates over the lust for splendour. *The White Devil* is a play without a single centre—its antinomies begin for me in that curious and, so far as I know, unexplained reference to 'so open and blacke a Theater' (*To the Reader*, ll.4–5)—but Vittoria, wrongly acted, might well usurp the position on stage.

After this initial cautionary note, I turn to discussing five aspects of *The White Devil* that I would expect to assume particular prominence in performance.

(i) *Isabella*. The part of Isabella is not without its attractions in the theatre. She exerts over the events of Act I a pressure which is brought to the level of a threat by Cornelia's angry address to Brachiano:

> Where is thy Dutchesse now, adulterous Duke?
> Thou little dreamd'st this night shee is come to Rome.
>
> (I.ii.275–6)

Her first appearance emphasises, by contrast, her gentleness:

> I do beseech you
> Intreate him mildely, let not your rough tongue
> Set us at louder variance. (II.i.10–12)

We are ready now for the necessary confrontation with Brachiano, but Webster carefully delays it for a further 130 lines, during which the violence of Brachiano's verbal battle with Francisco ends in the promise of a reconciliation to which Giovanni is the gentle spur. Brachiano's half-line:

> You have charm'd mee. (II.i.149)

immediately precedes his dialogue with his wife, and proposes for it a happy outcome, so that Brachiano's wilful misinterpretation of Isabella's 'devotion' (II.i.153) is a further unexpected reversal. Nevertheless,

Isabella maintains her part of the dialogue with some spirit, and her
final generous willingness to carry the blame for Brachiano's violation
of their marriage veils a strong and unanswerable reproach:

> I will make
> My selfe the author of your cursed vow.
> I have some cause to do it, you have none. (II.i.219–21)

She plays the part of the angry wife well enough to convince Francisco
that she is 'a foolish, mad/And Jealous woman' (II.i.266–7), but there
is a nice point of stagecraft here. Her fury is most convincing where it
is most genuine. She does not need to *act* her blistering hatred for
Vittoria. This scene required from its first actor a specific style of
acting, a formal representation of 'the Fury'. The same style is called
for from Cornelia and Vittoria.

> What fury rais'd thee up? (I.ii.260)

asks Flamineo when Cornelia interrupts the lovemaking of Vittoria and
Brachiano; and Monticelso, on the receiving end of Vittoria's vehe-
mence in the arraignment scene, comments,

> She's turn'd fury. (III.ii.289)

So here the startled Francisco asks,

> What? turn'd fury? (II.i.247)

There is much meat for both actress and critic in a comparison of
these three 'Fury' scenes. Webster's skill in the creation of Isabella will
be vindicated by it. Her death in dumb-show gives a contrastingly
silent indication of her generosity.

(ii) *The murder of Marcello.* Immediately before the quarrel between
Flamineo and Marcello that gives Flamineo the pretext for his experimental murder of his brother, there is a brief and startling incident:

> *Enter Cornelia.*
> *Cornelia*: Is this your pearch, you haggard? flye to'th stewes.
> [*Strikes Zanche.*]
> *Flamineo*: You should be clapt by th'heeles now: strike i'th Court!
> [*Exit Cornelia.*] (V.i.178–9)

It seems to me that the sudden entry through one stage door, the striking of an almost unprefaced blow, and the immediate exit through another stage door is exactly and ghoulishly parodied by Flamineo in the murder of Marcello:

> *Enter Flamineo.*
>
> *Flamineo*: I have brought your weapon backe.
>
> *Flamineo runnes Marcello through.*
>
> *Cornelia*: Ha, O my horrour!
>
> *Marcello*: You have brought it home indeed.
>
> *Cornelia*: Helpe, oh he's murdered.
>
> *Flamineo*: Do you turne your gaule up? I'le to sanctuary,
> And send a surgeon to you. [*Exit Flamineo.*] (V.ii.14–19)

The similarity of the two incidents can hardly fail to strike home on stage. For Flamineo it involves a maximalising of the sensation of murder, with an additional sardonic twist. In this further mutilation of the family, his imitative action implies, the blame is as much Cornelia's as his.

(iii) *Kissing—a figure in action.*[32] Our first reference to Brachiano and Vittoria is made by Lodovico, who immediately establishes the nature of their relationship.

> Vittoria, she that might have got my pardon
> For one kisse to the Duke. (I.i.43–4)

When they come together on stage they go to it with no more than a nod towards the preliminary courtesies. The commentary on their first kiss is provided by Zanche:

> See now they close. (I.ii.204)

So that when, in reply to Isabella's modest enquiry,

> Doth not my absence from you two moneths,
> Merit one kisse?   (II.i.159–60)

Brachiano claims that,

> I do not use to kisse.

we have the evidence of our own eyes to declare him a prevaricator. The *not*-kissing of Isabella should, in the gesture of a competent

---

[32] The phrase is taken from H. T. Price, 'The Function of Imagery in Webster', *PMLA*, LXX (1955), 717–39.

actress, be as visually outstanding as was the kissing of Vittoria, but the language will do the work if the actress doesn't. Isabella evokes the memory of 'pure' kisses in the past:

> You have oft for these two lippes
> Neglected Cassia or the naturall sweetes
> Of the Spring-violet.   (II.i.168–70)

The imagery adds bitters to the tainted kissing of Vittoria and the Duke. Brachiano's response is to increase the shrillness of his invective, and finally—in action a significantly villainous reversal of the proper function of kissing—he seals with a kiss his resolution to end all bodily contact with his wife:

> Your hand I'le kisse,
> This is the latest ceremony of my love,
> Hence-forth I'le never lye with thee.   (II.i.195–7)

He makes a kiss, the first ceremony of love, love's last rite. Isabella's death from kissing his picture is a cruel confirmation of the death of her marriage.

The figure of kissing recurs at the end of the play. In his anger at Vittoria's seeming duplicity, the action of kissing creates in Brachiano a moment of remorse:

> That hand, that cursed hand, which I have wearied
> With doting kisses! O my sweetest Dutchesse
> How lovelie art thou now!   (IV.ii.99–101)

It is with a half-humorous eye for the fittest punishment for the now repentant 'kissing Duke' that Vittoria answers his, 'Is not this lip mine?' with,

> Yes: thus to bite it off, rather than give it thee. (IV.ii.135–6)

But Flamineo is standing by with wise advice for the preservation of his sister's dishonour:

> Hand her, my Lord, and kisse her.   (IV.ii.170)

The reconciliation is arrived at precisely in that order. Brachiano first takes Vittoria's hand, and then, with further encouragement from Flamineo:

Stop her mouth, with a sweet kisse, my Lord. (IV.ii.195)

kisses her, this time with Flamineo providing the commentary:

So—now the tide's turned the vessel's come about.
Hee's a sweet armefull.   (IV.ii.196–7)

The fitting of punishment to crime, threatened by Vittoria, and prefigured in the poisoning of the portrait's lips, is carried out by Francisco. In a moment of rare altruism that recalls Isabella's generous care for others at her death, Brachiano warns Vittoria:

Do not kisse me, for I shall poyson thee. (V.iii.27)

The plight of the kissing Duke who cannot kiss is savagely ironical.

(iv) *Laughter—a paradoxical figure.* In the dumb-show presenting Isabella's death Julio and Christophero[33] wash the lips of Brachiano's portrait with poison and 'putting off their spectacles they depart laughing' (II.ii.23). In a play so radically concerned with the divergence of appearance and reality, it is scarcely to be expected that simple laughter will find a place. Laughter in *The White Devil* is generally the product or the cause of disturbance. On-stage laughter can enclose the actors in a world suddenly more markedly separate from that of the audience, just as nothing more certainly isolates two people in public than the sharing of a private joke. Something like this happens in the confusing and, I think, confused III.iii of *The White Devil*. Flamineo's feigned distraction gives him the liberty of a licensed fool, the instigator of dangerous laughter. When Lodovico joins him in striking a studied posture of melancholy, the spectacle provokes laughter in Antonelli and Gasparo; but the posturing is a flimsy disguise for the real cause each has for melancholy. When Lodovico receives news of his pardon, he laughs in earnest, Flamineo in the absurdity of his servitude. Lodovico now assumes the fool's license:

Lodovico: Your sister is a damnable whore.
Flamineo: Ha?
Lodovico: Looke you; I spake that laughing. (III.iii.105-6)

The text suggests that Flamineo is more offended by Lodovico's joy than by his insult; and with the same experimental sensationalism that governs his murdering of Camillo and Marcello he turns the tables very deliberately on Lodovico:

---

[33] Lucas retains Q's inclusion of this character. Without much conviction, so do I.

> This laughter scurvily becomes your face,
> If you will not be melancholy, be angry. *Strikes him.*
> See, now I laugh too. (III.iii.118–20)

I write without conviction about this scene, since it continues to puzzle me. I do not believe that it could be saved from confusion in performance. But we must, I think, recognise in the dramatist who prefaces Ferdinand's fateful entry with the merry making of the Duchess, Antonio, and Cariola a peculiar interest in the sound and action of laughter. 'Me thinkes I see her laughing', says the Ferdinand who has just discovered the Duchess's remarriage; and the verb unexpectedly confounds the sound with the sight of laughter. (II.v.52). In the final scene of *The White Devil* Lodovico remembers how Flamineo once struck him, and turns Francisco's vengeance into his own:

> Sirha you once did strike mee, Ile strike you
> Into the Center.   (V.vi.191–2)

But Flamineo repeats the laughter of the earlier scene:

Lodovico: Dost laugh?
Flamineo: Wouldst have me dye, as I was borne, in whining?
                                        (V.vi.195–6)

Flamineo's bitter wit, flung in the teeth of life throughout the play, turns laughter into a weapon against human pretensions. Faced with 'An everlasting could', he dies with his best joke.

(v) *The Ambassadors*. Having discussed four notable Websterian achievements, I end with what looks to me distinctly like a failure. The Ambassadors first appear in the play in a passage over the stage during which they are belittlingly described by Flamineo and the courtly Lawyer (III.i.67–79). Only five of them are mentioned in the stage directions to III.i, but six are present in court for the arraignment of Vittoria. The purpose of their presence is briefly explained by Francisco and Monticelso (III.i.1–8), who call them 'grave' and hope that their being convinced of Vittoria's guilt,

> shall make her infamous
> To all our neighbouring Kingdomes.

Their comments at the trial suggest only that this hope of Monticelso's is disappointed. After the Cardinal's fierce 'character' of a whore, the

French Ambassador's, 'Shee hath lived ill', calls from the English Ambassador the moderate comment,

> Trew, but the Cardinals too bitter. (III.ii.110-11)

and the English Ambassador seems at this stage to be speaking for the audience. It is perhaps a sign of Vittoria's self-conscious femininity that she should be so much more aware of the presence of the Ambassadors than anyone else. Is it as sexually vulnerable old men that she addresses them?

> Humbly thus,
> Thus low, to the most worthy and respected
> Leigier Embassadors, my modesty
> And womanhood I tender.   (III.ii.134-7)

Certainly the appeal is effective:

> *Eng. Emb.*: Shee hath a brave spirit.
> *Monticelso*: Well, well, such counterfet Jewels
> Make trew [ones] oft suspected. (III.ii.144-6)

After this telling metaphor of Monticelso's it is no longer clear that the English Ambassador speaks for the audience; and when Vittoria turns on Monticelso with a gesture towards the Ambassadors, it is clear that she is confident of their interest:

> if you bee my accuser
> Pray cease to be my Judge, come from the Bench,
> Give in your evidence 'gainst me, and let these
> Be moderators.   (III.ii.233-6)

Monticelso's rush to judgement, a sudden redirection of the arraignment, is, then, an admission that the duel of wits has gone against him; and the important evidence of this is the behaviour of the Ambassadors. But in what follows they show up very weakly, remaining silent until they are abruptly ushered off stage by Monticelso, still without a word, when the news of Isabella's death is received. In the scene that follows they are reduced to acting as feed-men for the 'distracted' Flamineo's bitter wit. It would be virtually impossible for an actor to endow with dignity the successive entries and single lines of the Ambassadors from Savoy, France, and England. Their part in the papal election is too slight to alter what has been previously established. Crowd scenes are never easy for an actor, who is likely to settle for repeating mannerisms that his earlier appearances have justified. But it is these Ambassadors who enter with Giovanni on the scene of final slaughter, and it is the English Ambassador's resourceful order,

Keepe backe the Prince, shoot, shoot—(V.vi.282)

that prevents a further desperate fight by Lodovico. Surely even Webster doesn't intend order to be restored by six doddering old men and a juvenile.

After the poisoning of Brachiano, Flamineo has a curious single-line reference:

I feare the Embassadours are likewise poyson'd. (V.iii.12)

Why? I cannot escape the feeling that Webster attempted more with the Ambassadors than he has managed to bring off.

NOTE. Productions of *The White Devil* at the National Theatre, the Everyman Theatre, Liverpool and the Stables Theatre Club, Manchester all opened in 1969 *after* the York Symposium.

The Duchess of Malfi *on the Stage*

ROGER WARREN

The Duchess of Malfi *on the Stage*

Ferdinand: Who took the ring oftenest?
Silvio: Antonio Bologna, my lord.
Ferdinand: Our sister duchess' great master of her household?
    Give him the jewel: . . .
    How do you like my Spanish jennet?
Roderigo: He is all fire.
Ferdinand: I am of Pliny's opinion, I think he was begot
    by the wind; he runs as if he were ballasted with
    quicksilver. . . .
    You are a good horseman, Antonio—you have excellent
    riders in France; what do you think of good horsemanship?
Antonio: Nobly, my lord—as out of the Grecian horse issued
    many famous princes, so, out of brave horsemanship,
    arise the first sparks of growing resolution, that
    raise the mind to noble action.
Ferdinand: You have bespoke it worthily.

(*D.M.*, I.i.88–147)[1]

T H I S   I S   N O T one of the more celebrated passages of *The Duchess of Malfi*, but it is important in helping the director to establish the 'tone' of much of the play, for there is a surprising amount of this kind of writing in the text, a poised and elegant, often witty, expression of sociable courtly activities which frames the action, and within which the horrors are unfolded. This spirited discussion of horses and riding has a vigour and vitality which suggests a very different court atmosphere from, for example, that of *The Revenger's Tragedy*, where Vindice's railing satirical tone reduces the other characters from the start to macabre grotesques:

---

[1] All quotations are from J. R. Brown, ed., *The Duchess of Malfi*, The Revels Plays (1964); afterwards referred to as 'Brown, *Duchess*'.

Duke; royal lecher; go, grey-hair'd adultery;
And thou his son, as impious steep'd as he;
And thou his bastard, true-begot in evil;
And thou his duchess, that will do with devil.
Four excellent characters. (*R.T.*, I.i.1–5)

Clifford Leech contrasts this with Webster's method, 'which has the flux of life in it'.[2] The question for the director is 'What *kind* of life?' It is a different kind even from that of *The White Devil*, opening with a frenzied 'Banish'd?' from a character who is said to have been 'begotten in an earthquake' and as early as line 52 promises,

> I'll make Italian cut-works in their guts
> If ever I return.

It seems to me of great importance that, by contrast, we only come to Ferdinand's savagery by degrees, and that, even then, we are constantly reminded of other considerations.

Professor Leech also thinks it right to 'begin with a commentary on an imagined performance'.[3] To some extent I shall attempt this, but without any laborious scene-by-scene assessment of 'stage requirements', aiming rather to establish the basic approach required, 'what is important in't'. This involves, primarily, as J. R. Brown observes, 'a study of [Webster's] use of language and his dramatic technique—a study of the kind of dramatic experience he communicates to an audience'.[4] But at the same time, I shall try to establish the precise impact of this technique on an audience, with particular reference to the 1960 Stratford production. Professor Brown feels that because 'the Five-Act structure was ignored' in this production, because 'there was no presence-chamber', and because of one particularly damaging cut (Bosola's last couplet), there resulted 'such neglect' that the 'tragedy cannot be said to have had a fair chance in the theatre'.[5] But I was not alone[6] in finding much of the essence of the play brought out in what

---

[2] 'Webster: *The Duchess of Malfi*', *Studies in English Literature*, 8 (1963), 11; afterwards referred to as 'Leech'. Gunnar Boklund, *The Duchess of Malfi: Sources, Themes, Characters* (Cambridge, Mass., 1962), p. 82, also points this contrast.

[3] Leech, p. 7.

[4] *The White Devil*, The Revels Plays (1960), pp. xliii–xliv.

[5] Brown, *Duchess*, p. lix.

[6] See the press notices quoted below, especially T. C. Worsley, *The Financial Times* (16 December 1960).

one critic called 'this very straightforward and direct production', and particularly in Peggy Ashcroft's demonstration that there is more to the play than the macabre. Further, I do not share Professor Brown's conviction that it is essential for the producer to emphasise the presence-chamber; together with the other Jacobean rituals which embody meanings (the Cardinal's investiture, the masque elements in the madmen scene), these are the hardest things to make significant for a modern audience, since, without modern equivalents, they can easily become mere decoration, what Donald McWhinnie, the 1960 director, consciously shunned: 'no elaborate naturalism, to amuse and mislead the eager eye'.[7] Rather, the atmosphere of this proud, aristocratic world must be established by emphasising the *significant* in its sets and costumes, and above all by the speaking and acting—by a particular attention to language and to the rhythms of 'the speaking voice', for, as J. R. Mulryne has it, the play's 'peculiar tone is . . . deeply influenced by the quiet, uninsistent rhythms of conversation', 'a more leisurely manner'[8] than in *The White Devil*. This kind of approach preserves us, I think, from what Professor Brown calls the rigorous search 'for a unified "moral vision" ' which has simply 'divided opinion',[9] for it places emphasis on specifically dramatic features like those which H. T. Price draws attention to: 'Webster's . . . use of contrast, and . . . his superb timing'.[10] These together create a world which shows men as more than Rupert Brooke's 'writhing grubs in an immense night',[11] as more varied even than Professor Leech allows: 'there is no world imaginable but that of the fearful and the mad'.[12]

The best description of Webster's world in this play is Professor Brown's: 'a dark sensationalism and menace, contrasted with softness'.[13] 'Set in the courts of princes', there is often air and light and gaiety as well as the more famous waxwork horror. It is dramatically advantageous that this should be so, for the tortures, the corruptions, and the Duchess's heroic end, all have the more impact by being contrasted with a more normal mode of behaviour. That is why the discussion of

[7] All quotations from Donald McWhinnie are from *Plays and Players* (February 1961), p. 6.

[8] '*The White Devil* and *The Duchess of Malfi*', *Stratford-upon-Avon Studies 1: Jacobean Theatre* (1960), pp. 214, 216; afterwards referred to as 'Mulryne'.

[9] Brown, *Duchess*, p. xlix.

[10] 'The Function of Imagery in Webster', *PMLA*, LXX (1955), 720.

[11] *John Webster and the Elizabethan Drama* (1916), p. 158.

[12] *John Webster: A Critical Study* (1951), p. 31.

[13] Brown, *Duchess*, p. xlix.

horses at the start is important. It has to establish an atmosphere of aristocratic vitality which can be corrupted:

> but if't chance
> Some curs'd example poison't near the head,
> *Death, and diseases through the whole land spread.* (I.i.13–15)

Ferdinand refers to 'a rank pasture here, i' th' court' (I.i.306), but it is necessary to stress that it is he who makes it so. Nor should even he appear outwardly sinister. One review of the Stratford production was disappointed because

> The brothers are outwardly ordinary. Max Adrian's Cardinal is, in aspect, just a Cardinal. Mr Porter's Ferdinand is not made to look exotically fearful. . . . the Cardinal's mistress . . . is alone in present-ing the sinister orchid-like outward show in keeping with the Web-sterean atmosphere.[14]

But the truth is that there is not one 'Websterean atmosphere', but two. Antonio stresses that the Duchess and her brothers are 'three fair medals, Cast in one figure' (I.i.188–9); it is in 'temper' that they are different. Webster opens out his view of the court: as well as the grace and wit of the Duchess and Antonio, there is the vigorous conversa-tion of the lords in the horse scene or in the mockery of Count Mala-teste—thereby serving to stress Antonio's own qualities by contrast[15]—and the honesty of the Marquis of Pescara. Dr Mulryne condemns this scene as 'almost childishly naive',[16] but it works perfectly well on the stage, though, it must be admitted, lacking the verbal power or wit of most of the other scenes. And in the scene of the Cardinal's investiture, the formal ritual is commented on by pilgrims: 'the cardinal/Bears himself much too cruel' (III.iv.26–7). Do not mistake me: I am not trying to play down the horrors, or to claim *The Duchess* as a 'balanced' morality, or to question for a moment Professor Brown's claim that 'certainly the main effect of the tragedy is the terror, pity, and admira-tion aroused by [the Duchess's] death';[17] but the tragedy gains, not loses, impact on the stage in that, more than most Jacobean plays, it shows us the domestic and the gentle as well as the horrific.

[14] *Theatre World* (February 1961).
[15] Cf. III.i.39–45.
[16] Mulryne, p. 219.
[17] Brown, *Duchess*, p. liv.

I

Doth not the colour of my hair 'gin to change?
When I wax gray, I shall have all the court
Powder their hair with arras, to be like me:—
You have cause to love me; I enter'd you into my heart
Before you would vouchsafe to call for the keys. (III.ii.58–62)

Norman Rabkin notes that 'to judge from the testimony of the critics the image that lingers longest is that of the poignant hairbrushing scene, with all its implications of the explosion of the world of innocence'.[18] The dramatic critics in turn reinforce this impression, several of the most responsible singling out from the Stratford version this scene or the wooing scene, or both, for as much praise as the scenes of torture.[19] And indeed the Duchess's wooing of Antonio is a masterpiece of happy confidence, wit, gaiety, and tenderness; and if allusions to death linger beneath the lines, that deepens rather than detracts from the feeling conveyed, just as the abundant Elizabethan vitality and relish for life seem to have been sharpened by their constant awareness and reminders of Death:

You do tremble:
Make not your heart so dead a piece of flesh
To fear, more than to love me: sir, be confident—
What is't distracts you? This is flesh, and blood, sir;
'Tis not the figure cut in alabaster
Kneels at my husband's tomb. Awake, awake, man!
I do here put off all vain ceremony,
And only do appear to you a young widow
That claims you for her husband, and like a widow,
I use but half a blush in't. (I.i.450–59)

Robert Ornstein makes a relevant comparison: 'In temperament she is a heroine of Shakespearean romantic comedy, graceful, witty, wanton

---

[18] *Twentieth Century Interpretations of the Duchess of Malfi* (Englewood Cliffs, N.J., 1968), p. 7.
[19] Cf. *The Times* (16 December 1960); T. C. Worsley, *The Financial Times* (16 December 1960); Philip Hope-Wallace, *The Guardian* (17 December 1960); Robert Speaight, *The Tablet* (23 December 1960); H. A. L. Craig, *The New Statesman* (24 December 1960).

and innocent at the same time, who woos and wins her husband.'[20] If
the actress will capture Webster's rhythms, the half-jesting tone, and
the imagery which makes a great plea for happy life, contrasting the
warmth of her flesh with the chill of the alabaster on the tomb, she will
start to build up one aspect of the Duchess to set against the tormented
figure, and a no less vivid one. This is precisely what Peggy Ashcroft
achieved, as T. C. Worsley recorded in detail:

> The beauty of Dame Peggy's performance was in the long prepara-
> tion that leads up to [her] death scene. . . . She is not content merely
> to make the Duchess good. She defines with any number of touches
> the nature of the goodness. As we see her first the Duchess is a
> woman of high natural spirits and vitality, and it is that buoyancy of
> heart that it is so terrible to see being desolated. This buoyancy is
> beautifully expressed in the early scene where she proposes to her
> Antonio, and it swells in confidence and ease as their love-play
> develops.[21]

This development matches Webster's own as the happy intimacy between husband and wife is expressed in confident wit:

Duchess: You get no lodging here tonight, my lord.
Antonio: Indeed, I must persuade one:—
Duchess: Very good:
   I hope in time 'twill grow into a custom
   That noblemen shall come with cap and knee,
   To purchase a night's lodging of their wives.
Antonio: I must lie here.
Duchess: Must? you are a lord of mis-rule.
Antonio: Indeed, my rule is only in the night.
Duchess: To what use will you put me?
Antonio: We'll sleep together:—
Duchess: Alas, what pleasure can two lovers find in sleep?

                           (III.ii.2–10)

In these scenes, Antonio has as important a part to play as the
Duchess; he matches her in wit and in elegance, contrary to some
critical views.[22] In the wooing scene, he is quick to compliment her

---

[20] *The Moral Vision of Jacobean Tragedy* (Madison, Wisc., 1960), p. 147.
[21] *The Financial Times* (16 December 1960).
[22] e.g. Robert Ornstein, op. cit., pp. 144–5.

'*beauteous* excellence' (and she no less quick to take up the compliment); it is he who first mentions the sacrament of marriage; and he is not slow to carry her words and actions to their logical conclusion:

> *Duchess*: One of your eyes is blood-shot—use my ring to't,
> They say 'tis very sovereign—'twas my wedding ring,
> And I did vow never to part with it,
> But to my second husband.
> *Antonio*: You have parted with it now.
> *Duchess*:   Yes, to help your eyesight.
> *Antonio*: You have made me stark blind.
> *Duchess*:   How?
> *Antonio*: There is a saucy, and ambitious devil
> Is dancing in this circle. (I.i.404-13)

His confident urbanity shows most clearly when he advises Cariola to marry:

> O fie upon this single life! forgo it!
> We read how Daphne, for her peevish flight,
> Became a fruitless bay-tree; Syrinx turn'd
> To the pale empty reed; Anaxarete
> Was frozen into marble. (III.ii.24-8)

Here the lightness of touch ('*peevish* flight', '*fruitless* bay-tree', '*pale empty* reed') is a fine example of that self-assured wit which indicates awareness and confidence, not frivolity; this is what courtliness really means, not pomposity or self-display; and in this, Antonio's poise has something in common with a much greater evocation of these metamorphoses:

> The *Gods*, that mortal Beauty chase,
> Still in a Tree did end their race.
> *Apollo* hunted *Daphne* so,
> Only that She might Laurel grow.
> And *Pan* did after *Syrinx* speed,
> Not as a Nymph, but for a Reed. (Marvell, *The Garden*, 27-32)

The mood which Antonio's speech establishes most resembles, I think, the gaiety of Florizel as he likewise uses humorous transformations of the gods to persuade Perdita to set aside her fears and be cheerful:

> The gods themselves,
> Humbling their deities to love, have taken
> The shapes of beasts upon them: Jupiter
> Became a bull, and bellow'd; the green Neptune
> A ram and bleated; and the fire-rob'd god,
> Golden Apollo, a poor humble swain,
> As I seem now. (*The Winter's Tale*, IV.iv.25–31)

The effect is that Antonio joins with the Duchess to provide a warmly human contrast to the sterner scenes later on. And as with the Duchess, the actor of Antonio must be able to capture the wit and poise of these lines; one critic noted how Derek Godfrey in 1960 'did it so softly, with such . . . poise, that he was a good match for the Duchess'.[23] Fresh from presenting, some months earlier, the most complete Orsino I have seen, the only one to realise both the aristocratic grace *and* the humour of the part, Mr Godfrey was then able to show how much vital gaiety *The Duchess* in fact contains. But he did more. He was also (rightly) commended for 'ris[ing] to the sighing Echo scene',[24] thereby showing that Antonio's wit, like that of the Duchess, is a sign, not of frivolity, but of sensitivity.

The Echo scene is another impressive contrast to the horror scenes, so beautifully written that F. L. Lucas goes so far as to claim, 'If we ask what Webster could do that his contemporaries could not, the answer lies not in horror-scenes, but in such things as this'.[25] Certainly, Antonio 'brooding . . . over the ruined church at Milan'[26] and hearing his wife's voice has to be given maximum emphasis, for two reasons. First, the still gravity of Antonio's speech indicates a thoughtful awareness which was suggested by different means in his courtly wit earlier:

> I do love these ancient ruins:
> We never tread upon them but we set
> Our foot upon some reverend history.
> And questionless, here in this open court,
> Which now lies naked to the injuries
> Of stormy weather, some men lie interr'd
> Lov'd the church so well, and gave so largely to't,

[23] H. A. L. Craig, *The New Statesman* (24 December 1960).
[24] J. C. Trewin, *The Illustrated London News* (17 December 1960).
[25] *The Complete Works of John Webster*, 4 vols. (1927), ii, 20
[26] ibid.

They thought it should have canopy'd their bones
Till doomsday; but all things have their end:

(V.iii.9–17)

Even more important, of course, is that the Duchess's voice in the echo
indicates that, as Professor Brown says, she 'is seen as clearly as possible to influence the action after her death'.[27] The keyword here is
'seen', for he notes further that 'Antonio's words seem to imply a
lighting-effect that reveals the duchess herself within a grave',[28] and he
refers to a similar device required in *The Second Maiden's Tragedy* of
1611. This is one place where the staging needs physically to reinforce
the verbal delivery; with modern lighting techniques, the physical
Duchess should be made visible to give extra impact to some of the
most beautiful and touching lines of the play:

Antonio: Echo, I will not talk with thee,
       For thou art a dead thing.
Echo: *Thou art a dead thing.*
Antonio: My duchess is asleep now,
       And her little ones, I hope sweetly: O heaven,
       Shall I never see her more?
Echo: *Never see her more.*
Antonio: I mark'd not one repetition of the echo
       But that; and on the sudden, a clear light
       Presented me a face folded in sorrow. (V.iii.38–45)

It is at such moments as these—at once beautiful as lyricism and
hauntingly effective when realised fully on the stage—that one marvels
afresh at the sheer insensitivity of William Archer and at the 'numb
palate' with which one dramatic critic with superb accuracy has charged
him.[29] This 'numb palate' is what the director and actors can least
afford when tackling Webster. 'During a performance the audience
must . . . be held by strong, intelligent speech',[30] says Professor
Brown; he might have added witty, elegant speech as well. For the
scenes involving the Duchess and Antonio, and to a lesser extent
the rest of the court also, require an evocation of the 'courts of princes';
but this does not mean pomposity or what Professor Brown calls

[27] Brown, *Duchess*, p. xxix.
[28] ibid, p. xxxv.
[29] Hilary Spurling, *The Spectator* (14 October 1966).
[30] Brown, *Duchess*, p. xlv.

'the fancy-dress roundabout of modern stage-settings',[31] but rather
the suggestion of an attitude of mind, the elegance and poise which
comes of confidence, and wit which expresses awareness. Webster's
text has provided the material for this; the director must create a
frame which will allow such moments of lyrical gaiety or tender quiet-
ness to have their full effect. Donald McWhinnie, directing the Stratford production, was well aware of this:

> The horrors don't need underlining . . . but the gaiety and delicacy of
> the first part of the play do. . . . remind the audience of the sunlight
> outside whenever you can; the glare of the market-place, the warmth
> of the square where Antonio and Delio meet Pescara in the midst
> of the carnage.

And though he was not wholly successful in conveying the full 'light'
of the play, he did provide an appropriate setting for the courtly
beginning—a fountain on a honey-coloured flagged floor (see Plate 2)—
and for the Pescara and Echo scenes. Above all, in Peggy Ashcroft and
Derek Godfrey he had players whose intelligence and vocal control
could realise the essence of their courtly world, not just its outward
trappings.

II

It would be a gross misrepresentation of the play to claim that these
Duchess–Antonio scenes dominate. Of course they don't; but the point
is that they have a grace and vitality of their own which must not be
neglected in performance, otherwise the contrast which Webster *has*
achieved will be lost. Yet even so, the scenes of corruption and torture
have a fire and vigour about them which hardly justifies Rupert
Brooke's 'writhing grubs' or Harold Hobson's 'invariable filthiness'.[32]
Donald McWhinnie emphasised how 'strangely vital' the 'corrupt'
society of the play is, and this, again, stems from Webster's imagery,
phrasing, and rhythm. Travis Bogard shows how Webster's 'tragic
satire' which 'confronts the audience with the loathsome reality of the
processes of natural decay' is expressed through 'comparisons of men
with animals, insects, and rapacious birds'.[33] But it is important to note

---

[31] Brown, *Duchess*, p. xxxix.   [32] *The Sunday Times* (18 December 1960).
[33] *The Tragic Satire of John Webster* (Berkeley and Los Angeles, 1955), pp.
133–4.

the vigour with which each of these comparisons is made: the audience is held by the 'economy and sharpness of phrase'[34] with which Webster conveys the corrupting influences of his aristocratic world. From the first scene, the actors can hold attention with the most pointed and edged comparisons: the Cardinal is 'a melancholy churchman; the spring in his face is nothing but the engendering of toads' (I.i.157–8). The brothers 'are like plum-trees, that grow crooked over standing pools; they are rich, and o'erladen with fruit' (I.i.49–51). Later in the play, the courtiers use similarly arresting images to indicate the more-than-human anger of the brothers:

> *Pescara:* Mark Prince Ferdinand:
>   A very salamander lives in's eye,
>   To mock the eager violence of fire.
> *Silvio:* That cardinal hath made more bad faces with his oppression
>   than ever Michael Angelo made good ones; he lifts up's nose,
>   like a foul porpoise before a storm—(III.iii.48–53)

Here again, the more normal the brothers appear in outward show, the more strikingly such comments may focus attention on the evil in their minds. This vitality and sharpness enables Webster to characterise the evil figures so that they are not cardboard villains—indeed, rather to the perplexity of some of the commentators. But these characters work well on the stage, so long as the actors respond to *all* the lines they are given.

The most obvious case is the Cardinal: the character becomes considerably more interesting when, again in a curiously arresting speech, this cold, evil man, villain and poisoner, is shown to be troubled by matters of the conscience:

> I am puzzled in a question about hell:
> He says, in hell there's one material fire,
> And yet it shall not burn all men alike.
> Lay him by:— how tedious is a guilty conscience!
> When I look into the fish-ponds, in my garden,
> Methinks I see a thing, arm'd with a rake
> That seems to strike at me: (V.v.1–7)

This is another place where Webster has immensely sharpened one of his famous borrowings. R. W. Dent cites Lavater's *Of Ghostes and*

---

[34] H. T. Price, 'The Function of Imagery in Webster', *PMLA*, LXX (1955), 719.

Spirites Walking by Nyght,[35] where Pertinax, 'for ye space of three dayes before he was slayne by a thrust, sawe a certayne shaddowe in one of his fishepondes, whiche with a sword ready drawen threatened to slay him', and claims that, 'should we some day discover a version . . . employing both "thing" . . . and "rake" . . . , our admiration would be still further qualified'. I fail to see why. In the first place, imitation or not, a rake is a much more suitably startling object for attack than a sword, and greatly adds to the menace and disquiet of the 'thing'; it communicates the Cardinal's spiritual disturbance perfectly, and would still do so if Webster had stolen *all* the details. In the second place, it suggests the way in which the Cardinal, like the other characters, sees life in terms of his material surroundings, needs to establish whether hell is a 'material' fire or not, and is most readily disturbed by apparitions seen in terms of his own palace garden. And this, in turn, emphasises the need to place the Cardinal, like the others, in a civilised Jacobean world—a world of gardens and fish-ponds as well as coffins and madmen. Whether or not Webster stole the entire passage, rake and all, he inserted it at a point where it would have maximum dramatic surprise, just before the close, and provided the director with yet another pointer to the world he has created.

Webster presents these moments of awareness or shifts of character with bold strokes and heightened language; they are not subtle effects, but they work if the actors are unafraid of them. This applies particularly to Bosola. His mockery of the deceptions of courtly life, the other side of the coin from Antonio and the Duchess, is expressed by combining vivid comparisons with conversational rhythm:

> There was a lady in France, that having had the smallpox, flayed the skin off her face to make it more level; and whereas before she looked like a nutmeg-grater, after she resembled an abortive hedgehog. (II.i.26–9)

But Webster does not let Bosola's extensive acid mockery remain unfocused: his sharp phrases reveal an awareness of what lies behind the 'rich tissue' worn by Ferdinand:

> Thus the devil
> Candies all sins o'er; . . . what's my place?

[35] See R. W. Dent, *John Webster's Borrowing* (Berkeley and Los Angeles, 1960), pp. 32–3; and also R. K. R. Thornton, 'The Cardinal's Rake in *The Duchess of Malfi*', *Notes and Queries*, ccxiv (August 1969).

The provisorship o' th' horse? say then, my corruption
Grew out of horse-dung: (I.i.275–87)

At the same time, he anticipates Ferdinand's view of the court as a
'rank pasture', and turns the vigorously healthy discussion of horses at
the start of the play to a corrupter use. Professor Brown comments that
'Webster seems to have been unafraid of the psychological problems
occasioned by joining . . . many rôles, but gave his Bosola the marks of
an ambitious malcontent'[36] as well as murderer and general factotum.
As with the Cardinal and Ferdinand, contrary or hidden motives are all
part of the variety of the characters. Ferdinand, in particular, is an
extraordinarily early example of what we like to think of as a modern
invention—the character with half-suggested, understated motivation:
'Do not you ask the reason: but be satisfied, I say I would not'
(I.i.257–8). Critics have complained about something which is part of
the essential make-up of the play: I apologise for traversing much-
trodden ground, but the very variety of the characters is only really
evident in performance, where scrupulous consistency is not essential,
and where hints and suggestions can be as—or more—potent than bald
statements. In another context, Professor Brown has said: 'Possibly
new plays like . . . Pinter's *The Dwarfs*, which use fantastic happenings
to present the fantastic unrealities of half-conscious thought, have
accustomed actors to playing unrealistic situations boldly.'[37] Pinter is
especially apposite here because, like Webster, he writes with such
immediacy and power that if motives in either are unclear, it is unlikely
to be the fault of muddled or incompetent writing: they are intentional.
For a modern actor, used to parts like Ruth in *The Homecoming* or the
entire cast of *The Collection*, where much is suggested but nothing
made specific, a part like Ferdinand should cause no trouble, particularly since Webster has provided so much detail.

To start with, Ferdinand's tendency to sudden moods and remarks
which conceal what he really feels is established at the outset when
he suddenly turns a joke sour, a passage I deliberately omitted when I
quoted the discussion of horses at the beginning:

Why do you laugh? Methinks you that are courtiers should be my
touch-wood, take fire, when I give fire; that is, laugh when I laugh,
were the subject never so witty—(I.i.122–5)

---

[36] Brown, *Duchess*, p. xxviii.
[37] *Shakespeare's Plays in Performance* (1966), p. 189.

Professor Brown rightly comments that this emphasises Ferdinand's
'control' and 'the precarious life of attendance at court',[38] but it also
does more: it accustoms us to the volatile outbursts of one who has
hidden thoughts lurking beneath his courtly manner. (It is the necessity to establish this court atmosphere that makes me doubt Professor
Brown's conjecture that 'ring' and 'tilt' in the horses passage may be
bawdy references, though this of course would help to make clear the
sexual preoccupation of Ferdinand's thoughts.) But there can surely be
no doubt of the 'half-hidden sexual urgency'[39] of the dramatic first
clash between the Duchess and Ferdinand, where the Duchess's sharp
reaction to Ferdinand's obscenity results in a quick shift of meaning on
his part which only serves, as always in the theatre, to emphasise his
original innuendo:

> *Ferdinand*: A visor and a mask are whispering-rooms
>   That were ne'er built for goodness: fare ye well:—
>   And women like that part which, like the lamprey,
>   Hath ne'er a bone in't.
> *Duchess*:   Fie Sir!
> *Ferdinand*:   Nay,
>   I mean the tongue: variety of courtship;—
>   What cannot a neat knave with a smooth tale
>   Make a woman believe? Farewell, lusty widow. [*Exit.*]
> *Duchess*: Shall this move me? If all my royal kindred
>   Lay in my way unto this marriage,
>   I'd make them my low footsteps: (I.i.334–43)

This encounter is very important for two reasons. First, it implies
firmly Ferdinand's sexual obsession; second, it brings the two central
characters together in a vigorous clash and emphasises the Duchess's
defiance. This clash recurs in similar terms in the middle of the play,
and also at the climax, when the Duchess makes her last defiance, and
Ferdinand's obsession with her (now dead) body drives him mad. This
clear dramatic opposition of these two must be brought out in performance, so that Professor Bradbrook must have seen some pretty lop-
sided productions for her to claim that Bosola 'so dominates any presentation of the play that the loves and crimes of the House of Aragon
seem but a background to his tragedy'.[40] For length of commenting

---

[38] Brown, *Duchess*, p. 16.   [39] Brown, *Duchess*, p. xlvi.
[40] 'Two Notes Upon Webster', *MLR*, XLII (1947), 289.

speeches, though it gives Bosola special status, does not make him dominate Ferdinand or the Duchess: the very *mysteriousness* of Ferdinand's remarks and actions gives him an extra impact in performance; and if Bosola has an interesting double attitude to life—murdering and repenting and murdering again—so has the Cardinal or Ferdinand himself. Certainly, as Dr Mulryne puts it, Webster's 'subtle insight into turns of mind, the fluctuations of speech and varying of rhythm give us some grounds'[41] for the incestuous interpretation; as those rhythms and verbal emphases are what the actor has to go by, the evidence must be briefly stated.

Significantly, the first reappearance of Ferdinand after the 'lamprey' conversation is with the wild and startling cry 'I have this night digg'd up a mandrake' (II.v.1). That the cry is 'puzzling' is all part of Webster's creation of a nobleman whose impressive outside, including his speech, conceals sinister preoccupations. Since the mandrake was supposed to resemble the human form, this obsession with the Duchess's *body* is implied, but not stated directly: as Professor Brown puts it, 'his reaction involves, in some fantastic way, horror, violence and sex'.[42] This is developed by his hysterical, vigorously imaginative visualising of his sister making love:

> Excellent hyena!—talk to me somewhat, quickly,
> Or my imagination will carry me
> To see her, in the shameful act of sin.
> *Cardinal*: With whom?
> *Ferdinand*:   Happily with some strong thigh'd bargeman;
> Or one o' th' wood-yard, that can quoit the sledge,
> Or toss the bar, or else some lovely squire
> That carries coals up to her privy lodgings.
> *Cardinal*: You fly beyond your reason. (II.v.39–46)

The Cardinal's moderating comment makes Ferdinand's obsession as clear as any implication can; and the violence of his attitude is emphasised by contrast with the intimate gaiety and lack of obsession in the Duchess–Antonio scenes, a happy security stressed by Cariola's confident jest about the Duchess as 'the sprawling'st bedfellow'. This contrast is a further reason for underlining the gaiety and human warmth of these scenes in performance. Both Ferdinand's violent instability

[41] Mulryne, p. 223.
[42] Brown, *Duchess*, p. 63.

and his sexual preoccupation develop when, after his desire to 'know who leaps my sister' (II.v.77), he goes to enormous lengths to avoid seeing Antonio in the Duchess's bedroom, using language which lingers both on lustful enjoyments and the waning of these with old age:

> Whate'er thou art, that has enjoy'd my sister,—
> For I am sure thou hear'st me—for thine own sake
> Let me not know thee: . . .
> Enjoy thy lust still, . . .
> . . . And for thee, vile woman,
> If thou do wish thy lecher may grow old
> In thy embracements, . . . let not the sun
> Shine on him, till he's dead. (III.ii.90–104)

Clifford Leech concludes that Ferdinand 'identifies himself with [her]first husband because he feels sexual jealousy':[43]

> . . . thou hast ta'en that massy sheet of lead
> That hid thy husband's bones, and folded it
> About my heart.   (III.ii.112–14)

It is reasonable for Professor Leech to conclude that 'the implication of incestuous feeling seems evident'. The twice-repeated 'I will never see thee more' at the end of the scene is the farewell of a distracted lover rather than a brother; it summarises the significance of their second confrontation. This is one of those moments when one of Webster's compressed, vividly suggestive lines summarises a whole area of the play; and it is the kind of effect which can be appreciated to the full on the stage: two critics[44] have borne testimony to John Gielgud's delivery of that line, long after the event; and a third to its 'unmistakable psychological twist'.[45]

However, the reasonable question, 'Why do Ferdinand's motives need to be concealed?' needs answering. I think it is in fact a cunning and successful device to suggest a mind verging on the brink of madness, unstable from his first volatile silencing of the courtiers' laughter. And it is his last confrontation with the Duchess that tips his mind into madness. Hysteria overcomes him as he looks down at her dead face, manifested by his sudden burst of unconvincing explanations—until

---

[43] Leech, p. 17.

[44] Kenneth Tynan, *The Observer* (18 December 1960); Harold Hobson, *The Sunday Times* (18 December 1960).

[45] Audrey Williamson, *Theatre of Two Decades* (1951), p. 285.

the rhythm breaks down and the tell-tale 'her marriage!' explodes as he
passionately remembers that she married someone else:

> For let me but examine well the cause:
> What was the meanness of her match to me?
> Only I must confess, I had a hope,
> Had she continu'd widow, to have gain'd
> An infinite mass of treasure by her death:
> And that was the main cause: . . . her marriage!—
> That drew a stream of gall, quite through my heart.
> (IV.ii.281–7)

And he leaves with the first cry of real madness,

> I'll go hunt the badger, by owl-light:
> 'Tis a deed of darkness. (IV.ii.334–5)

Here again, Webster uses sharpness of phrase to suggest the frenzy of
passion—this time, the onset of madness, brought about by looking at
the Duchess's dead face.

In performance, this part must, as I suggested, be at the centre of
attention, linked, and so contrasted, with the Duchess throughout.
There are two obvious points. First, those sudden fluctuations of
phrase, tone, and rhythm in Ferdinand need a large-scale performance
unafraid of big effects, yet able to accommodate the sharp verbal twists
and turns. Indeed, the varying response of critics to the tremendous
power with which Eric Porter's Ferdinand opposed Peggy Ashcroft's
Duchess in fact testifies to his presentation of both aspects. For *Punch*'s
characteristic 'barking mad'[46] and Robert Speaight's 'a clearly incestuous motive to Ferdinand'[47] isolate what Mr Porter combined, simply
by responding to Webster's rhythms and pointing. Second, one point
neglected by Stratford was a requirement made clear enough by Webster, when he gives extra substance to the famous 'Cover her face: mine
eyes dazzle: she died young' by adding:

> She and I were twins:
> And should I die this instant, I had liv'd
> Her time to a minute. (IV.ii.267–9)

It will surely add to the impression of two characters linked by blood
yet contrasted in character if they look alike. A similar incestuous

---

[46] Eric Keown, *Punch* (28 December 1960).
[47] *The Tablet* (23 December 1960).

situation, in Act I of *Die Walküre*, was recently made particularly effective in that not only the voices but also the sensuous physical similarity of Gwyneth Jones and James King brought out the crucial point made by the orchestra time and again as brother and sister feel more and more at one as they recall that they have heard each other's voices in echoes and seen each other's faces in reflections. Wagner uses incest to convey the passionate one-ness of Siegmund and Sieglinde, Webster to convey the contrast between the Duchess and Ferdinand; but either way, physical similarity obviously helps to make the musical or verbal points. In the climactic scene of the Duchess's death, this contrast and many other strands of the play meet.

III

What in fact is the dramatic heart of this famous scene? This?

> Thou art a box of worm-seed, at best, but a salvatory of green mummy:— what's this flesh? a little crudded milk, fantastical puff-paste; our bodies are weaker than those paper prisons boys use to keep flies in; more contemptible, since ours is to preserve earth-worms. (IV.ii.124–8)

For Professor Bradbrook this speech 'epitomises what the play is really concerned with';[48] but while fully acknowledging that this fine speech ranks in power with 'Be absolute for death' or the language of the Book of Job, I would emphasise that it is *one* of the things which the play is concerned with. For if this speech terrifyingly reduces man to a worm, within seconds the Duchess makes her great affirmation of the human spirit—'I am Duchess of Malfi still'—and even Bosola allows sweet-ness[49] to enter his language ('Didst thou ever see a lark in a cage', etc.) which, even as it condemns man, in its vitality proclaims Bosola himself more than a tomb-maker. And as the dialogue develops, the spirit of witty jesting returns from the earlier Duchess to establish her courage and presence of mind:

> *Duchess*: And thou comest to make my tomb?
> *Bosola*: Yes.

---

[48] 'Two Notes Upon Webster', *MLR*, XLII (1947), 290.
[49] Cf. Travis Bogard, *The Tragic Satire of John Webster* (Berkeley and Los Angeles, 1955), p. 141.

Duchess: Let me be a little merry—of what stuff wilt thou make it?
Bosola: Nay, resolve me first, of what fashion?
Duchess: Why, do we grow fantastical in our death-bed? do we affect
    fashion in the grave?
Bosola: Most ambitiously. (IV.ii.149–56)

With the reference to fashions in tomb-making, the courtly world re-
enters the play, to remind us that while Bosola mocks it, the Duchess
shows us its strength. She uses the diamonds and pearls of that world
to express her aristocratic heroism, which surprises even Bosola:

Bosola: Yet, methinks,
⠀⠀The manner of your death should much afflict you,
⠀⠀This cord should terrify you?
Duchess:⠀⠀⠀⠀⠀⠀⠀⠀⠀⠀Not a whit:
⠀⠀What would it pleasure me to have my throat cut
⠀⠀With diamonds? or to be smothered
⠀⠀With cassia? or to be shot to death with pearls?
⠀⠀⠀⠀⠀⠀⠀⠀⠀⠀⠀⠀⠀⠀⠀⠀⠀⠀(IV.ii.213–18)

And then, after the typical Websterian effect of using the surprising
'geometrical hinges' to increase the tension by an extra call to attention,
he indicates how great an ordeal the Duchess's wit and presence of
mind is concealing as she almost cracks with 'any way, for heaven-
sake,/So I were out of your whispering'. But within seconds she has
rallied and is able to be humorous again:

⠀⠀I would fain put off my last woman's fault,
⠀⠀I'd not be tedious to you. (IV.ii.226–7)

The phrasing and rhythm, in turn conversational, mocking, defiant, and
tense, chart every development of this astonishing scene with the
total control of tone which Dr Mulryne remarks: 'a sense of the parti-
culars of the actual situation (the executioners' whispering) is evidence
of a supreme dramatic awareness.'[50] The variations of pace and mood
in the Duchess's speeches mean that the human spirit rises above the
grisly apparatus with which the character is surrounded; and that spirit
triumphs by developing those varied aspects of the Duchess's character
that Webster so fully reveals in the early scenes, as Peggy Ashcroft
beautifully demonstrated in her performance, to which H. A. L. Craig
testifies: she gave

[50] Mulryne, p. 217.

the part the lightness of charm. . . . Only with the noose round her neck and circled by her assassins did she fulfil the tragic strictures of the Ayrton drawings which, until this production, had been my only visualisation of the play. She was fire, air and duchess then; not until her last rites . . . did she kick off the woman.[51]

Notice that Mr Craig found that he had to revalue his previous exclusively sombre visualising of the play because Peggy Ashcroft's complex performance, responding to *all* the demands of the text, allowed light to penetrate even this darkness. This stage experience seems to me to establish 'what the play is really concerned with'. The Duchess's grace and humanity contrasts with the abject, ignominious, or desolate deaths of her persecutors, a contrast strengthened by the lyrical beauty of the Echo scene.

It also causes Ferdinand's madness, 'the madness', as Professor Leech says, that 'he wanted to see in his sister, the madness she avoided'.[52] This death scene is the last confrontation of Ferdinand and his sister in more senses than one; for while the (presumably masked) Bosola carries out Ferdinand's purposes with his own vigorous individuality, the aim—'To bring her to despair' and to damn 'that body of hers' (IV.i.116–21)—is clearly Ferdinand's. The masque of madmen is peculiarly appropriate to the mad tormentor, not just to make her despair, but to celebrate a kind of weird 'wedding in madness' between the two of them. That I take to be the real point of the ceremonial, epithalamium-like form of the madmen scene that critics have thoroughly investigated;[53] and of all the points of staging in the play it is the most difficult to bring off, because a modern audience no longer associates spectacle with meaning. Donald McWhinnie's solution—to play the horrors 'straight and spare and cold as the slaughter house'—of course could only make half the points, as some reviews noticed. But it is very hard to see how the formal meaning of the scene can be made clear, short of 'organising' the madmen in a formal way which robs them of their essence as madmen, or of having Ferdinand on or above the stage, physically directing the action, which might work—just.

But for the rest, there is nothing which a detailed and imaginative response to this particular courtly world of Webster's should not be

[51] *The New Statesman* (24 December 1960).   [52] Leech, p. 25.
[53] Cf. Inga-Stina Ekeblad, 'The "Impure Art" of John Webster', *RES*, N.S. IX (1958), and Brown, *Duchess*, pp. xxxvi–xxxvii.

able to bring off on the modern stage. For as T. C. Worsley said after the Stratford production,

> it works fully only in performance, and then only if the performance matches the grandeur of the conception. The staging, the design and the acting must finally combine to carry us out of the trivialities of gangsterdom into the world of good and evil on a transcendentally grand scale.[54]

This a production will achieve most surely if it responds to the vivid detail of Webster's world in *The Duchess* which I have tried to outline, a world containing wit and gaiety and beauty as well as madness and death and savage torture. Professor Brown stresses the 'reiterations' of 'dark' and 'darkness';[55] but there are also great moments of light and elegance and courtly splendour, both deceptive and real. The designs must accommodate these contrasts, and Donald McWhinnie, well aware of this, succeeded to some extent, placing on his warm stone floor (which could also light 'cold' for the torture scenes) a series of 'super-props', a fountain, a tombstone for the graveyard, and 'a twelve-foot high chair in gold and red velvet [for] the Cardinal's palace in Rome'. But though he aimed at 'maximum pace of scene-changing', he lost valuable court atmosphere by using 'the insolent and sloppy serving-men of Malfi, Rome and Milan to shift the furniture'. This, though, is one stratum of court life that the text scarcely emphasises, and the device fragmented, instead of building up, Webster's world. I suspect that a permanent set sufficiently varied to suggest different aspects of the court world—a stately home which turns into a prison, the ruins of a once proud abbey, a formal palace garden—may be the answer here. Further, though Mr McWhinnie's dictum 'clothes, not costumes' is the right attitude, and axiomatic nowadays in any responsible production of Shakespeare and his contemporaries, they want to be elegant rather than, as Leslie Hurry's were, oppressive. They made the first half seem unnecessarily ponderous in movement, and so went against what Dr Mulryne rightly calls Webster's 'alert, observant, witty' mind and 'agile' intellect.[56] Most important of all, the courtly atmosphere I have insisted upon has to be a matter of playing—rhythm and pacing, a versatility that can cope with the elegant and the terrifying side by side; for that is what Webster himself manages to do.

[54] *The Financial Times* (16 December 1960).
[55] Brown, *Duchess*, pp. xliv–xlv.   [56] Mulryne, p. 202.

T. S. Eliot[57] claims for Webster above all the gift of style. While agreeing, I would prefer to clarify the situation as far as *The Duchess* on the stage is concerned by saying 'styles'. Together the two parts of the play constitute what Professor Leech calls 'writing at the level of a masterpiece'.[58] Without claiming that every scene is perfect, there is enough masterly writing in both 'styles' of the play to make it particularly effective on the stage. For me, the only Jacobean play which is so *consistently* effective is *Women Beware Women*. At Stratford this summer, the Royal Shakespeare Company will be mounting its second new production of *Women Beware Women* in eight years. I very much hope that they will give *The Duchess of Malfi* the same attention in the near future.

[57] 'The Duchess of Malfi', *The Listener*, XXVI (18 December 1941).
[58] Leech, p. 49.

The Power of The White Devil

A. J. SMITH

The Power of The White Devil

I'D LIKE TO start by looking at two scenes from *The White Devil*.
The first is Act III, scene iii. This is a passage between Flamineo and
Lodovico, the hatchet-men of the opposing factions in the play. It's a
chance encounter, but it's loaded from the start by the situation that
puts them in hostility to each other, most of all by the recent death of
Isabella. And that's how it is introduced: either of them has a carefully
placed aside, contemptuous of the other, which sets them to use the
meeting for intelligence or some factional end:

> *Lodovico* [*aside*]: This was Brachiano's pander, and 'tis strange
> That in such open and apparent guilt
> Of his adulterous sister, he dare utter
> So scandalous a passion. I must wind him.[1]
> *Flamineo* [*aside*]: How dares this banish'd count return to Rome,
> His pardon not yet purchas'd? I have heard
> The deceas'd Duchess gave him pension,
> And that he came along from Padua
> I'th' train of the young prince. There's somewhat in't.
> Physicians, that cure poisons, still do work
> With counterpoisons.

These opposite statements of the same intent neatly balance each other,
and set a pattern of tension which the scene will ironically modulate.
Moreover the episode itself is offered as a kind of theatrical flourish:

> *Marcello*: Mark this strange encounter.

Flamineo's brother Marcello, who points the prodigy for us thus, is
planted to oversee events and to intervene and arrest things once the
immediate effect is made.

---

[1] My quotations are taken from the New Mermaid edition, Elizabeth M.
Brennan, ed. (second impression, 1967).

The encounter opens in abrasive antagonism, a mood of savage burlesque-hyperbole:

Flamineo: The god of melancholy turn thy gall to poison,
And let the stigmatic wrinkles in thy face,
Like to the boisterous waves in a rough tide
One still overtake another.
Lodovico: I do thank thee
And I do wish ingeniously for thy sake
The dog-days all year long.

Then by a curious sleight of tone and reference their fencing brings them together, and they drift rapidly into a brotherly pact of melancholy:

Flamineo: How croaks the raven?
Is our good Duchess dead?
Lodovico: Dead.
Flamineo: O fate!
Misfortune comes like the crowner's business,
Huddle upon huddle.
Lodovico: Shalt thou and I join housekeeping?
Flamineo: Yes, content.
Let's be unsociably sociable.
Lodovico: Sit some three days together, and discourse.
Flamineo: Only with making faces;
Lie in our clothes.
Lodovico: With faggots for our pillows.
Flamineo: And be lousy.
Lodovico: In taffeta linings; that's gentle melancholy;
Sleep all day.
Flamineo: Yes: and like your melancholic hare
Feed after midnight.

This is very much more a shared attitude and manner than a real agreement for no issues have been canvassed. The entry of Antonelli and Gasparo, laughing, confirms the bizarre *rapport*, binding them together in common derision of the kind of world that reacts thus to Isabella's death—'We are observed: see how yon couple grieve'. For them, it seems, it is the same world that has kicked them around and kept them down—even set them at odds by making them creatures of the great adversaries who control the hemispheres of the play:

Lodovico: Precious girn, rogue.
We'll never part.
Flamineo: Never: till the beggary of courtiers,
The discontent of churchmen, want of soldiers,
And all the creatures that hang manacled,
Worse than strappado'd, on the lowest felly
Of Fortune's wheel be taught in our two lives
To scorn that world which life of means deprives.

There's a good deal of skill, as well as theatrical life, in the way the immense speed of the broken dialogue carries off this *rapprochement* of tone and attitude.

Then quite abruptly comes news of Lodovico's pardon at the hand of the dying Pope. And it produces an immediate convulsion. Lodovico's attitude reverses as abruptly as the news arrived; he laughs, turns on Flamineo's objections with blunt and mocking insults, and in a mounting flurry of slighting exchanges Flamineo strikes him. Marcello steps in to drag Flamineo off and end the episode, and the two desperadoes don't face each other again in their own persons until the final showdown.

The scene, I think, shows the liveliest sense of theatre, though it's very hard to say what it adds up to. What one notes about it at once is its clear-cut movement of reversal, which turns on the abrupt shock of that unmotivated announcement. They start off hostile, draw together, and end with blows in an explosive revel of sardonic railing.

One isn't asked to take sides or adjudicate between the two men, least of all in relation to Isabella's murder. Webster aims, it would seem, to play off the adversaries in the audience's judgement so that one doesn't commit oneself to either but is forced to take a relative view of them. It's particularly hard to judge them because their motives aren't apparent. The characters don't tell us why they behave as they do; they merely follow out arbitrary attitudes and whims and seek to uphold their will to do that. The pact of melancholy, so rudely reversed, seems to be based on nothing more substantial than a shared sense of general grievance. And the attitudes they strike are comically posed, like grotesque play-acting. The moment Lodovico hears of the pardon he drops altogether his contempt of the world and swings to the opposite extreme; no doubt Flamineo would have done the same had his fortune suddenly improved thus. But then the issue itself is trivial. We see the characters as simply determined to act out with grotesque ferocity the humour of the moment, to show their will at random and impose it if they can.

One can't question the dexterity of the writing or the sheer sense of the stage it shows. Yet finally the episode is hardly important to the plot and only marginally relevant. The insulting blow leads on to Lodovico's later butchery of Flamineo; but Francisco's gold is a wholly adequate motive for that. And if the quarrel here is supposed to prepare the event then it is another such *ad hoc* stroke as Lodovico has to carry off when he tells us, just once in a casual afterthought, of his thwarted lust for the poisoned Isabella.

Overall the scene makes a curious impact of randomness, momentary force. Its vivid complex life comes out of nowhere, is abruptly broken off, and then sinks back into unimportance. One might think it a gimmick or a mere *coup de théâtre*. But even if there were no more to it than that the evidence is that it's been carefully plotted as such. We have to reckon with the force of a calculated randomness.

*   *   *

My second example is Act V, scene i. In the midst of the preparation for the ceremonial barriers, under cover of which the plot to poison Brachiano is working up, there are some ironical broken exchanges between Brachiano's courtiers and the feigned foreigners—the plotters. A little action develops, and drifts in and out of the confused stir, between Flamineo, Marcello, and the Moorish courtesan Zanche. This turns on the way Zanche hangs amorously about Flamineo, a pursuit which produces a good deal of sceptical talk about lascivious women, delivered in a spirit of cold clinical reductiveness.

Flamineo's family now try to force Zanche away from him for the sake of the family honour—which one might think was already too deeply compromised to be much affected by this. Cornelia finds her with Flamineo and beats her away; Marcello kicks her. A quarrel suddenly flares up between the two brothers, abruptly transforming their previous attitudes to each other. They exchange savage words, and Flamineo leaves; Marcello draws his sword and sends it after his brother by way of challenge.

Zanche now sets herself amorously at the disguised Francisco whom she takes to be a Moor like herself, boldly protesting love and desire for him. Cornelia enters with Marcello, having heard news of a fight he is to have with some unnamed adversary. As they talk, Flamineo comes briskly in with Marcello's sword and runs Marcello through—

I have brought your weapon back.

The quarrel itself seems trivial. Indeed the episode is elaborately arranged to let us see that while Flamineo doesn't give a damn about Zanche (or about any kind of enslavement to a woman) and seeks to shake her off, Zanche herself has no great care for Flamineo either beyond the immediate prospect of pleasure, and at once offers herself to Francisco. The issue for Flamineo is plainly not love or solicitude for Zanche but self-will—he won't be dictated to. And the peculiar irony of the incident, carefully set up around the conflicting reactions of Cornelia, is that these are brothers. We see that what matters aren't the issues themselves but one's arbitrary and indifferent will to pursue them; they represent one's humour (and therefore one's will) for the moment. The episode puts human attachments in a relative light when brotherly regard is so subject to whim and love so easily transferred. But then every gesture in this scene stands in pawn to the ironies that run right through and mock the wanton will, as when Zanche offers love to the disguised Duke of Florence, the plotter who'll ultimately have her killed.

Above all though it's the way the episode moves that gives it force. The sudden act of violence arrests and points the drifting casual action between which this little plot interweaves itself, coming as if at random, suddenly out of nowhere. It isn't the craftsmanship that's casual. The theatrical point of the action seems to be just this unmotivated abruptness, or convulsive spasm: not here—*here*—gone . . . and Marcello lies dying. And it lies with the sense of the play. The pervading relativism allows such a breach between brothers without its raising issues of consequence or a Lear-like appeal to imperatives of kin. Moreover there are the ironies, brutally exploited in the talk of the crucifix Flamineo broke as a baby, and in the quick exchange of the momentary scuffle. Shock is the effect of the event in the theatre, with the explosive entry and blow, Cornelia's scream, Marcello's retching, the blood: but it's a shock quickened with a kind of wit. The special quality of the scene comes from the way it combines an assault on the sensibilities with a sharp mental life. And it's a mental life that suggests

a wider context of understanding for this revelation of the instantan-
eous onset of death, opening up a prospect of arbitrary horror.

The narrative relevance of this episode, too, is in question. Nothing
in the action turns on it. It leads to Cornelia's lament over Marcello's
corpse and the picture that passage presents of the world we live and
die in; it gets Marcello himself conveniently out of the way, if that
matters; it gives an extra turn of irony or so to Brachiano's poisoning
which immediately follows—'The last good deed he did, he pardon'd
murther'. Why shouldn't one write it down as a random if pungent
theatrical *coup*?

But if these scenes are mere sensation-mongering then it's the play
itself that stands in question, for they are wholly typical of the way the
action moves. What makes *The White Devil* more than a loose-knit
sequence of theatrical effects? The attempt to resolve that is a search
for the real power of a play which is more in the end than the sum of
its diverse parts. One can be confident of the judgement without any
prior assurance of one's ability to substantiate it. The proof is the
single impact the play makes where it matters, in the theatre. To think
of staging it is to see how much the effects are of a piece, and how far
they grow out of a single imaginative apprehension.

*   *   *

What makes *The White Devil* inherently elusive is that the speeches
themselves, pungent as they are, offer one so little to grip on. To try
some reading of a character or motive against the lines themselves is to
see how little they actually show us of inner life. For one thing, they
never offer us a coherent argument; as the action overall doesn't
develop a consistent dialectic. One can find passages that seem to carry
on a debate:

> Pray what means have you
> To keep me from the galleys, or the gallows?
> My father prov'd himself a gentleman,
> Sold all's land, and like a fortunate fellow,
> Died ere the money was spent. You brought me up,
> At Padua I confess, where, I protest,
> For want of means, (the university judge me,)
> I have been fain to heel my tutor's stockings
> At least seven years. Conspiring with a beard

Made me a graduate, then to this Duke's service;
I visited the court, whence I return'd—
More courteous, more lecherous by far,
But not a suit the richer; and shall I,
Having a path so open and so free
To my preferment, still retain your milk
In my pale forehead? No, this face of mine
I'll arm and fortify with lusty wine
'Gainst shame and blushing.

This is just the delineation of a set character, or a world. It's clear that there's no genuine argument here because there's nothing really at issue; there may be principles involved, of a kind, but no vision emerges of a coherent context of values to be contested dynamically in a man's life.

The first problem of the play is what the speeches actually do say, and how they work. One sees that far from building an argument they tend to put one thing by another in a kind of gnomic discontinuity, looking to adages and likenesses:

Oh my lord,
The drunkard after all his lavish cups,
Is dry, and then is sober; so at length,
When you awake from this lascivious dream,
Repentance then will follow; like the sting
Plac'd in the adder's tail: wretched are princes
When fortune blasteth but a petty flower
Of their unwieldy crowns;

Such language works not to take us into a speaker's consciousness but to distance people; it partly accounts for the sense one has that the characters resist one's attempts to pin them down:

O gold, what a god art thou! and O man, what a devil art thou to be tempted by that cursed mineral! Yon diversivolent lawyer; mark him; knaves turn informers, as maggots turn to flies; you may catch gudgeons with either. A cardinal;—I would he would hear me,—there's nothing so holy but money will corrupt and putrify it, like victual under the line.

The violent energy of the writing doesn't simulate the life of a working mind; the lines point outward to the world often by some relatively impersonal and public manner of reference such as proverbial lore. These speeches work above all to offer a context of reference and action, present a certain account of the world; through them the characters of the play are always offering to define the kind of world they inhabit, or the kind of world they think they know and can manipulate. The discontinuity of the movement argues that the only coherence most of them can hit on is the settled attitude of sceptical mistrust itself, a sense enforced by the steadily reductive tendency of the language and assumptions as they play upon the common motives of the world and men's actions. Webster's supposed method of commonplace composition follows out this disposition. But it vastly overdoes the case to speak of *The White Devil* as a work of imitative art like Tasso's *Aminta*, that delicate *cento* of other men's splendours marvellously rewoven into a novel texture. Reweaving of that kind isn't Webster's interest; the common matter lies about here and there in nuggets, enlarging the sense of an atomised world:

> We see that undermining more prevails
> Than doth the cannon. Bear your wrongs conceal'd,
> And, patient as the tortoise, let this camel
> Stalk o'er your back unbruis'd: sleep with the lion,
> And let this brood of secure foolish mice
> Play with your nostrils; till the time be ripe
> For th'bloody audit, and the fatal gripe:
> Aim like a cunning fowler, close one eye,
> That you the better may your game espy.

Webster's borrowings in this play present themselves in random effects and sentences, all his people can offer us by way of developed thought or sustained moral purpose. They allow the characters a pungent local life without tying them down to settled principles, or at any rate without making their principles explicit. We can speak only of attitudes people strike.

The notorious ambiguity of the motives and characters of *The White Devil* comes back to the language and the way it pushes one away; we can't place these people because they don't tell us about themselves. Critical readings of the play amply demonstrate the difficulties one gets into if one tries coolly to get at the real motives on which the main characters act. Webster himself seems less concerned with motives—

which he takes for granted—than with conduct and its consequences, or with humours strikingly assumed. What does Brachiano amount to? How indeed does one get at him? His language offers us no play of mind or consciousness but only a series of impulses. We mark his love for Vittoria—'Quite lost Flamineo'; his barbaric rejection of Isabella yet willingness to use her; his sponsoring of the murders and relish for them; his boldness and sharpness too in the arraignment of Vittoria; his statesmanlike courtesy in welcoming the 'foreign' visitors; his wild misery and emptiness at the last; and so on. The character is nothing more than the sum of the various scenes in which he appears, the several attitudes he strikes. The same holds for Vittoria, and we waste time as literary critics speculating about what the play itself pointedly withholds. These characters are not given to scrutinising their own impulses; they are viewed from the outside, and Webster seems no more interested in moral discrimination than in psychological exposure. Whatever one makes of *The White Devil*, it's no drama of consciousness.

What then moves the characters to action? Love and hate are the poles on which revenge plays turn, and amorous enslavement is the special animus of *The White Devil*. Family love gets a distinctive showing here, which one needs to place. Hate is another matter, and nothing in the play that I can see gives human indifference that moral stature. Yet if we take sexual love, the initiating impulse of the play, what do we really see of it? There are versions enough: Brachiano's passion for Vittoria (and hers for him?); Lodovico's lust for Isabella; Zanche's pursuit of Flamineo and then of Francisco; Brachiano's former love of Isabella, now turned to loathing. But no episode displays the passion or anything Webster wanted to make of it. The love dialogue in Act I is the striking case, especially if one puts it by the great paradigms in Wagner or Shakespeare or Chaucer. Webster has learned from Shakespeare how to counterpoint lovers' exchanges against the commentaries of onlookers but the difference here is that the commentators really control the scene. The dialogue wittily keeps our attention on external circumstances. So love itself is passed off in an exchange of gifts, turned by Flamineo's innuendoes into a figure of lovemaking—'That's better; she must wear his jewel lower'—and by Vittoria's narration of her dream allegorising the removal of the impediments to their love.

Or there's the long and violent quarrel between Brachiano and Vittoria in Act IV brought on by Francisco's feigned protestations of love for Vittoria in the politic letter sent to the House of Convertites.

This does sharply hit off a familiar amorous motive, a jealousy which turns on its object but converts to abject penitence when the woman's countering anger threatens the relationship itself. Yet the enormous vitality here hasn't to do with a special insight into thwarted love. As so often in the play the violence has its ludicrous side. The episode gets punch from the irony of the quarrel in such a false cause, more from the vast reversal on which it turns. Flamineo mockingly mediates to us the clubroom wisdom which is as much as Webster wants to make of love:

> Fie, fie, my lord.
> Women are caught as you take tortoises,
> She must be turn'd on her back.—
> . . . What a strange credulous man were you, my lord,
> To think the Duke of Florence would love her?
> Will any mercer take another's ware
> When once 'tis tows'd and sullied?

Brachiano rejects his wife's love in Act II out of a sharply defined erotic impulse—the revulsion of jaded appetite—which isn't in itself the point of the scene but compounds the irony of their reversal of roles to placate Francisco. The sexual motive, so vehemently carried through, is a given humour which we're asked to assume from a few harsh phrases. Brachiano can put so extreme a disposition because it's not to be tested; it emerges as dramatic expedient, or a confirmation of the way the world goes, rather than for any special interest Webster takes in the condition.

Family regard gets a better hearing in the play and to that extent is still more cavalierly deployed. Webster sets up these domestic episodes with elaborate care for their effect, which is usually a compound of irony and pathos: Isabella's loyal response to her husband's loathing; Cornelia's mourning over Marcello and conflicting impulses towards his murdering brother; Giovanni's inquiries after the condition of the dead when his mother has just been poisoned. These homely affections are all that stand against the callous self-will of the world, and it's especially striking that the one such regard which leads to important action, Francisco's care for his sister, isn't displayed pathetically at all after she is poisoned but assumed, just at the moment when the scene is set up for its expression. Francisco himself brusquely brushes aside any expression of regard for his sister as an obstacle to his witty revenge:

> Remove this object,
> Out of my brain with't: what have I to do
> With tombs, or death-beds, funerals, or tears,
> That have to meditate upon revenge?

None of these pathetic attitudes is developed in itself; they are all simply displayed for an immediate stage effect, leading nowhere but always painfully vulnerable. Isabella is poisoned by the loving kiss she gives Brachiano's portrait, Cornelia torn apart by love of all three of her dissident children, Marcello stabbed unarmed by his brother over his care for their family honour. It's the victims alone who act out of unselfregarding concern, and that is what makes them victims.

Are we to see these people as expendable pawns of the policies of great men? The world the play offers us revolves round the corrupting whims of men of power and its characters tend to see themselves as betrayed to it by their poverty. The condition of late Renaissance courts defines if it doesn't limit an action which persistently reminds us that this is what happens in such places and with such people, this is the fate of princes as well as their parasites:

> To see what solitariness is about dying princes. As heretofore they have unpeopled towns; divorc'd friends, and made great houses unhospitable: so now, O justice! where are their flatterers now? Flatterers are but the shadows of princes' bodies, the least thick cloud makes them invisible.

But the piece is no more a mirror for magistrates than it's a warning to aspiring courtiers. Nor does it play up the forms of greatness, political power or an etiquette of honour, so much as its freedom from external constraint and the larger scope it gives to self-will. If Webster had a point to make about courts and great men then he has taken care to let us see that this world of power is a special case only in its writing large of human will, in the freedom it gives men to do as we would.

The instability of such a world must have some bearing on the unorthodox articulation of the play. Webster seems to have conceived the work less as an organic development than as a series of set pieces. The notorious shortcomings of construction themselves partly account for one's sense of the emergent character of events and occasions in the play. For controlling climaxes we get only a mounting succession of *coups*. Motivation seems contemptuously sketchy even when we know that the thing really happened thus, as with Monticelso's animosity towards Vittoria and Brachiano because his nephew is Vittoria's wronged husband. Striking theatrical effects seem irrelevant to the course of the action, with contrivances that get nowhere, episodes that come to nothing, characters who peter out. Why the elaborate plot between Monticelso and Francisco to get Camillo out of the way, so that Brachiano may dishonour himself publicly with Vittoria? Its pointlessness is built in since Camillo gets his neck wrung before he can even set foot outside Rome. Why the dumb-shows, and the comic flummery of the conjuror and poisoning doctor? Why the culinary arrangements at papal elections? And why the election itself? What of Cornelia's curse upon Vittoria and Brachiano when she finds them together? of Monticelso's book of all the villains in Rome? of Monticelso himself after he's elected Pope and dissuades Lodovico from the revenge to which he himself had earlier prompted Francisco? These scenes are effective in themselves and they are of a piece in their variously ironic commentary on men's actions. Indeed the surprises and the ironies are so carefully plotted, so dexterously contrived to shock, that one might suspect Webster of erecting theatrical effect into a dramatic principle and of seeking no more in his source material than a bagful of opportunities for sheer stage tricks (as Shaw thought Shakespeare did). One thing these contrivances don't suggest is that the characters are in full command of their affairs or the consequences of their wills; they are all flashing around in the dark, to some little purpose or none.

If their scattered professions suggest motives which the action itself makes nothing of, that needn't impugn Webster's craftsmanship. It might show his cool concern to frustrate our attention to motives and to keep us outside them. The *ad hoc* motivation is a condition of the play's peculiar power in the way it exploits the sudden unexpectedness and violent randomness of events in a world of dislocated energies. One sees something of the special character of the tragedy by the inappropriateness to it of the orthodox categories of Aristotelean criticism, say heroic steadfastness or tragic choice. This is hardly a play in which a hero elects to press through with things to the end on some principle or driving design. What it shows us instead are characters moving by emergent expedients to self-regarding ends, whose tragedy lies just in their inevitable collisions with the emergent wills of others. The singularity of this view of greatness is that in the end it's the absence of choice that's marked, beyond the limited choice of reaction to others' infringements of one's own will. For the paradox of the movement is the way that a sense of the inevitable pulls the very randomness into coherence.

If this is gimmicky there's a consistent method in it, and a consistent apprehension of life. One noted feature of the play is the relativeness—ambiguity if one likes—of its values and attitudes, a character so persistently plotted for that it looks like a leading principle of the construction. Nothing is ever allowed to stand absolutely, or unquestioned. Vittoria's accusers are themselves viciously tainted. Monticelso's catalogue of criminals was compiled to a dubious end and is used to a corrupt one. Francisco puts the right pious objections to Monticelso's promptings to revenge but discloses his own sinister designs the moment Monticelso is gone.

Every moral posture is undermined, if not in our regard then in the eyes of the characters themselves; as when Lodovico forswears his revenge at Monticelso's dreadful admonition, but is immediately pulled back to it again with double force by the arrival of Francisco's gold, sent as from Monticelso:

> Why now 'tis come about. He rail'd upon me;
> And yet these crowns were told out and laid ready,
> Before he knew my voyage. O the art,
> The modest form of greatness! that do sit
> Like brides at wedding dinners, with their looks turn'd
> From the least wanton jests, their puling stomach
> Sick of the modesty, when their thoughts are loose,
> Even acting of those hot and lustful sports
> Are to ensue about midnight: such his cunning!
> He sounds my depth thus with a golden plummet;
> I am doubly arm'd now. Now to th'act of blood;

One thinks above all of the sequence of violence that clinches the action, which doesn't enact or fulfil some effective morality but unfolds, one behind the other, a series of relative gains. Brachiano poisons Isabella, and Francisco has him poisoned; Flamineo goes to kill Vittoria and Zanche, who then think they have killed him; Flamineo, Vittoria, and Zanche are butchered by Lodovico and his crew, criminal assassins in the pay of Francisco, who are shot down by the guards under Francisco's young nephew Giovanni; Francisco himself is roundly condemned as a murderer by Giovanni. Is it the condemnation that's in question here, or is revenge itself wrong? Or who is wronged and who justified in this action? And if one thinks to take Giovanni himself as a juvenile Fortinbras who will restore right order then his position has already been undermined by Flamineo's pointed delineation of the selfseekers great men inevitably grow to be when they feel their power secure. In the end it's only the passive victims who have an unequivocal claim on our esteem.

If relativeness is one principle of the arrangement another seems to be shock. The very succession of scenes has a startling discontinuity which the theatre ought to bring up. Repeatedly a situation develops in which casual traffic is abruptly transformed by sudden violent action. Not only the main events but quite incidental effects work this way, such as Cornelia's bursting into the love dialogue in Act I, or the brusque cataclysmic announcement of Monticelso's election to the papacy, or the turnabout shifts of the several quarrels. These sudden reversals, violent swings from extreme to opposite extreme, give this world of the play its most alarming aspect.

The last episode is a virtuoso exercise in this kind of plotting with Flamineo's assault on the women, then theirs on him and his mock death, and his confounding of their triumph as well as our expectation when he rises so blandly:

> O cunning devils! now I have try'd your love,
> And doubled all your reaches. I am not wounded:
> The pistols held no bullets: 'Twas a plot
> To prove your kindness to me;

The held-off shock of the knifings is itself shatteringly outdone as the guards rush in to shoot down the murderers in their turn. There's an accelerating tempo of incident and riposte, a mounting series of assaults on one's nerves and senses, ironic twist upon twist in the unresolved mutations of this play.

But the scene whose peculiar pungency lies in the shock of ironic reversal is the enactment of Brachiano's dying and death. Here's a chance of a real theatrical *tour de force*, to show by degrees a man's disintegration and death of poison. If the movement of the play continually works to hold the doubtful ground between a given state and its opposite extreme then the issue here is the supreme irony, the metamorphosis of life itself into the state of not being (as Montaigne calls it), and what follows from that cataclysm for the sense our lives make.

The fearful world of this vision presents itself in theatrical terms and one's imagination needs to encounter it there. The action gradually resolves out of the scattered preliminaries for the tournament with the preparations for the murder, the conspiratorial side-mutterings and embracings, the sense of wire-taut peril more finely drawn with every fresh move (the plotting has an odd kinship with Jonson's *Alchemist*). Lodovico's sprinkling the beaver with poison comes as a casual parenthesis in the sequel of Marcello's murder, though it's pointed out by Francisco's melodramatically sinister aside—'He calls for his destruction.' Then out of the random confusion of the barriers there's the Oedipus-like entry itself, a sudden eruption of shrieking agony, 'An armourer! Ud's death, an armourer!', that at once transforms the scene into one of those images of hysterical disorientation which Webster apprehended with peculiar force and controlled so brilliantly. The circumstance itself is held in this mood of panic, even extended over an arbitrary stage-exit; so that one gets the further shock of the rapid degeneration at the re-entry—'There's death in's face already'—as well as the multiple ironies of Flamineo's conversation with the disguised Francisco about the deaths of great men:

O speak well of the Duke.

It's characteristic of the play to reverse the moral alignment thus ironically as the murderer sees his own condition in the fate of his victim; and to leave one uncertain whether he means it or is just acting out his role.

An ironic reversal is implicit in the fearsome vision of misery caught so vividly in the staging of a lonely death amid a collapsing world—the coming and going of physicians and holy men, the howling of women offstage, the dying man's delirious visions of horror, the muttered gibes of courtiers already emboldening into open detraction, the total overthrow of everything that gave sense to the man's life. There's little to console one here, and it's a grotesque parody of pious consolation that the death-bed scene seizes, with its picture of the last rites turned into a fiendish mockery of the dying man and of death, a farce directed above all to showing him as he dies the fearful indignity of his own dissolution, and the absurdity it makes of his existence. Brachiano's last shriek of 'Vittoria! Vittoria!' terrifies more than all, for it brings home to us that he has grasped this ultimate vision of horror, his secular hell and final human degradation. The clinching irony comes pat—

Lodovico: My lords he's dead.
Omnes: Rest to his soul.

—a piety which Vittoria's aside savagely places—'O me! this place is hell!'

If my account has force then it's clear that *The White Devil* isn't a play of the order of *The Spanish Tragedy* or *The Revenger's Tragedy*, where the moral alignment follows the obligation of revenge and allows one to talk of heroes, Machiavellian villains, avenging justice, and the like. Nor has it anything in common with a work like *Hamlet*, whose action develops some settled concern into a dialectic to which every speech dynamically contributes. The counterpointing of scenes in *Troilus and Cressida* may be the nearest thing Shakespeare affords to the relativism of *The White Devil*, but Webster's play has little in common with a movement which allows as much scope to the heart's drastic gestures as to the world that keeps giving them the lie. Webster's far more limited sense of human possibility allows no such insights as Troilus or Hector or old Shallow incarnate, and consequently no such effective moral scourge as Thersites. A closer comparison might be John Donne. *The Progress of the Soul*, written in the same decade as this play, is an exuberant attempt to carry through a thoroughgoing sceptical relativism in an account of the economy of fallen nature. But its vision of the civic jungle has—and assumes—an assured purposeful-ness that's quite missing from Webster's play, and one simply can't take the action of *The White Devil* as predicating man's predatoriness, or the relativity of our judgements in respect of absolute truth. Donne's is a menacing world but we know just where we stand in it. Webster's is desperate because that's just what no one who inhabits it can know.

The decisive matter is what the characters make of their world, and perhaps what they don't or can't make of it. For all the furniture of counter-reforming zeal, inquisitions of morals included, there's really no metaphysical dimension in the play at all. Effectively the characters don't admit in their lives anything beyond the here and now, which death simply negates:

> On pain of death, let no man name death to me,
> It is a word infinitely terrible.

> Turn this horror from me:

What then do they live by? Nothing in the play warrants our speaking

of 'a world of evil', or even of anything so revolved as Machiavellism.
Only the successful working of Francisco's plot suggests that people's
actions aren't all blind self-will and momentary expediency, mocked by
ironic circumstance. Even Francisco's devious control is pointedly
casual, and limited, so that however Webster meant it we see him not
as a Machiavellian but simply as the least vulnerable performer in a
game of pride, a self-justifying avenger whose justice is itself wholly in
question. The absence of a central moral focus makes it meaningless to
place him in relation to Brachiano or Vittoria or Flamineo, for all their
impulses present themselves as arbitrary attitudes and choices. If we
look for settled motives or principles we find only local values—wifely
loyalty, motherly love, family solicitude, the motions of the victim in
the world of this play. But the submissive virtues themselves aren't so
much coldly exploited as simply over-vulnerable in a world where men
are seeking to impose their wills at random, moving dimly round each
other like self-enclosed atoms whose reaction is the only check upon
action.

The inherent relativism, the ironic reversals and their persistent
unsettling of men's assurances, the annihilating shocks and débâcles—
whether designedly or not the action moves to fix our minds on the
kind of world these people face up to so confidently. The most fright-
ening thing about it is its denial of human dignity. This does seem
pointed. We hear much of both Brachiano and Francisco as politic
statesmen but we don't for a moment see them engaged in some public
concern beyond their own self-willed ends, never meet them in any
aspect that might seem to give their lives stature, point, settled sense.
What we do understand is that sycophancy is the due of power, and the
moment power is lost—as in death—then derisive indifference is all
that naked humanity can claim. The speeches themselves, which offer
us so little of the speaker, continually tell us about the world he appre-
hends. They point to a condition of petty corruptness in which humanity is prey—but prey less to calculated evil than to man's own animal
status, squalid and debasing cankers, poisons, decay, maggots, wolves:

> They are first
> Sweetmeats which rot the eater: in man's nostril
> Poison'd perfumes. They are coz'ning alchemy,
> Shipwracks in calmest weather! What are whores?

If the tone and texture of reference steadily hold life cheap, so do most of

the characters in their actions; ironically, since they set a high enough
value on their own lives:

> Excellent, then she's dead,—

The chilling disparity between people's evaluations of others' lives and
their own, their affront to human kind, comes out most pointedly in
the circumstances of Brachiano's death. Hamlet's graveyard democracy
of dust here turns to a grim levelling of men's lives and impostures in
the degradation of dying. Any live man can feel himself superior to a
dying prince and feed his pride that he has won the game. If the
eschatological *reductio ad absurdum* makes nonsense of tragic choice
then it also negates tragic heroism. Webster offers us an unheroic
tragedy which moves by expediency, men acting not on principles but
for immediate selfish gratifications. The tragic attitude stands, if at all,
in the teeth of their self-concern. Vittoria faces up to her death so
bravely only when she sees that she has no choice; until then she
wriggles, craftily and deviously with shameless unheroism, to evade
Flamineo's threats, and even when the assassins rush in she offers
herself to them or their master to save her skin:

> O your gentle pity!
> I have seen a blackbird that would sooner fly
> To a man's bosom, than to stay the gripe
> Of the fierce sparrow-hawk.

The bizarre irony of that clutching at her one power over men (specifically, I suppose, at Francisco's feigned offer of love in his entrapping
letter to her) pointedly lets us see that we aren't here dealing with a
Cleopatra or a Beatrice Cenci. The passing self-disclosure hardly holds
Vittoria up to our contempt but it does put her concern with her own
skin in a light of grim farce.

Elements of farce intermittently burlesque the traffic of lust and
blood, and not only because so much of it is mediated to us by sceptical
malcontents. Brachiano's lovemaking; the gulling of Camillo; the
dumb-show murders, and the passages with the poisoning doctor; the
arraignment; Brachiano's death-bed; the final killings—all of these
assume aspects that bring into derision the moral and human issues.
But ironic mockery is itself a moral posture in this play. Brachiano
mocks Monticelso; the diversivolent lawyer, grotesquely parodying the
law, makes a charade of the inquisition of morals before it starts;
Francisco's concern with the wit of his revenge is a desire to make

mock of his adversaries; Vittoria and Zanche turn to easy mockery of Flamineo when they think they have him down; he turns the mock against them when he rises. The urge to belittle one's fellow-creatures draws from an uneasy awareness how easily one may oneself be reduced a grotesque object of derision:

> O thou cursed antipathy to nature! Look his eye's bloodshed like a needle a chirurgeon stitcheth a wound with. Let me embrace thee toad, and love thee, O thou abominable loathsome gargarism, that will fetch up lungs, lights, heart, and liver by scruples.

For there is something inherently farcical both in the view that characters take to each other and in the playwright's attitude to all of them. We see them struggling to control their world by deriding it, while he persistently betrays their assurance with his ironies. Brachiano jests coarsely with Flamineo and the poisoner over the dumb-show murders, and himself dies horribly of poison; Flamineo acts out a grotesque parody of facing death and of death itself to heighten the wit of his gulling of Vittoria and Zanche, and is at once confronted with the actuality of both.

In a world where people respect each other so little our pity is not much in place. The characters hardly claim as much as our respect. For most of its course the play seems arranged to resist our sympathies, opposing intolerance and deviousness on the one hand to effrontery and headstrong self-will on the other—striking enough qualities but none of them especially admirable. If we feel that it does nonetheless allow people a kind of grandeur in the end it can only be the final episode which sublimates their scattered powers and at last offers us something in human nature to esteem. All the play allows us for our unreserved respect is the way the three meet their deaths when they see that they have to; and they invite our approval because it's only then that they acknowledge each other, and each other's defiant pride:

> *Gasparo*: Are you so brave?
> *Vittoria*:   Yes I shall welcome death
> As princes do some great ambassadors;
> I'll meet thy weapon half way.

> *Flamineo*:   Th' art a noble sister,
> I love thee now; if woman do breed man
> She ought to teach him manhood. Fare thee well.

The circumstance is contrived so that we see them caught up in play-acting, half menacing half absurd, right up to the moment when they recognise that there's no evading death. Our final concern with the play is with what emerges from then on, specifically, with what Webster gets out of this narrowing-down on inevitable death.

The denouement offers us two protracted enactments of death which seem to be set off against each other. The real singularity of the play's construction is the way the action is brought to fix the prospect of dying and to follow the process right up to the frontier itself:

> *Lodovico*:   What dost think on?
> *Flamineo*: Nothing; of nothing: leave thy idle questions;
> I am i' th'way to study a long silence
> To prate were idle; I remember nothing.

The violent abruptness of the reversal of fortunes—Brachiano's screaming metamorphosis from vigour to dying torment, the entry of the murderers to Vittoria and the others, the moment of the dagger-thrust—throws back on the passions of the play to show life poised unpredictably on a knife-edge. Something of the frenetic energy the characters display may draw from that felt precariousness, as it expresses for us the lurking apprehension of people who live wholly for this world in an action that never remotely suggests there's anything else. The power of Brachiano's death-scene is that it so devastatingly shows us all that frenzy of will and pride coming to senseless nothing. The death it offers is the ultimate horror, that mocks our lives and dignity by reducing them to meaninglessness before we even die.

The deaths of Vittoria and Flamineo might have done no less, and Webster sets up his inquiry as rigorously as for Brachiano, holding the scene there right up to the blow and then beyond it to take the victims' responses at each step:

> I do not look
> Who went before, nor who shall follow me;
> No, at myself I will begin and end.
> *While we look up to heaven we confound*
> *Knowledge with knowledge.* O I am in a mist.

The absence of choice makes this tragedy a study of reactions to what is inevitable. For it's here that the deaths of Vittoria and Flamineo and Zanche pull the whole action into perspective, suggesting a possible human sublimity for the first time where the earlier deaths only negated life and dignity. This shared confrontation of death (shared with the assassins too, in the end) gives us the one stable point of reference the play affords, an absolute and admirable human attitude. Only here, thus narrowly concentrated, do we see human will take on an ennobling dignity and reach out in fellow feeling, intelligence find some better employment than wittily preying on its own humanity. For the only heroism the play allows is the refusal to capitulate in the face of inevitable death, when there's nothing to lose or gain or hold on to save self-respect, and pride. They act out their own exaltation:

> Let no harsh flattering bells resound my knell,
> Strike thunder, and strike loud to my farewell.

Lodovico when his turn comes sustains a heroic pride which defies his captor's invocation of heaven's justice:

> I do glory yet
> That I can call this act mine own. For my part,
> The rack, the gallows, and the torturing wheel
> Shall be but sound sleeps to me; here's my rest:
> *I limb'd this night-piece and it was my best.*

A proud self-will is the condition of this limited grandeur, as it's the agent of the moral wilderness we encounter in the play. Men's capacity to impose their wills gives their lives a sense only in their unwillingness to let even death defeat them. The prospect of the world Webster holds out to us may be bleak, even desperate, but it isn't in the end mean.

Intelligence in The Duchess of Malfi

NIGEL ALEXANDER

Intelligence in The Duchess of Malfi

'I AM DUCHESS of Malfi still.' Once heard in the theatre, or even
encountered in a lecture or work of criticism, the line seems unforget-
table. The words, of course, are easy to repeat. What makes them
unusually memorable, however, is their capacity to sum up the tragic
action of John Webster's play in a way that relates it firmly to our own
experience. It is an assertion that reaches out beyond the theatre and
takes possession of the imagination. It does so because it is one expression of that continual declaration of human independence which proclaims the unique value of a particular human existence in the face of the
inevitable and eternal triumph of death. This self-assertion is both
necessary and vain. It is vain because one unquestionable truth about
human life is that it is a slow but irreversible process of decay. The
symptoms of this disintegration, with the addition of more or less
intricate detail, may be dwelt upon with disgust or delight by those of a
moral, satiric, or merely morbid disposition. It is a necessary assertion
because the consciousness of his own existence is one of a human
being's most precious possessions. This consciousness is not yet understood and there is at present no really adequate way of describing an
individual's sense of self-identity. Yet the operations of this sense may
be observed, although they cannot be completely explained. One interesting manifestation of this consciousness is the way humans entertain
each other by dramatic representations which combine every attainable
expression of the muddy knowledge of mortality with the strongest
possible affirmation of the importance and independent value of human
action. This representation of man's aspirations in the context of his
infinite decrepitude has been called tragedy.

It is evident that Webster was 'much possessed by death' but, at the
centre of *The Duchess of Malfi*, two co-existent but incompatible attitudes are brought into direct and fatal conflict. Death gains its victory
but the words of the Duchess remain in Webster's verse to dispute the
dominion of the imagination. When he wrote this play John Webster

saw a good deal more than the skull beneath the skin. The words are spoken by the Duchess during the second, and final, attempt by her brother to drive her to despair and madness before her death. In the first of these torture scenes she has been given what she takes to be the severed hand of her husband with her wedding-ring upon its finger. She has seen what she believes to be his mutilated body hanging beside that of their eldest child. At this moment, in the second torture scene, she has been tormented by a masque of madmen and is now in conversation with an old man. This sinister figure declares himself a tombmaker and is contemptuous of the world of the flesh. His contempt dwells more upon the details of the body's dissolution than upon any compensating flight of the soul:

> *Bosola:* Thou art a box of worm seed, at best, but a salvatory of
> green mummy: what's this flesh? a little cruded milk, fantastical
> puff-paste: our bodies are weaker than those paper prisons boys
> use to keep flies in: more contemptible; since ours is to preserve
> earth-worms: didst thou ever see a lark in a cage? such is the soul
> in the body: this world is like her little turf of grass, and the heaven
> o'er our heads, like her looking-glass, only gives us a miserable
> knowledge of the small compass of our prison. (IV.ii.123 ff.)[1]

The speech is a *memento mori* which, if it is considered too curiously, is liable to make the reader or listener more mindful of his own mortality than is altogether comfortable. Suffering and death are not necessarily ennobling experiences and the courage with which the Duchess emphasises the claims of life is possibly commoner in fiction than in fact. It is perhaps for this very reason that we cling so strenuously to her assertion of bravery. This seems to me a reasonable and proper critical response because the attitude of the Duchess is not a bravura flight of fictional fancy on the part of the dramatist but is based upon observation which is conveyed to the audience in a dramatic work of art that is a brilliant piece of artistic craftsmanship.

'The conception of a certain young woman affronting her destiny' is the subject of *The Duchess of Malfi* if one may be permitted to borrow the phrase from the preface which Henry James wrote to the New York edition of *The Portrait of a Lady*. The subject, as he remarked, is not an uncommon one. 'Millions of presumptuous girls, intelligent or

---

[1] My quotations are taken from the New Mermaid edition, Elizabeth M. Brennan, ed. (second impression, 1967).

not intelligent, daily affront their destiny, and what is it open to their destiny to *be*, at the most, that we should make an ado about it?' It is, however, an important subject and a difficult one to handle. In comparing his own artistic problem to the way in which Shakespeare or George Eliot had attacked the same problem James observes that

> their concession to the 'importance' of their Juliets and Cleopatras and Portias (even with Portia as the very type and model of the young person intelligent and presumptuous) and to that of their Hettys and Maggies and Rosamonds and Gwendolens, suffers the abatement that these slimnesses are, when figuring as the main props of the theme, never suffered to be sole ministers of its appeal, but have their inadequacy eked out with comic relief and underplots, as the playwrights say, when not with murders and battles and the great mutations of the world.[2]

James insists that the adventures of his heroine are to be 'mild' in that they are to be independent 'of flood and field, of the moving accident, of battle, murder and sudden death', that 'without her sense of them, her sense *for* them, as one may say, they are next to nothing at all'. The adventures of the Duchess of Malfi are clearly not 'mild' in this sense since it is precisely murder and sudden death which form her great adventure. The great mutations of the world may, perhaps, be allowed to form a part of Webster's subject but it is the way in which they affect the fortunes of the Duchess, her sense for life and her attitude to death, which here makes the intensity of the drama. The most persuasive of modern critics appear to agree that the Duchess is herself the centre and subject of the play, however they then choose to interpret that subject. The cry 'I am Duchess of Malfi still' matters because John Webster has somehow braved the deep artistic difficulty of presenting the consciousness of his presumptuous, intelligent, and high-spirited heroine to the audience. The creation of that consciousness was not a matter of happy accident or even the result of the systematic ransacking of other men's hoards of language. Dramatic creation depends upon a conjunction of qualities rare in themselves and rarer still in combination. It requires insight and sensitivity to allow the dramatist to detect interesting and essential features of the human situation and it then requires a high degree of technical accomplishment

[2] Henry James, *The Art of the Novel: Critical Prefaces of Henry James*, R. P. Blackmur, ed. (1934), 49–50.

to translate these features into a conventional dramatic code which is flexible enough to cope with fairly complex ideas and yet sufficiently easily learnt for an audience sitting in a theatre three hundred, or three thousand, years later to detect and appreciate these essential features.

The point is worth insisting on because critics are still slightly uneasy at R. W. Dent's conclusive demonstration that Webster wrote with his commonplace-book open beside him and that the jagged cadences of his verse sometimes owe more to his reading than his own invention. In discussing the famous image of the 'thing, arm'd with a rake' which the Cardinal of Aragon sees in the fishponds of his garden Dent points out that the image originally comes from Capitolinus' life of the virtuous Pertinax, and may have been found by Webster in either Lavater or Lodowick Lloyd's *The Pilgrimage of Princes*. Dent argues that

> we recognise the peril of praising Webster's genius in specific passages without taking into consideration his method of composing them. The realization that he was adapting material to his own use should not disturb our admiration for the dramatic effectiveness of the Cardinal's speech, but it must obviously alter the grounds of our admiration for the dramatist.[3]

Dent finds adequate grounds for his admiration in praising 'the clarity and humanity of his governing conception' in *The White Devil* and has recently given that conception the attention that it deserves.[4] John Webster evidently composed in the same way in which Bernard Shaw's fictitious William Shakespeare composes in that satirical but serious plea for a national theatre, *The Dark Lady of the Sonnets*. Waiting on the terrace of the Palace at Whitehall for Mary Fitton, Shakespeare has continually to reach for his tablets in order to record the conversation of the attendant Yeoman of the Guard which consists of such phrases as 'Angels and ministers of grace defend us' or 'There, indeed, you may say of frailty that its name is woman'. Shaw's claim for the importance and the power of the theatre, however, was wholly serious. The structure of *The Duchess of Malfi* could not be borrowed but had to be created and it is that which makes it a dramatic masterpiece.

---

[3] R. W. Dent, *John Webster's Borrowing* (Berkeley and Los Angeles, 1960), p. 33.

[4] R. W. Dent, 'The White Devil, or Vittoria Corombona' in *Renaissance Drama* (1966), ed. S. Schoenbaum, pp. 179–203.

The action of the play, and consequently the presentation of the consciousness of the Duchess herself, depends upon the efforts made by the characters to conceal or discover two secrets. These secrets, the marriage of the Duchess to Antonio Bologna, the master of her household, and her subsequent secret murder at the hands of her brothers, are revealed almost immediately to the audience. The plot of the play is concerned with the way in which the knowledge of them is slowly dispersed in an ever-widening circle of awareness among the characters on stage until, in Bosola's last speech, they are defiantly proclaimed to the world. It is one of the play's most interesting features that while its subject is the mind of the Duchess, the technical 'centre of consciousness'—the character who knows most about the events of the plot and acts as an interpreter of the actions of the other characters to the audience—is Daniel de Bosola. He is responsible first for acting as the agent or 'intelligencer' who penetrates the secrets of the Duchess. He reports the birth of her children, discovers the identity of her husband, and is the actual author of her destruction. He experiences an abrupt reversal of fortune when his master, Ferdinand, Duke of Calabria, refuses to reward his murderous services. Indeed the Duke is so disturbed by the sight of his sister's dead body that he warns Bosola that he is lucky to escape with his life. This 'neglect' turns Bosola into an enemy and avenger who destroys both the brothers and reveals their secret murder to the world. In this action, however, he accidentally kills Antonio and is himself mortally wounded by Ferdinand.

Bosola is therefore both the instrument of murder and the agent of revenge. He is concerned with the revelation of a hidden crime, whether that crime is the marriage or the murder of the Duchess. In the commission of these actions he stumbles over other secrets—the violent reaction of his master which eventually turns into genuine madness and the liaison between the Cardinal of Aragon and his mistress Julia. Bosola actually witnesses her poisoning by the Cardinal after he has confessed to her that he has murdered his sister. By the end of the play all of the actors in these events are either dead or dying upon the stage and Bosola's 'Revenge' speech is thus an accurate description of the outward plot of the play:

> Revenge, for the Duchess of Malfi, murdered
> By th'Aragonian brethren; for Antonio,
> Slain by this hand; for lustful Julia,

Poison'd by this man; and lastly, for myself,
That was an actor in the main of all,
Much 'gainst mine own good nature, yet i'th'end
Neglected. (V.v.80–86)

In the double 'revenge' action—the revenge which the Cardinal and
Ferdinand take upon their sister for offending their family honour and
the retribution which overtakes them—Bosola has the part of a double-
edged weapon that cuts both ways. His position in the play is perhaps
best symbolised by the dagger which Ferdinand hands to his sister in
her chamber:

Duchess: He left this with me.
Antonio: And it seems, did wish
You would use it on yourself?
Duchess: His action seem'd
To intend so much.
Antonio: This hath a handle to't,
As well as a point: turn it towards him, and
So fasten the keen edge in his rank gall. (III.ii.149–53)

In employing Bosola to strangle the Duchess, Ferdinand is also prepar-
ing the sword-thrust which ends his own life. From his experience as
'familiar', 'intelligencer', and executioner, Bosola draws a final moral
which Webster uses to return the attention of his audience from the
plot to the subject of the play:

We are only like dead walls, or vaulted graves
That, ruin'd, yields no echo. Fare you well;
It may be pain: but no harm to me to die
In so good a quarrel. Oh this gloomy world,
In what a shadow, or deep pit of darkness
Doth, womanish, and fearful, mankind live?
Let worthy minds ne'er stagger in distrust
To suffer death or shame for what is just:
Mine is another voyage. (V.v.96–104)

Bosola's voyage to oblivion is a more terrible version of the 'everlasting
cold' (V.vi.267) caught by Flamineo at the end of *The White Devil*.
Flamineo describes his life as 'a black charnel' while Bosola describes
the human body as being itself a 'dead wall' or 'vaulted grave'. Web-

ster's vision of hell always seems to be associated with a crippling cold that paralyses the will as certainly as it afflicts the body with *rigor mortis*. The terrible certainty of oblivion receives repeated expression at the end of the play. The Cardinal hopes that he may be 'laid by, and never thought of' (V.v.89) while Delio describes the fame of both Ferdinand and the Cardinal as no more enduring than if a man should 'Fall in a frost, and leave his print in snow' (V.v.114). Bosola's pessimism is entirely justified but the very words in which it is expressed are designed to remind the audience that the play contains more secrets than can be dreamt of in the limited vessel of Bosola's consciousness.

The reference to the body as a tomb is a traditional proverb and an equally traditional part of a puritan psychology that regarded the entire world of the senses as a deceitful mirage. The doctrine of σῶμα—σῆμα 'the body is a tomb', mentioned by Plato in *Cratylus* 400c, conceives of the body as 'a tomb wherein the *psyche* lies dead, awaiting its resurrection into true life which is life without the body'.[5] Bosola had expressed this attitude before when he told the Duchess that the soul in the body is like a lark in a cage. The Duchess accepts death as a release from prison and an entry into a better world and tells her executioners:

> Pull, and pull strongly, for your able strength
> Must pull down heaven upon me: (IV.ii.226–7)

but her hopes of heaven are not unconnected with the belief that she will meet her husband there. For the Duchess the 'eternal Church' will be a place where 'we shall not part thus' (III.v.68–9) and is thus contrasted with the Church served by her brother the Cardinal which has forced them to part, as they suspect for ever, on the road that leads from Ancona. The Duchess has expressed her love for her husband and children through her body and its senses in life. In death she hopes that heaven will grant her that freedom to love which the world controlled by her brothers is determined to deny. Even Bosola seems aware that the condition that he describes is not man's inevitable destiny since he seems to suggest that 'worthy minds' may possibly extract themselves from the 'shadow, or deep pit of darkness' in which 'womanish and fearful' mankind lives. This description is taken from the fifth book of Sidney's *Arcadia*:

[5] E. R. Dodds, *The Greeks and the Irrational* (Berkeley and Los Angeles and Cambridge, 1951), pp. 152, 169 n.87.

in such a shadow or rather pit of darkness, the wormish mankind
lives, that neither they know how to forsee, nor what to fear: and are
but like tennis balls, tossed by the racket of the higher powers.

R. W. Dent, in noting the passage, asks the pertinent question, 'In this
play, where the Duchess displays more courage than any of the male
characters, one wonders if Webster changed "wormish" to "womanish" for any reason other than metre'.[6] Bosola's dying speech expresses
his own pessimistic view of an absurd universe in which men are the
'stars' tennis balls'. The imagery in which this pessimism is expressed
recalls to the audience's imagination the death of the Duchess and
therefore reminds them of human behaviour which may have been
'womanish' but was certainly not fearful. Bosola's very assertion
that the human body is a vaulted grave 'That, ruin'd, yields no echo'
must serve to remind the audience of the spectacular stage effect of the
echo from the tomb and that suggests that Bosola's dying words are not
a complete explanation of the dramatic facts. It is a dramatic triumph
to make Bosola, the agent of death and a 'wretched thing of blood'
(V.v.91) the dramatic catalyst who is responsible for revealing to the
audience the unshaken resolution and independent integrity of the
Duchess. He has striven to ignore these qualities in life, and in death he
sees death and shame as their only reward. There is, therefore, an
imaginative gap between the dramatic facts of the play as perceived by
the audience and the interpretation of them, and of the world, offered by
Bosola. In the scene of execution, Bosola tells the Duchess 'I am come
to make thy tomb' (IV.ii.115) but the dramatist has employed him to
make the entire play her monument. She has used her body to express
rather than to bury her soul and from her stage tomb she breaks out
into the only after-life that the critic can predict for her—an existence
in the imagination of the audience. What matters, then, for our understanding of the play, is not the depth to which we succeed in penetrating Bosola's motives. His masks and disguises, however sinister or
extraordinary, are a reflection from the standing pool of policy round
which he moves and which, as the Cardinal later suggests, reaches as
deep as hell itself. This reflection provides the background against
which the audience can perceive and judge the quality of the Duchess.

Webster uses this imaginative gap to suggest that there may be
another order of existence, an approach to life based upon a love which

[6] *John Webster's Borrowing*, p. 265.

is a high adventure of the human spirit, that is totally beyond the comprehension of Bosola, or Ferdinand, or the Cardinal. This failure of intelligence destroys them because in attempting to crush that power in the Duchess they compass their own ruin. Ferdinand's reaction, and the way in which the Cardinal treats Julia, are perhaps an indication that the denial of the instincts of love is a clear case of self-destruction. These are comforting thoughts but the dramatist does not allow them to obscure the evident fact that the Duchess is dead and that Bosola's report on his own life and the mist and pit of darkness in which he finds himself is, as far as it goes, an accurate one. The balance between love and self-destruction in human affairs is a delicate one and there are no easy solutions. The problem for the dramatist, as the author of *A Delicate Balance* pointed out in a recent interview, is:

> getting people to listen to the words. They will listen only to what they want to hear and then translate it into something they can live with. I don't like to let them off the hook: which is one of the reasons I get criticized for not having the catharsis in the body of the play. I don't think that's where the catharsis should be any more. I think it should take place in the mind of the spectator some time afterwards—maybe a year after experiencing the play. One thing I don't like about the naturalistic theatre in general is that it usually gives answers instead of asking questions.[7]

Catharsis is itself a confusing and inexact term which Aristotle appears to have used in an attempt to describe or justify the disturbing pheno-menon that we cannot yet claim to understand—the fact that an audience receives pleasure from the representation of scenes of death and horror. Albee is, I believe, redefining the term in order to point out that the events represented upon the stage are not designed by the author as an 'answer'—they do not represent a stimulus which must produce an involuntary and predictable reaction upon the part of the audience. Instead they are an array of sensations designed to draw attention to observations about the world which the author believes to be interesting or important but whose structure and significance may take time to perceive. The play is a process which educates the attention of the audience to the distinctive features of the play but which must also appeal to their own judgement and experience of the world.

[7] Irving Wardle, 'Edward Albee looks at himself and his plays' *The Times* (18 January 1969).

Although the audience sitting in the theatre appear to be merely passive, their participation in the events of the play is, at least in some sense, an active one requiring the exercise of perception and judgement. This accounts not only for the great variety of literary opinion but for the bitterness with which the matter is disputed, since to attack a man's opinions about a play may be to assault the quality of his perception of the world.

John Webster has been called decadent or obsessed with death because his plays do frequently resemble a charnel-house of the imagination in which the audience cannot escape the knowledge of their own death and therefore react, on occasion, with the disgust and disbelief that are naturally aroused by this uncomfortable thought. Webster forces his audience to regard this unpalatable fact because it is only once it has been accepted that the full value of the other elements of his composition can be appreciated. The intricate spider's web of intrigue, 'policy', and death which surrounds the Duchess creates a darkness both in the language and the lighting of the stage which concentrates attention upon her own perspective of the world.

This darkness, which engulfs the entire play by the fifth act, is established early in the action. Although the immediate concern of the plot will be the secret marriage, the first information that the audience receives is designed to suggest that the conduct of Bosola, the Cardinal, and Ferdinand conceals events whose disclosure will certainly be discreditable and may be dangerous. In the course of the first act, this sinister information is slowly expanded but no explicit account of their past is given. These hints and details, therefore, represent a threat for the future which Bosola defines more clearly in the character-sketch of the brothers which he gives to Antonio:

> He and his brother are like plum trees, that grow crooked over standing pools, they are rich, and o'erladen with fruit, but none but crows, pies, and caterpillars feed on them. Could I be one of their flatt'ring panders, I would hang on their ears like a horse-leech, till I were full, and then drop off. (I.i.49–54)

The poisonous atmosphere associated with a standing or stagnant pool is a deliberate extension of Antonio's description of a prince's court as 'like a common fountain' (I.i.12) and a contrast is already established between the pure spring of the French court and the possibility of a polluted source in Italy. The image is one of sterility since the fruit produced by crooked plum-trees serves only to fatten scavenging birds and noxious insects. Bosola describes himself as a horse-leech and Antonio later compares him to a moth which breeds in unused clothes and destroys them. This sense of the court as a standing pool which breeds nothing but poisonous and preying forms of life is reinforced by the continuing recurrence of such images in the language of Delio and Antonio. The Cardinal is described as 'a melancholy churchman. The spring in his face is nothing but the engend'ring of toads' (I.ii.80–82), while Ferdinand uses the law 'like a foul black cobweb to a spider' (I.ii.100). Beneath these assertions of a general threat lies the one certain piece of information—that Bosola has served seven years in the galleys for 'a notorious murther' (I.i.70) which had probably been committed at the instigation of the Cardinal. It is, therefore, a matter of infinite menace when he is left behind in order to act as Ferdinand's intelligencer. Bosola's prediction of his own intentions comes true in a rather unexpected fashion. Intending to behave like a horse-leech to the brothers he finds himself latched on to the Duchess as her master of the horse. He begins her destruction by offering her unripe fruit which had, so he says, been forced on in horse-dung. He thrives on the information which he sucks out and transmits to his master, and he does not drop off from the Duchess until he has drained her of life.

The intelligence which Bosola slowly gains about the marriage of the Duchess is carefully designed and structured to convey information about two other important matters to the audience. The Aragon brothers' concern at the conduct of their sister reveals more of their hidden nature than they suspect or intend, while the steadily mounting pressure that they put on her reveals a way of life which they are incapable of appreciating but whose elimination will cause their own destruction. Ferdinand thus begins to give himself away to the audience at the very moment that he gives Bosola his commission as secret agent:

Ferdinand: I give you that
    To live i'th'court, here: and observe the Duchess,
    To note all the particulars of her haviour:
    What suitors do solicit her for marriage
    And whom she best affects: she's a young widow,
    I would not have her marry again.
Bosola: No, sir?

Ferdinand: Do not you ask the reason: but be satisfied,
    I say I would not. (I.ii.172–9)

Ferdinand's reason is never revealed in the play. What the audience is offered is a series of hints and suggestions which is more effective than direct statement since they combine to suggest a totally psychopathic personality. He is evidently fascinated by his sister's sexuality. He objects to her taste for masques and revels and advises her that:

... women like that part, which, like the lamprey,
Hath nev'r a bone in't. (I.ii.255–6)

When he learns that she has had a child, his response is not merely to demand revenge for injured honour but to inflame himself into a murderous rage by filling his mind with images of his sister in the act of copulation with a variety of partners. Rebuked by his brother he threatens to 'kill her' symbolically by murdering the Cardinal or stabbing himself—a threat which he later fulfils in madness. This combination of prurient interest in the details of the sexual encounter together with puritanical and fanatical expressions of horror at the act is an acute report of a common and wearisome condition of humanity. It has led critics to assert that Ferdinand was 'really' afflicted by an incestuous love for his sister. The matter has perhaps been most succinctly expressed by William Empson:

Elizabethans believed that Lucrezia Borgia went to bed with her brothers because, owing to her intense family pride, which was like that of the Pharaohs, she could find no fit mate elsewhere. The incestuous reflections of Ferdinand would thus be obvious to the first audiences, as a standard expression of the insane pride which is almost his only characteristic (at the start of the play, he forbids his courtiers to laugh unless he laughs first); no wonder he turns into a wolf in the last act, as one hoped he would.[8]

In the absence of any definite or unequivocal indication by the dramatist, the matter can hardly be settled. The play does not require its audience to settle it because what is at issue is not the indicated sexuality of Ferdinand's passion but the way in which his love for his sister has been poisoned at its source and turned into violence. The 'explanation' of Ferdinand in terms of incestuous desires is perhaps popular

[8] William Empson, 'Mine Eyes Dazzle', *Essays in Criticism*, 14 (1964), 80–86.

because it is supposed to account for his violence. The phenomenon observed by Webster is, however, rather more complex than can be accounted for by the inadequate labels of our still primitive psychology. If his perception of her sexuality drives Ferdinand to murder, it is the beauty, even in death, of her body that restores him for a terrible moment to his senses:

> Cover her face. Mine eyes dazzle: she di'd young.
>
> (IV.ii.259)

In the intelligence which he had received from Bosola, Ferdinand had seen only a hidden crime against his family honour which must be punished if necessary by death. As he looks upon the sister whom he has destroyed he perceives, for the first time in the play, the world of love which he has been unable to comprehend and from which he has now banished himself for ever. His attempt to confine the Duchess in prison and send her to her grave succeeds, but at the cost of his own reason. The condition of lycanthropy, in which he imagines himself to be a wolf, is not simply the 'fatal judgment' (V.ii.83) that Bosola calls it but the result of a strenuous and unreasonable attempt to deny the other information carried by Bosola's intelligence—the existence of passions which humanity shares with the animals but also, perhaps, with the angels and which cannot be extinguished except by a flight into madness and death.

These passions receive one of their most remarkable expressions in the scene in which Ferdinand, visiting the Duchess under cover of darkness in order to preserve his vow never to see her again, hands her the dead hand which she is intended to mistake for Antonio's. When she first feels it she assumes that it is Ferdinand's:

> *Duchess*:   You are very cold.
> I fear you are not well after your travel:
> Ha! Lights: Oh horrible!
> *Ferdinand*:   Let her have lights enough.
>
> (IV.i.51-4)

The scene is comic as well as horrible and could become the form of macabre farce that arouses wild laughter instead of the pity and terror traditionally associated with tragedy. If the Duchess is merely passive in this scene then the leaving of the hand is simply a joke, though a horrible one, which makes a mockery of her and her hopes. The note of pity, the care for her brother in spite of everything, provides an actress with the opportunity, which she must value and seize upon, to be actively and compassionately engaged in the scene. The mockery of her situation and her hopes is no less, but the quality of her mercy cannot be laughed away. It is this note which seems to me the key to Webster's treatment of the Duchess. She may describe herself as

> ... acquainted with sad misery,
> As the tann'd galley-slave is with his oar.
> Necessity makes me suffer constantly.
> And custom makes it easy. (IV.ii.28–31)

but unlike Bosola who, although he has been released from the galleys is still the slave of fate and chance, she is never one of the stars' tennis balls but operates upon her environment up to what is literally her last breath. When she is dead it emerges that she has in fact changed the course of the action.

The way in which this effect will be achieved is revealed in her first interview with her brothers. They warn her expressly against the dishonourable dangers of a second marriage and season their advice with explicit threats.

> *Cardinal*:   You may flatter yourself,
>   And take your own choice: privately be married
>   Under the eaves of night—
> *Ferdinand*:   Think't the best voyage
>   That e'er you made; like the irregular crab,
>   Which, though't goes backward, thinks that it goes right,
>   Because it goes its own way: but observe:
>   Such weddings may more properly be said
>   To be executed, than celebrated.
> *Cardinal*:   The marriage night
>   Is the entrance into some prison. (I.ii.236–44)

A few lines later the Duchess reveals to the audience that even as she listened to these words she had already chosen her course. She is well aware that her marriage may seem irregular and that her own way is now a perilous one

>   —wish me good speed
>   For I am going into a wilderness,
>   Where I shall find nor path, nor friendly clew
>   To be my guide. (I.ii.277–80)

As a free spirit she chooses with both her blood and her judgement. Within the framework of the poisoned fountain or standing pool which is the world ruled by her brothers, and the 'deep pit of darkness' which is the fifth act, Webster has provided the Duchess with six major scenes. These are the wooing and winning of Antonio, the scene of her pregnancy and the labour induced by Bosola's apricots, the 'merry' evening with Cariola and Antonio in her chamber the night that Ferdinand enters and finds her talking to herself while brushing her hair at the mirror, the banishment from Ancona and her parting from Antonio, and finally the two scenes of torture and death. In the plot of the play these are scenes which reveal more and more of her secret to her brothers and appear to place her completely in their power. They also, I believe by deliberate dramatic design, span the major events of a woman's life—marriage, childbirth, disaster, parting, and death. As the tension increases so the courage of the Duchess rises to meet it—a frame of mind which is as heroic in her circumstances as it is when expressed by the poet of *The Battle of Maldon*. Courage, good humour, and consideration for others are the unvarying characteristics which Webster is careful to attribute to her in these changing circumstances and therefore produce that sense of identity that allows us to talk about a dramatic 'character'. Gradually her brothers, and their instrument Bosola, remove from her everything that has made life worth living until she is left with nothing but her courage. Yet she encounters her executioners with the same wit and determination that had carried her into the 'wilderness' of her love. Her 'voyage' may be accused of swerving from the decorum proper to her rank and birth but 'like the irregular crab' she remains convinced that her way is right. In the world of the play it is the behaviour of her executioners that is irregular and unnatural. They are themselves aware of this the instant that they have killed her, and Ferdinand and Bosola begin the long and deadly process of mutual recrimination over her still warm corpse. It is a mistake to regard the fifth act as the conventional but dull execution of 'poetic justice' upon the evildoers. It is a working model of the world of 'policy' unredeemed by human love which the characters extinguished in themselves when they murdered the Duchess upon the stage.

The secret which the Cardinal and his brother must now conceal from the world is the 'present from your princely brothers' (IV.ii.163) conveyed to the Duchess by Bosola. Death is, as the Duchess says, the best gift that they can give and Webster uses all of the macabre resources of the masque of madmen, the coffin, cords, and Bosola's bellman speech to reinforce this sensation for his audience so that it strikes with maximum effect. The lunatic fantasies of the masque of madmen are interesting because their obsessions cause them to misinterpret the events of the world and confuse them with their own fantasies of lust and power. The view that 'Hell is a mere glass-house, where the devils are continually blowing up women's souls on hollow irons, and the fire never goes out' (IV.ii.78–80) is ominously close to the opinions shared by Ferdinand and the Cardinal. This is the mad world which Bosola controls and in which he is himself 'an actor in the main of all', although he is not yet conscious of the insane part that he is playing. Bosola's actions are based upon the belief that Ferdinand is a competent Machiavellian.[9] It turns out that he is lunatic and dangerous. The act which should satisfy Ferdinand and bring Bosola his reward has, therefore, an entirely opposite effect. Ferdinand half realises that, whatever he may have intended, he was not prepared to endure the true consequences or effect of his actions. This makes him 'ungrateful' to Bosola and that act of ingratitude seals his own fate. Bosola is forced to realise that his own interpretation of the world has been wrong. He realises it too late—there can now be no turning back for any of the characters—but in showing the secret of death to the Duchess he has prepared the way in which this same secret is slowly revealed in the last act, claiming another death at every step. The coffin, the cords, and the tolling bell are the rites of passage for all the characters in the play. If they have paid attention to Bosola's words the audience may be slightly chilled by the realisation that the bell tolls for them.

This knowledge does not terrify the Duchess. There is a distinct danger that the calmness with which the Duchess accepts her death may leave the audience unmoved by its terror. The fear and agony of Cariola, biting and scratching as the cord goes round her neck and struggling to avoid the inevitable by a vain succession of increasingly improbable pleas for a stay of execution, remind them that death is, at the last, still terrible. For Cariola life itself is still a thing of value and she properly fights in its defence. If the Duchess does not struggle it is because only her love for Antonio has made her life of value to her and

---

[9] The best account of the masque's function in the structure of the play is the often reprinted article by Inga-Stina Ekeblad, 'The "Impure Art" of John Webster', *Review of English Studies*, N.S. IX (1958), 253–67.

the acceptance of death has now become the only available expression of that love. It is the only expression left because her marriage with Antonio cannot observe the 'degree, priority and place' of a world ordered by Ferdinand and the Cardinal. The Duchess appeals beyond the customs of her society to the natural world where the birds in the fields are free to choose their own mates. Her family is an expression of that natural order and her courage in its defence provides a hint of the power which might translate it into a new political reality. The Renaissance court now seems a devious labyrinth which obstructs the very human nature it had once liberated. It can still crush the Duchess but it cannot control indefinitely the power which she represents. Webster's observation of the troubles which afflicted his society is both accurate and prophetic.

In *Beyond Psychology* Otto Rank has written of the need for

a new evaluation beyond our moral classification of masculine and feminine which shall take into account the more fundamental difference concerning the functioning of the will in the personality of the two sexes. Whereas man's will in its free expression is simply 'wanting', in woman's psychology we meet the paradoxical will phenomenon of wanting to be wanted. Such reversal in the expression of the will raises the question as to whether we are to see in it another perversity of human nature or a genuine expression of woman's natural self. This latter assumption would then presuppose that there always was and still is a woman-psychology, which has not only remained unrecognized through the ages but has been misinterpreted religiously, socially and psychologically in terms of masculine ideologies.[10]

Rank is himself drawing attention to a problem rather than attempting to offer an exact description of an admitted scientific truth. If *The Duchess of Malfi* is concerned with a 'woman-psychology' then Julia exists as a reminder that it is neither simple nor necessarily admirable. Some of the difficulties inherent in the situation are perhaps reflected in the way in which many critics have condemned Antonio, especially when he is presented as on his way to appeal to the Cardinal's sense of humanity, as lacking in masculine decisiveness. The play is a carefully constructed dramatic equation whose 'solution' depends upon the value

[10] Otto Rank, *Beyond Psychology* (New York, 1958), pp. 240–41.

that we are ourselves prepared to assign to some of its unknown quantities. The structure and the imagery both seem to suggest that within the framework of the poisoned fountain or standing pool of the opening and the deep pit of darkness which is its end, John Webster has succeeded in presenting one woman's psychology which is misinterpreted, religiously, socially, and psychologically in terms of the masculine ideology of her brothers. The problem is not one that requires an answer since what is being dramatised is the unresolved clash between vital and competing human instincts and the imperfect control exercised by man's turbulent intelligence. Webster does not offer us a solution but a report in which the growing darkness of the 'sensible hell' perceived by Bosola is lit for a moment by the flash of 'I am Duchess of Malfi still'.

1   Vittoria Accoramboni, the 'White Devil', a portrait attributed to Alessandro Allori

2   The Court of the Duchess of Malfi. Leslie Hurry's design for the
1960-1 Stratford/Aldwych production. *From centre:* Eric Porter as
Ferdinand, Peggy Ashcroft as the Duchess, Max Adrian as the
Cardinal, Sian Phillips as Julia, Derek Godfrey as Antonio

3   *Das Wappen des Todes*. Engraving by Albrecht Dürer, 1503

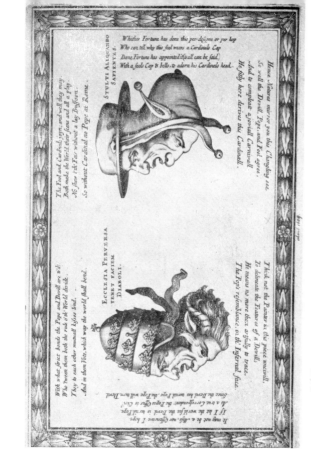

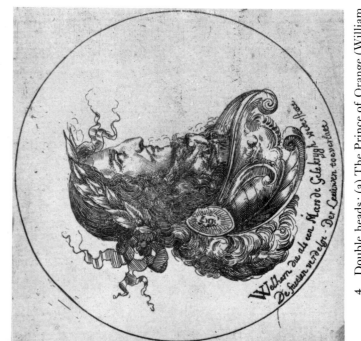

ECCLESIA PERVERSA
TENET FACIEM
DIABOLI.

STVLTI ALIQVANDO
SAPIENTES.

It may not be a whit more Obscene I Ape,
As a true Correspondent the Pope Ape is Cut,
If I like the world so the Devil is no like Pope.
Since the Devil his world Pope, the Pope with turn Devil.

With what sweet hands the Pope and Devill are ti'l,
Who between them both the rule o'th' World devide,
They to each other mutuall kisses bend,
And in them Vote, which way the world shall bend.

Think not the Painter is the piece uncivill,
To delineate the Traitor of a Devill,
He meant no more than arguily to trace,
The Pope resemblance, to th' Infernal face.

Whither Fortune has done this per-desinne or yer hap
Can tell why this fool wears a Cardinals Cap
Done Fortune has appointed it is all can be said,
With a fools Cap & bells to adorn his Cardinals head.

The Fool and Cardinall joyn, and well they may
Both make the World their foote and all 's a play
We show 'tth Few without a lay Buffoon,
So without Cardinall no Pope at Rome.

Hence Nature mirrs you this Changling see,
So well the Devill Pope and Fool agree,
And to compleate a jeerall Carnivall
He subly here derives this Cardinall.

4 Double heads: (a) The Prince of Orange (William
   III) in two aspects (Catalogue of British Museum
   Satires, I, no. 1222)

   (b) Pope/Devil and Cardinal/Fool (ibid., no. 1230)

5 [opposite] 'Perspective' woodcuts by Erhard Schön:

   (a) Equivocal scene, entitled 'Aus, du alter Tor!'

   (b) Landscape with portraits of Charles V, Ferdinand I, Pope
   Paul III, and Francis I, c. 1535

7　The Great Paranoiac, by Salvador Dali

6　The Last Judgement, by Hermann Tom Ring, 1555

8 *Damned Souls*, from Rogier van der Weyden's *Last Judgement*

9 *Death and the Lovers.* Engraving by Albrecht Dürer

The Devil's Law-Case—*an End or a Beginning?*

GUNNAR BOKLUND

The Devil's Law-Case—*an End or a Beginning?*

T H E   T I T L E   T H A T   I have chosen is not supposed to indicate an attempt to establish a new chronology of Webster's plays. I shall not be concerned with works printed later than 1623, which for one reason or another have been ascribed to Webster, nor shall I argue in favour of a change of the generally accepted order of the three familiar plays, and propose *The Devil's Law-Case* first, *The White Devil* second, and *The Duchess of Malfi* third, attractive though this order would be from the moralist's point of view. It would be pleasant to end a consideration of the significant part of Webster's career by making the dramatist himself conclude that

> *Integrity of life, is fames best friend,*
> *Which noblely (beyond Death) shall crowne the end.* [1]

It would, however, be perilous to base chronology on such vague internal evidence as a gradual change of moral attitude or religious convictions. I shall instead be cautiously conservative and accept the old order of the three plays—*The White Devil, The Duchess of Malfi, The Devil's Law-Case*—not only, to be sure, because it is old or for the sake of the argument, but because it still appears the most reasonable one, having the support both of Webster himself in the Dedication to Sir Thomas Finch and of R. W. Dent with his convincing kind of internal evidence.[2] The end and the beginning with which I shall be concerned are, then, only incidentally matters of chronology.

Although Professor Dent has not been able to identify anything like the same number of borrowings in *The Devil's Law-Case* as he has in

---

[1] *The Duchess of Malfi,* V.v.145–6. My Webster quotations are all from Lucas's edition (1927).

[2] R. W. Dent, *John Webster's Borrowing* (Berkeley and Los Angeles, 1960), pp. 57–9.

The White Devil and *The Duchess of Malfi*, he seems fairly confident
that 'it was composed in the same imitative fashion as were the tragedies'.[3] More or less familiar proverbs are indeed quoted or distorted,
passages from Matthieu, Montaigne, and above all Sidney are similarly treated, and *Sejanus* and *The Devil is an Ass* join Sir William
Alexander's tragedies among the few dramatic sources of Webster's
inspiration. Granted that Professor Dent's admission that he 'investigated so little of the popular literature from 1615 on' largely accounts
for the paucity of verbal parallels to passages in *The Devil's Law-Case*
thus far discovered, we may still be able to make a valid distinction
between Webster's workmanship in the tragicomedy and in the tragedies.[4] It has been my experience—and I daresay not a unique one—
that every time one reads through the bulk of English drama written,
say, between 1600 and 1612, one encounters passages and exchanges
which recall *The White Devil* and *The Duchess of Malfi*, often in the
most unexpected places. I am not referring to proverbial expressions
such as the stars' tennis balls, which as frequently appear as footballs,
or even to death's doors that open two ways—nets to catch the wind
are, after all, spread in many an early play apart from *The Devil's
Law-Case*—but to more unpredictable echoes. It is surprising to find
the following observation in Cooke's *Greene's Tu Quoque*:

> Poor wretched man! thou'st had a golden dream,
> Which gilded over thy calamity;
> But, being awake, thou find'st it ill-laid on.[5]

Or the following one in the anonymous *Trial of Chivalry*:

> I tell you, madam, I shall shortly have
> His whole proportion cut in Alabaster,
> Armd as he was when he encountred here,
> Which kneeling shall be set upon his tombe.[6]

It is equally surprising to come across a fair sprinkling of evocative
passages in *Charlemagne*, including a gordian knot and a venture in one
poor shallow boat, and the wonder grows when in William Rowley's *A*

---

[3] Dent, op. cit., p. 59.
[4] ibid., p. 59.
[5] J. Cooke, *Greene's Tu Quoque*, p. 277 (in R. Dodsley and W. C. Hazlitt, *A
Select Collection of Old English Plays* (1874–76),XI).
[6] *The Trial of Chivalry*, IV.i. (in A. H. Bullen, *A Collection of Old English
Plays* (New York, 1964), II, 325).

Shoemaker a Gentleman Sir Hugh and his beloved Winifred meet mar-
tyrdom in a fashion that has a familiar ring to it:

> *Hugh*: The storme of death now comes,
>   Beare up brave saile.
> *Win*: I feele no storme; but even the merriest gaile
>   That ever life was driven with.[7]

Earlier in the same play we have been treated to a wooing scene between Leonora, the emperor's daughter, and Crispianus, supposedly a
squire of very low degree, a scene that comes astonishingly close to the
Duchess's wooing of Antonio:

> *Leon.*: . . . but these are petty Arts, no Ile shew thee by speculatory
>   magick, her face In this glass; kneele sir, for't must be done with
>   reverence I tell you: now tell me what thou seest?
> *Crisp.*: I see a shadow Madam.
> *Leon.*: 'Tis but a shadow, hold up thy right hand and looke agen, What
>   seest thou now? any substance yet?
> *Crisp.*: I know not madam, I am inchaunted with your Magick.
> *Leon.*: 'Tis too long to dally, away with shadowes, and imbrace the
>   substance, introth I love thee; nay doe not feare . . . Ile share
>   all dangers with thee.[8]

I have not come across any passages in the drama before 1618, apart
from proverbial expressions, which with similar immediacy suggest
The Devil's Law-Case, and the play may thus represent an actual slack-
ening of Webster's imitative tendencies and, in spite of Professor
Dent's *caveat*, be somewhat further removed in workmanship from the
tragedies than at first appears.

The difference in plot-structure between *The Devil's Law-Case* on
one hand and *The White Devil* and *The Duchess of Malfi* on the other
has of course long been obvious. As Lucas and long before him Stoll
explained, Webster may have found a useful version of how a mother
tries to disown her son by proclaiming him a bastard in any one of half
a dozen works, from Johannes Magnus' *History of the Swedish Kings* to
the anonymous play *Lust's Dominion*, to which list Professor Dent has
more recently added Warner's *Continuance of Albion's England*.[9] But no

---

[7] W. Rowley, *A Shoemaker a Gentleman* (1638), I1r.
[8] ibid. E2r.
[9] See Lucas, op. cit., ii, 215–21; and Dent, op cit., pp. 308–9.

matter 'from what particular tree in the forest Webster picked his chestnut'—to use Lucas's phrase—this did not provide him with more than one important element of his plot; he had nothing like the solid framework supplied by Belleforest in the case of *The Duchess of Malfi* and by the story of Vittoria Accoramboni in the case of *The White Devil*, to which he could add and from which he could subtract as he saw fit, but which still gave his plot substance and direction. In *The Devil's Law-Case* we have to do with several elements of roughly equal significance to that of the law-case itself. We have Goulart's story of how a would-be murderer manages to cure his enemy by bleeding him to health instead of to death; we have the story dramatised in *The London Prodigal* of how a father, appearing in disguise, announces his own death in order to be able to study the reactions of his profligate son; we have the episode in *The Malcontent* of the wounded Ferneze, presumed dead by friends and enemies alike; we may have the abortive duel between Ingen and Lord Proudly in Field's *Amends for Ladies*; we certainly have the names of Leonora, Crispianus, and Winifred in William Rowley's *A Shoemaker a Gentleman*.[10] Since a more systematic search for similarly pertinent episodes will undoubtedly uncover others, it would seem indicated that Webster pieced together the plot of his tragicomedy in a manner closely related to that in which he perfected the verbal structure of the tragedies. He had neither the natural continuity of an exciting story nor the elemental problems of a familiar *exemplum* to fall back on, and was apparently not able to bring his disparate ingredients together to a convincing dramatic whole. For *The Devil's Law-Case* moves along in an undeniably jerky fashion, even though it begins and ends with Romelio at the centre of interest. The original conflict between Contarino, Ercole, and Romelio over Jolenta, cleverly envisaged and effectively presented as it is, seems most con-clusively solved when the duel has been fought. Then Romelio's attempt to recoup himself for his commercial losses, first by murdering Contarino and then by having Jolenta masquerade as pregnant, is devel-oped in almost loving detail, whereupon Leonora's plot to revenge herself on her son leads to the elaborate and centrally located trial scene, with its not altogether unexpected reversals of fortune. The combination of schemes and accidents that brings the play to a conclu-sion must, however, be said to defy prediction; the last act of *The*

[10] For Goulart's story see Dent, op. cit., pp. 304–5, and for the Ferneze episode Elizabeth M. Brennan, 'An Understanding Auditory' in the present volume.

Devil's Law-Case is technically a worthy counterpart to the last act of *The Duchess of Malfi* in its apparently capricious and melodramatic design. Whether it serves an equally worthy purpose is a question to which I shall return. Let it suffice to say now that if Webster was trying to write a tragicomedy in the fashionable Fletcherian manner— and this may be what he was doing—he ran into considerable difficulties, particularly but far from exclusively in his final act.[11]

To the Websterian it must seem almost sacrilegious to treat Webster from a technical point of view, as if he were a disciple of John Fletcher, and I shall not continue in this vein without having tried a more catholic approach: to study *The Devil's Law-Case* in a Websterian sense, i.e. in the critical light shed on it by *The White Devil* and *The Duchess of Malfi*. Does the play make sense or, perhaps rather, does it make Websterian sense? In order to answer these questions I shall have to take a fresh look at the tragedies, where this distinction may not be without its validity either.

As I interpreted *The White Devil* years ago, from my own rather unusual vantage-point, the tragedy undoubtedly made sense, particularly if the dramatist's ever admirable intentions could be taken into account when his execution did not come up to expectations. I still manage to live comfortably with this hybrid, this Websterian *White Devil*, and in spite of a growing distrust of interpretations I still find myself in basic accord with mine own. I still cannot see *The White Devil* primarily as a 'tragic satire', since the tone of Webster's comments is to me sardonic rather than satirical and their aim to generalise on human nature rather than criticise individual aspects of it. Although the play has no tragic hero or heroine in any meaningful sense of the word, it is by no means lacking in tragic effect, since it evokes in the susceptible audience its own peculiar kind of pity. This is a pity not for the ineffectually virtuous men and women who go mad or are killed off after having tried halfheartedly to prevent the success of evil from being absolute. Nor is it a pity for the obnoxiously vicious ones, who either perish or know how to withdraw to the relative safety of high offices. It is at the most a pity for the general state of mankind, mankind which embraces both categories and does not seem able to produce any practically valid alternative between the two.

---

[11] For the tragicomic aspects of *The Devil's Law-Case* see J. R. Mulryne, 'Webster and the Uses of Tragicomedy', in the present volume.

This pity for the 'busy monster man unkind' is, I still maintain, alto-gether more important than the notorious vitality of Webster's 'glorious villains', without which, however, it could not have been created. The triumph of the will that so many critics discover when Flamineo and Vittoria prepare themselves to die, is presented by Webster as real enough but also as a shallow triumph, barely concealing the emptiness underneath, as the self-sufficient victims are made to realise in their ultimate moments. Compared to the calculating amoralism of the Grand Duke, who directs the final operation, the flamboyancy of mur-derers and victims alike amounts to little but a grand gesture, not far removed in effect from Cornelia's and Marcello's moralising and the young Giovanni's pious promise to punish 'all that have hands in this'. What has proved most disturbing about *The White Devil* may, however, be the impression that the gestures are at least not despicable.

So far so good. It is always pleasant to come across a play that is so nicely balanced thematically as *The White Devil*. The balance is, however, also precarious, which a comparison with the quite similar but much more secure balance of *Volpone* will bring out. At almost any given moment of Webster's tragedy and particularly during the last act, the intensity with which individual episodes and individual speeches are developed threatens to tear the play apart and turn it into a ram-bling melodrama. Flamineo's running commentary is not the safest guide to the meaning of *The White Devil*, and after the rapid sequence of horror, mockery, and violence that one is exposed to in the Paduan scenes, it may well be impossible to gather one's wits sufficiently together during Lodovico's and Giovanni's final exchange of words to realise what the end of the play actually tries to achieve. We have ample evidence that there are people who find it difficult to appreciate the 'impure art of John Webster', who refuse to accept the Websterian sense of *The White Devil* as at all adequately expressed, and it is only sensible to admit that there may be good reasons for this.

The Duchess of Malfi has always been an easier play to come to terms with, and not only because 'its hero and heroine are more worthy of our moral approbation', as Lucas once in some disgust put it.[12] Up to the murder of the Duchess Webster spins a very simple plot indeed, a plot virtually without distracting ingredients once Bosola's strange intelligencing capers at Amalfi are taken for granted. In contrast to *The White Devil*, *The Duchess of Malfi* has also got at its centre an easily

---

[12] Lucas, op. cit., i, 100.

defined but extremely dynamic moral issue, which is kept alive at least as long as the heroine is alive. It would actually seem as if, while we are mainly concerned with Webster's treatment of Belleforest's *exemplum*, we are in no significant difficulties, whereas when the dramatist begins to operate on his own he soon manages to confuse at least the casual spectator.

For in spite of her passivity the Duchess provides her tragedy with a definite centre, not only from the point of view of plot but above all thematically, as her stature changes from that of the exclusively private individual, bent upon her personal enjoyment, to that of a plausible symbol of all that suffer without having recourse to either force, justice, or mercy. It is a development of which we slowly become aware, not yet when the Duchess is brought on to the stage big with child, perhaps not even when she appeals to the law of nature which the birds that live in the field are allowed to obey, but certainly when she says farewell to Antonio and their eldest child in a vain attempt to save as many as possible 'from the Tiger'. It is all achieved with remarkable restraint and lack of sentimentality. No matter what a Jacobean audience may have thought about the Duchess's conduct in the first act, at the moment when she and Antonio part and—as I once put it—for ever afterwards she is certainly innocent, and the combination of nature, innocence, and defencelessness seems to prepare the ground for the apotheosis of the Duchess and the repentance or punishment of her murderers, which would bring the tragedy to a truly satisfying moral close.[13]

But, as I still maintain, this is not Webster's way. By making the Duchess to an increasing extent share the limelight with Bosola, he has made it possible for us to understand properly the nature of his repentance and the extent of his reformation. That Webster has made Bosola himself express complete faith in the goodness of his quarrel should not mislead anyone, since we here have to do with the most convincing inventor of subterfuges and rationaliser of motives that ever cut throat on the stage. It is really a most unlikely combination of circumstances that brings about the extermination of evil in the last act. Julia's promiscuity, Antonio's naïvety, the Cardinal's sudden stupidity, Ferdinand's madness, and Bosola's own murderous habits interfere with his

---

[13] For an interpretation of the Duchess's preparation for death along what seems to me rigidly Christian lines see D. C. Gunby, '*The Duchess of Malfi*, A Theological Approach', in the present volume.

good intentions, with the inevitable result that the significance of the Duchess's death somewhat recedes into the background of darkness and confusion where both the virtuous and the vicious lose their way. Although the appalled spectators on the stage have no choice but to accept Bosola's interpretation of the events and are thus able to discover some glimmer of hope in them, as is right and proper when children are listening, there is really very little hope to discover. Remorse has driven one murderer mad and made another fearful of a thing armed with a rake, but for all of Bosola's blustering there has been no effective reformation, and consequently the assertion of virtue is very quiet indeed. For better or for worse, intentionally or not, the ultimate effect of Webster's deliberately created confusion may well be: 'The Duchess is dead. There is no more to say.' Her influence after death may, if some of the implications of the last act are taken seriously, not last longer than that of the Cardinal who desires to be 'layd by, and never thought of', or of Sejanus' children whose fate is forgotten as soon as their story is told. If we think of the outcome in terms of 'the eternal Church', where the Duchess hopes never to have to part from Antonio, her death is indeed a victory and her salvation assured, but here and now radically different considerations prevail. This double perspective may be confusing, since Webster does little to clarify it, but I believe that the Websterian must insist upon it.

In spite of the moral and/or religious significance of the heroine's endurance *The Duchess of Malfi* is in the final analysis a much sadder play than *The White Devil*, and this is not primarily a matter of a pervading mood.[14] It is one thing to find, as we do in *The White Devil*, first insipid moralism and then jolly amoralism wanting as codes of human conduct; very few social and religious systems worth the name have been founded on such concepts. It is, however, something quite different to reach the same conclusion about a concept so dear to prophets and reformers alike as the redeeming or at least inspiring power of passive suffering. The level on which the glorious villains of *The White Devil* operate may, after all, be unnecessarily elevated, and sordid egoism without pretences, in the fashion of *Volpone* and *The Alchemist*, the only rational way of life. Perhaps *The Devil's Law-Case* will provide an answer to the question in which direction Webster's thought was travelling.

[14] 'A profound, unalterable sadness' is Lucas's familiar description of the atmosphere of the play (ii, 21).

Any critical treatment of *The Devil's Law-Case* will inevitably be hampered by the lack of a critical tradition on which to fall back. Few scholars have found the play worth serious consideration, and nothing like a generally accepted interpretation has consequently been achieved. What follows should then be looked upon as an interim report on *The Devil's Law-Case*, an attempt to view it in Websterian terms and see what sense it makes. One way of doing this is to treat Romelio as its hero or at least protagonist, since it is his conflicts with the four other major characters that give the play both direction and nerve. When confronted with his natural egoism and superior knowledge of the world, two such 'complete gentlemen' and 'perfect lovers' as Contarino and Ercole appear veritable babes in the wood, a situation which recalls the difficulties under which the virtuous characters in *The White Devil* labour. To make a declaration of one's financial needs or one's intimate feelings, to demand that this declaration should be treated with the respect that one's rank and honour require, and to fight a duel if it is not . . . such chivalric principles are not likely to keep anyone alive in Romelio's—and Webster's—world of dark corners, into which Contarino and Ercole are suddenly introduced. This is not to say that their values are laughed out of court, since Ariosto too has his rules to follow, by means of which he is supposed to bring order into the 'indirect proceedings' which constitute the strange cases he has to judge. But order is not restored in his legal way, nor in the gentlemanly way of trial by combat. In a highly characteristic fashion Webster twists the solution around, and it is not until Contarino and Ercole, imperfectly aware of what has actually happened, disguise themselves and try to play the same game as Romelio that he is first brought to bay and then restored to something of his original status. After such machinations of their own, not to mention Contarino's declaration of his love for Leonora, it is perhaps right and proper that they are dismissed rather perfunctorily in the final settlement. Their parts do indeed fall a little towards the end, and not only for the sake of decorum.

Since she is Romelio's sister Jolenta quite properly finds it much easier than her lovers to realise what her brother is up to, particularly since he does not bother to keep his motives hidden from her. Whereas the contrast between Romelio on one hand and Contarino and Ercole on the other is, at least roughly, one between a commercial and a feudal code of conduct, the conflict between brother and sister is viewed in purely ethical terms. What he calls 'A piece of Art' is to her 'Rather a damnable cunning, / To have me goe about to giv't away, / Without consent of my soule', and all the comfort that she can teach herself when she has been contracted to Ercole is that 'There is a time left for me to dye nobly, / When I cannot live so'.[15] It is only when she has heard of Contarino's death and his supposed unfaithfulness to her that she agrees with her brother's proposal to 'dissemble dishonestie', which attempt, however, comes to nothing, since she has learnt from him not only to maintain a properly cynical attitude to the world but also to play her own game of deception. Having subjected Jolenta to this, Webster apparently felt that she deserved an elaborate restoration of moral status: thus the strange masquerade of the black and the white nun, with its dismissal of all 'vaine shew'—'Never mind the outward skin, / But the Jewell that's within'—followed by the ringing proclamation 'without controle' that 'There's no true beauty, but ith Soule'.[16] For all the rapidity with which 'all further scruteny' ceases, there can be no doubt about the seriousness of the whole episode.

In Leonora's case a similar symbolic restoration would be hard to achieve, since she is thoroughly familiar with Romelio's ways of operating from the very beginning of the play. Her arguments to convince Jolenta of the advisability to marry Ercole are of the same practical nature as her son's, with a few touches of her own worldly wisdom added: 'To be contracted / In teares, is but fashionable' ... 'Virgins must seeme unwilling' ... 'To be a little strange to one another, / Will keepe your longing fresh'[17], all instructions that recall Flamineo's familiar advice to Brachiano in the House of Convertites: 'Women are caught as you take Tortoises, / Shee must bee turn'd on her backe.' It is, however, apparently not such cynicisms that make Jolenta's resistance collapse but Leonora's recourse to the extraordinary measure of a mother's curse: 'Your Imprecation has undone me for ever.'[18]

Neither now nor when she receives premature word of Contarino's death with the Websterian exclamation 'O, I am lost for ever', is it perhaps possible to take Leonora's love for the young nobleman quite seriously. Hers is a predicament that is usually treated as ludicrous on the stage, and her interview with Contarino, in which, completely at cross-purposes, they exchange compliments with each other, is in fact a

---

[15] *The Devil's Law-Case*, I.ii.124–7, 259–60.
[16] ibid., V.v.45–56.
[17] ibid., I.ii.135–6, 139, 165–6.
[18] ibid., I.ii.117.

comedy scene. It is not until Romelio announces that he has killed her beloved that the full extent of her passion is revealed, and soon all comic touches are dispensed with:

> Come age, and wither me into the malice
> Of those that have been happy; let me have
> One propertie more then the Devill of Hell,
> Let me envy the pleasure of youth heartily,
> Let me in this life feare no kinde of ill,
> That have no good to hope for:[19]

In spite of the passion for revenge which now overwhelms her, she remains in control of the plot that she lays against her son; in court she speaks to the purpose, neither too much nor too little, and it is only the unlikely accident of Crispiano's appearance after so many years that spoils her game and proves her an honest woman. Her decision to seek oblivion within the walls of a convent is unaffected by the threat to Romelio's life; what she does for him is only to comprise for him within the framework of a 'dumbe Pageant' 'a right excellent forme / Of penitence'.[20] At the news of Contarino's survival, however, she throws repentance to the winds and wants to 'leape these Battlements, / And may I be found dead time enough, / To hinder the combate'.[21] Whereupon, in no uncertain fashion, she claims her own, i.e. the completely acquiescent Contarino. There may be comic undertones to all this, but Leonora herself should certainly be taken seriously. With her passion-dominated reactions she provides an effective contrast to the polite emotions of Ercole and Contarino and the lack of emotions of Romelio. What she has to do for her breach of the monastic vow is simply to do penance with Jolenta and Angiolella, to which penance is added the admonition that Ariosto finally bestows on the whole group of more or less remorseful sinners:

> —so we leave you,
> Wishing your future life may make good use
> Of these events, since that these passages,
> Which threatned ruine, built on rotten ground,
> Are with successe beyond our wishes crown'd.[22]

---

[19] *The Devil's Law-Case*, III.iii.298–303.
[20] ibid., V.iv.149–50.
[21] ibid., V.iv.211–13.
[22] ibid., V.v.98–102.

The most unlikely character to be included in this innocuous wish is undoubtedly Romelio. Even if we adopt a purely pragmatic attitude to his activities and emphasise that he really does not marry off his sister against her will but only tries to, that he really does not murder Contarino but only tries to, that he really does not acquire Ercole's and Contarino's property but only tries to—an attitude that may be essential for the proper understanding of tragicomedy—it is still somewhat hard to have the sun of forgiveness shine equally on him and on his intended victims.

For let there be no doubt about Romelio's villainy. When he realises that Contarino's death would be to his own great advantage, he is immediately ready with a plot that 'scornes Precedent' and will put an engine to work that 'shall weigh up my losses, / Were they sunke as low as hell'.[23] The glee with which he plays the murderous Jewish surgeon is so extreme that the shade of Barabas of Malta has been evoked, and the cynical comment with which he stabs his victim has an even more professional ring to it:

> Yet this shall proove most mercifull to thee,
> For it shall preserve thee
> From dying on a publique Scaffold, and withall
> Bring thee an absolute Cure, thus.[24]

It would seem ill-advised to let such a man loose again on the unsuspecting population of Naples.

The standard explanation of the apparent confusion of issues at the end of *The Devil's Law-Case*, and one that may still be dear to many Websterians, is of course that Romelio comes equipped with indomitable courage, the one redeeming feature in Webster's ugly world, the quality that supposedly turns Vittoria into a tragic heroine. It is not to be denied that Webster's Romelio has courage, even though it is not of the bravado kind that goes in search of a quarrel on a point of honour or self-esteem. Since there is no alternative to his duel with Ercole, he prepares himself for it in the best way he knows, refusing the solace of the Church, which will make him perform 'like a Dormouse', but accepting bodily food, which will make him fight 'with a good stomacke'.[25] Survival and not salvation is what the practical man must aim

---

[23] *The Devil's Law-Case*, II.iii.190–91; III.ii.90.
[24] ibid., III.ii.114–17.
[25] ibid., V.iv.82, 95–100.

at if—unfortunately—he has to fight, and Romelio is nothing if not supremely practical. This quality lies behind his attacks on gentility, that 'superstitious relique of time past', which he analyses as 'nothing / But ancient riches', and it also lies behind his refusal to believe in the significance of the 'most strange, most dreadfull, and / Unfortunate names' that he had given his wrecked ships:

> I am perswaded there came not Cuckolds enow
> To the first Launching of them, and 'twas that
> Made them thrive the worse for't. Oh your Cuckolds hansell
> Is praid for i'th Citie.[26]

Although Romelio makes very few references, whether in jest or in earnest, to the habits of the business world—he once compares Jolenta's marriage-contract to the 'thriftiest bargaines that were ever made' in the city—life to this 'Fortunate Young Man' is really a sequence of commercial ventures.[27] Some of them, such as forcing one's sister into a marriage, will yield satisfactory returns at moderate risks, whereas in more desperate situations, where immediate results are imperative, the risk of a murder will have to be taken. The risks must, however, always be calculated, balanced against the probable profits, which in its turn demands absolute honesty to oneself, if to nobody else. Not only honour but also religion is merely a superstition, to be used against those who profess it, as Romelio uses it to get rid of his troublesome mother before the duel. This honesty has its attractive side to it—F. L. Lucas was particularly fond of it—but not even if taken together with the courage that Romelio also demonstrates does it constitute the redeeming feature for which we have been looking.[28] Romelio is, after all, not a confidence man of the relatively minor calibre of Jonson's Face; in his uninhibited egoism he actually comes much closer to Volpone. And yet Webster allows the situation in *The Devil's Law-Case* to develop beyond what a Jonsonian verdict could be expected to handle, whereupon he brings everything to a close in a manner which indicates that all is supposed to be well that ends well.

It would be easy to dismiss the perfunctory nature of this ending and the disproportions it involves by accusing the shade of John Fletcher

---

[26] *The Devil's Law-Case*, I.i.41–3, II.iii.59–74.

[27] ibid., I.ii.154–7. I have restored Lucas's reading 'The Fortunate Young Man' (I.i.13) to that of the first quarto, since there is ample evidence of the existence of 'youngman' as a separate word in seventeenth-century English.

[28] Cf. Lucas, op. cit., ii, 226.

of it, or by supposing that the material proved too recalcitrant to the dramatist, who finally found the standard comedy solution impossible to achieve, the solution in which everyone gets more of less what he deserves, and instead preferred a more mechanical one, a solution of the kind to which Shakespeare, according to some critics at least, resorted when he brought *Measure for Measure* to a close. Be that as it may, it is, however, my self-imposed duty in this paper to disregard mechanical solutions and search for possible Websterian meanings, and I do believe that *Measure for Measure*, as I read it, may provide us with the key to *The Devil's Law-Case*, even though Ariosto is an even more unsatisfactory judge than Duke Vincentio. In Shakespeare's play, too, the situation has clearly developed beyond the point where leniency solves everything, and yet leniency is the order of the day. This is possible in Vienna, since the corruption that boils and bubbles in the city has its origin in sex, i.e. a force in nature that must indeed be considered productive, even to such extent that it makes dukes and novices alike acquainted with strange bedfellows. The balance between law and order on one hand and life and anarchy on the other would seem to require an accommodation rather than a solution, and thus *Measure for Measure* must end as it does.

But, it may be objected, the forces at work in *The Devil's Law-Case* can only in the obvious case of Leonora be associated with anything so vital as sex. The basic motivation of Romelio is of a curiously undramatic kind; since he is interested in neither power nor pleasure, he does not achieve the symbolic dimensions of a Volpone or a Sir Epicure Mammon but operates in a much more subdued and matter-of-fact manner. Not even a duel is an occasion for posturing or bravado; self-preservation is natural, and the equally natural extension of self-preservation is the continuous acquisition and augmentation of property. There is no doubt about it that Webster derives the commercial spirit from the basic selfishness of man, with which any society interested in its own preservation must make its compromises—as Ariosto does in *The Devil's Law-Case*.

The final accommodation of the play must consequently be understood to rest on very insecure foundations. It is good to know that 'There's no true beauty, but ith Soule'; Contarino and Ercole have been taught a lesson and are now associated with women who know more about the Romelios of this world than they can ever hope to learn, and Leonora's passion has, we must assume, been properly domesticated. Still, if we accept the terms in which the general conflict between the merchant of Naples and his adversaries is presented, it can only be a matter of time before Romelio will upset the accommodation, and then the former babes in the wood had better know their lesson. Natural egoism may be even more difficult to control than natural sex.

This is as far as I should like to carry my reading of *The Devil's Law-Case* at the present time. I have tried to extricate as much sense as possible from the play, and this sense has quite obviously been Websterian. Only by so doing could I now be in the position to answer part of the question that my title posed: *The Devil's Law-Case*—an end or a beginning? The play is firmly connected with *The White Devil* and *The Duchess of Malfi*, not only in style and workmanship but above all in theme. The characters and their problems have been cut down to everyday size, and the play as a whole is more concerned with the trivial side of life than the tragedies, but this does not make it a trivial play. It is possible to make a case for *The Devil's Law-Case* as the natural concluding statement of John Webster in the sequence of unpleasant plays which began with *The White Devil*. In the Websterian sense it appears to be an end and not a beginning.

But there are also other aspects to consider. The Websterian sense is not something which emerges effortlessly from the transparent structure of *The Devil's Law-Case*. The confusion of the play remains a problem, and although we may always say that this confusion is on the whole planned and achieves its dramatic purpose when you have the intelligence to recognise it, it will take some persuasion to convince not only anti-Websterians but also casual readers of *The Devil's Law-Case* of the validity of this Websterian point. The sensible attitude to this problem is certainly to admit that, exactly as was the case in *The White Devil* and *The Duchess of Malfi*, there are certain dramatic manoeuvres of Webster's that do not come off or that come off in so precarious a fashion as to create the wrong kind of effect. An additional explanation of this failure in *The Devil's Law-Case*—so much more obvious here than in the tragedies—may well be that Webster was trying to adapt himself and his motley material to the technique of Fletcherian tragicomedy, with its extreme emotional conflicts, unexpected reversals of fortune, and arbitrary final settlements.

And yet I feel that it would be a mistake to connect *The Devil's Law-Case* more than superficially with the emerging tragicomic fashions of the 1610s. The play is conversational rather than declamatory, the rhetorical patterns seem almost completely absent. In the historical sense it does not really point forward to anything in tragicomedy, neither to the high seriousness and deadly moralism of *The Maid of Honour* nor to the false pretences and tawdry thrills of *The Renegado*. Its connections appear almost exclusively with the past, not only with Webster's own tragedies but also with Ben Jonson's and Shakespeare's bitter comedies. It is with *Volpone* and *The Alchemist*, with *All's Well that Ends Well* and *Measure for Measure*, that *The Devil's Law-Case* should be associated, in terms of theme, overall seriousness, and the baffling neutrality which the dramatists prefer to maintain to the very end. That Webster's play cannot compete with the carefully contrived effect of Jonson's comedies nor with the truly double-edged one of Shakespeare's, goes without saying. If, however, the association can be made at all meaningful, it indicates that *The Devil's Law-Case* is well worth rescuing from critical oblivion.

Webster and the Uses of Tragicomedy

J. R. MULRYNE

Webster and the Uses of Tragicomedy

IT IS CHARACTERISTIC of the extreme self-consciousness of his writing that one of his own characters provides the appropriate epigraph for a look at some of the distinctive features of Webster's dramatic art. In Act IV, scene i of *The White Devil* Francisco parodies the dramatic experience of which he himself forms part:

> Come, to this weighty business.
> My tragedy must have some idle mirth in't,
> Else it will never pass. I am in love,
> In love with Corombona ... (IV.i.118–21)[1]

John Webster's 'case', his 'impure art', has proved 'elusive'[2] to critical discussion largely because of that feature to which Francisco's speech calls attention: the conflation of tragic and comic genres to which at once Webster seems profoundly committed, since it provides the life-blood of some of his major work, and yet towards which he maintains, it may be of necessity, an irreverence to which not only Francisco's words, but the very fact of his speaking them, bear witness. Webster's experiments with the uses of tragicomedy seem to me, as they may to others, the most puzzling and provoking aspect of his work, and the aspect most resistant to critical discussion. But they seem also to present the most challenging and relevant face of what he has to say.

To speak of *tragicomedy* is to invite J. L. Styan's rebuke that the term is 'spurious'.[3] Certainly I do not use the word in a way that Renaissance critics would have understood or approved. Yet among these critics there ran a strong instinct for naming and defining a type

---

[1] All quotations are from J. R. Brown, ed., *The White Devil* and *The Duchess of Malfi* (1960 and 1964 respectively), The Revels Plays.

[2] The phrases are from T. S. Eliot, *Selected Essays* (New York, 1950) and T. B. Tomlinson, *A Study of Elizabethan and Jacobean Tragedy* (Cambridge 1964).

[3] J. L. Styan, *The Dark Comedy* (2nd ed., Cambridge, 1968), p. vi.

of drama less even in mood and temper than most classical comedy or tragedy. Cicero was quoted again and again: 'in tragedy anything comic is a defect and in comedy anything tragic is unseemly'; but with a growing sense that his position was belied by experience in the theatre.[4] Classical precedent, together with contemporary French and Italian practice, helped to drive home the need for a third term; and if the definition of tragicomedy that emerged was somewhat meek and stilted, it did at least offer some acknowledgement of that flexibility of tone and attitude which has so much to do with the vitality of Elizabethan drama. In this paper, without I think too much singularity, I am borrowing those earlier critics' term—because I have no better—to focus through one writer one aspect, characteristic though also extreme, of the variousness, the uncommittedness, of Elizabethan drama. What I have in mind relates Webster to an Elizabethan genre— I call it a genre; it is at least a distinct direction of Elizabethan theatre—which reflects a permanent and quite distinctive habit of mind; one that makes itself felt in English medieval theatre, and one that has again, and this I want to pursue, become familiar in the theatre of the present century.[5] It is a genre that includes, on the Elizabethan stage, relatively few examples, or relatively few in 'pure' form; but it is one that intermittently affects the structure of feeling of a wide range of important plays. By tragicomedy I do not mean tragic plays into which a comic scene or scenes are inserted; though, to take classical instances, the Porter scene in *Macbeth* and the graveyard scene in *Hamlet*, as well as, in another vein, the equivocal last moments of *Antony and Cleopatra*, all take on a sharper meaning when seen in relation to this genre. Nor do I mean a comedy that turns serious like *Much Ado*; though to see the hesitations of feeling that characterise that play in the light of what I am calling tragicomedy is to go nearer the centre of the play's meaning. Nor am I thinking of the comedy-beyond-tragedy of Romance; though to take, for example, the bear-and-tempest episode of *The Winter's Tale* in its fully tragicomic sense is to appreciate the whole play more accurately. What I have in mind

---

[4] For an authoritative discussion of Renaissance ideas of tragicomedy see Marvin T. Herrick, *Tragicomedy: Its Origins and Development in Italy, France and England* (Urbana, Illinois, 1955).

[5] Styan, op. cit., p. 9, makes the connection with English medieval drama; see also M. C. Bradbrook's discussion of the debt owed by *The Jew of Malta* to *The Croxton Play of the Sacrament* in her *English Dramatic Form* (Cambridge, 1965), pp. 54–5.

is, rather, a form in which comedy and tragedy, the laughable and the appalling, are so composed that neither is predominant; where indeed the play's meaning demands that comic and tragic confront each other in a genuine dilemma of feeling. Wilson Knight and Jan Kott have shown us how, on a partial view, *King Lear* often conforms to this definition;[6] *Troilus and Cressida* might be said to reflect it in a less generous spirit; *Richard III* at its most vital moments is genuinely tragicomic. Outside Shakespeare, *Volpone* employs a large measure of the grotesque, as does *Bartholomew Fair*; and the grotesque is the affective equivalent of the (broadly) philosophical impasse tragicomedy dramatises. *The Changeling*, *The Revenger's Tragedy*, and *The Atheist's Tragedy* all approximate, in technique and feeling, tragicomic experience. But in all these cases, with the possible exception of *Troilus*, and in others that could be cited, tragicomedy is employed in the service of something not itself: a moral or social or other conviction that remains the play's ultimate focus of attention. For present purposes, we might say that only Marlowe and Webster among Elizabethan dramatists employ tragicomedy as the full dramatic equivalent of experience and conviction.[7] Some of the consequences for Webster's art will be discussed below.

We need a fuller definition of tragicomedy than the Renaissance provided, if we are to see the extent to which Webster's work conforms to what I am calling a distinctive habit of mind. If in seeking one we turn to critical writing of the recent past it will inevitably seem that we are distorting Webster's work to fit moulds quite alien to his own traditions of thought and feeling. Some distortion is I think inevitable; the theatre tempts us more persistently than other literary forms, because of the very conditions of performance, to remake earlier works in contemporary terms. And yet we can at least plead that other critics of Webster, with no especial axe to grind, have felt and commented on the remarkable 'modernity' of his major plays. Writers like H. T. Price, Travis Bogard, M. C. Bradbrook, J. L. Styan, and Norman Rabkin have all detected in Webster marked affiliations with recent

---

[6] G. Wilson Knight, '*King Lear* and the Comedy of the Grotesque' in *The Wheel of Fire* (1960), pp. 160–76 (first published in 1930); Jan Kott, '*King Lear* or Endgame' in *Shakespeare Our Contemporary* (1964), pp. 101–37.

[7] For a discussion of Marlowe in a similar light see J. R. Mulryne and Stephen Fender, 'Marlowe and the "Comic Distance"' in *Christopher Marlowe*, Mermaid Critical Commentaries (1968), pp. 47–64.

trends in literature and thought.[8] If analysis of Webster's uses of tragi-comedy does nothing else, it may at least bring into focus those aspects of Webster's art which require from a reader or audience of today the least adjustment of response. We shall also be able to see—and the experience may throw light in both directions—the parallels between Webster's dramatic practices and those of recent experiments in tragicomic form, some of them based, in varying ways and to vary-ing degrees, on Elizabethan drama: such work as Tom Stoppard's *Rosencrantz and Guildenstern are Dead*, the Marowitz *Hamlet*, and Peter Brook's *King Lear*.

It is commonplace that a large and still growing part of contempor-ary theatre—some would say too large—has been concerned to explore the area of theatrical experience I am calling the tragicomic, and which Martin Esslin has called the Absurd, Jan Kott the Grotesque, and J. L. Styan the Dark Comedy.[9] To survey the theory that has been devised to explicate or at least parallel this movement would clearly ask more space than is available. A useful shorthand may be to set side by side two definitions of the comic, one by a writer from before the era of renewed interest in the serious, or tragic, potential of comedy, the other by a writer very much a part of that era. Both share similar premises: that tragedy and comedy arise out of closely related per-ceptions—a view, incidentally, they share with Renaissance theorists, who refer the argument back to Plato.[10] But each of the modern writers follows his premises to very different, even opposed, conclusions; and from this disagreement we may appreciate the essentials of the modern view of the comic—or, in the term we're using, the tragicomic. The first writer, Kierkegaard, says that:

Wherever there is life, there is contradiction, and wherever there is contradiction, the comical is present.... The tragic and the comic are the same, in so far as both are based in contradiction; but the tragic is the suffering contradiction, the comic the painless contradiction.

---

[8] H. T. Price, 'The Function of Imagery in Webster', repr. *Elizabethan Drama: Modern Essays in Criticism*, ed. Ralph J. Kaufmann (New York, 1961), pp. 225–49; Travis Bogard, *The Tragic Satire of John Webster* (Berkeley and Los Angeles, 1955); M. C. Bradbrook, op. cit.; J. L. Styan, op. cit.; Norman Rabkin, ed., *Twentieth Century Interpretations of 'The Duchess of Malfi'* (Engle-wood Cliffs, N. J., 1968), pp. 1–8.

[9] Martin Esslin, *The Theatre of the Absurd* (1962); Jan Kott, op. cit.; J. L. Styan, op. cit.

[10] Herrick, op. cit., p. 9.

The comic is painless, Kierkegaard explains, because it envisages 'the way out'; whereas 'the tragic apprehension sees the contradiction and despairs of a way out'.[11] The extent to which we have seen in recent decades a reappraisal of the comic emerges very clearly when we cite against this Eugene Ionesco. For him, as for Kierkegaard, tragic and comic share a common source in contradiction; but they have become virtually identical, not contrasted, in the emotional experience they offer. Ionesco writes:

> The unendurable admits of no solution, and only the unendurable is profoundly tragic, profoundly comic and essentially theatrical. . . . It seems to me that comic and tragic are one, and that the tragedy of man is pure derision.[12]

Comedy, equally with tragedy, conveys the 'anguish' in which Ionesco's plays deal; both explore the same tight cul-de-sac, with no way through to reassurance. Comedy has become tragic, or anguished, because the contradictions are now seen as ultimate, and the only response to ultimate contradictoriness is comic or tragicomic; such laughter as points back to the insecurity, arising from a lack of knowledge, that gives rise to it. Ionesco explains how this tragicomic division of feeling may be reflected in the plays of this genre:

> these two elements [the comic and the tragic] do not coalesce, they coexist: one constantly repels the other, they show each other up, criticise and deny one another . . .[13]

Such coexistence, a precarious tension, defines the 'unstable equilibrium' of modern tragicomedy; and under some such rubric Webster's major plays may, I think, usefully be read. A study of the ways in which the two major plays reflect the techniques and outlook of tragicomedy will help us, not, certainly, to startlingly new readings of either play, but hopefully to a more natural, because more familiar and contemporary, sense of their integrity as dramatic statements.

The initial point of contact between Webster's play and modern tragicomedy is at once obvious and yet not easy to define. Both sets of plays are written, we might say, in the service of no identifiable absolute, whether political, moral, or religious; their tragicomic stance may

---

[11] Quoted in Cyrus Hoy, *The Hyacinth Room* (1964), p. 67.
[12] Eugene Ionesco, *Notes and Counter-Notes*, tr. Donald Watson (1964), pp. 18, 26.
[13] ibid., p. 26.

even be said to arise ultimately from their contemplation of man's rootlessness and uncertainty. The quotations from Webster fall pat enough:

> *Vittoria*: My soul, like to a ship in a black storm,
> Is driven I know not whither. (*W.D.*, V.vi.248–9)

> *Flamineo*: While we look up to heaven we confound
> Knowledge with knowledge. O I am in a mist.
> (*W.D.*, V.vi.259–60)

> *Bosola*:   O this gloomy world!
> In what a shadow, or deep pit of darkness,
> Doth womanish and fearful mankind live!
> (*D.M.*, V.v.100–2)

Such statements might easily be countered—the game is not difficult to play—by others in a contrary sense; but most readers may be willing to agree that the major impression made by either *The White Devil* or *The Duchess of Malfi* is of a deeply concerned, even anguished, agnosticism. But agnosticism does not mean in Webster, any more than in *Waiting for Godot*, or in Kafka, an unawareness of, or lack of interest in, the positives by which it refuses to be bound. Indeed in *The White Devil* (to consider that play for a few pages) we experience precisely that division of response, a genuine ambivalence of feeling, which characterises the 'absurd' work and gives rise to tragicomic laughter. Our reaction to the play is caught between two contrary and irreconcilable gestures of assent, just as in Beckett or Kafka we are caught between two irreconcilable assumptions about man's place in the universe. It is of the essence that we assent to neither while we assent to both. Just so in *The White Devil* our feelings are tugged between delight in the vitality and daring of the major figures (the romantic reading, we might say) and respect for the religious and social acceptances that they deny (the pious reading). Critics who insist we take seriously the repeated political and moral commonplaces, and the crucial interventions of figures like Isabella, Giovanni, Cornelia, and Marcello, are, of course, in the right. Except that we find that where our moral sense will and must follow, our more libertine instincts find nothing to attract. Nor is this merely a matter of duty against desire, conformity against daring; or rather it is this, provided we are willing to accept that our *feelings* may be as genuinely and powerfully engaged on one side as the other. We find ourselves caring just as much for Isabella's orthodoxy and Cornelia's and Giovanni's (even when we are not certain they are sincere in it) as for the vitality and permissiveness of Brachiano or Lodovico or Francisco. Equally, when a word such as 'charity' or 'nobility' becomes just a pawn in the power game, we delight in the intellectual and moral extravagance, without losing sight of, or ceasing to care for, the word's more orthodox applications. We might go further and say that, throughout the play, we find our interest maintained in direct proportion to the skill with which Webster exploits the gap between the romantic and the pious readings; we might almost say that the play's essential meaning, and, more particularly, its moral credibility, depend upon this tactic and this skill. The crucial instance is, of course, the Arraignment of Vittoria, a scene which has been described by critics unaware of the play's tragicomic structure as a confidence trick, 'a lie in the poet's heart'.[14] In fact it serves as defining eikon for the whole play: a trial that exercises throughout the prevailing division of assent. Further instances could be multiplied; almost every scene, if we are to relish its full piquancy, asks of us a simultaneous gesture of acceptance and rejection, a contradictoriness of feeling that runs the whole gamut of emotion from puzzlement, through a sense of the preposterous, and on to outrage and ultimately anguish. Eliseo Vivas, speaking of Kafka, defines very neatly the moral bearing, and moral responsibility, of Webster's outlook:

> Generally speaking, a [tragi]comic grasp of the world rests on the perception by the writer of a moral duality which elicits from the reader a 'comic' response as the only means of freeing himself from the conflict towards values to which he is attached and yet towards which he cannot justify his attachment satisfactorily.[15]

This basic moral duality, never resolved, accounts for the particular quality of Webster's 'agnosticism' and predicts the characteristic 'detached involvement' of modern tragicomedy.

The divided allegiances of *The White Devil* are familiar enough, though I do not think critics have sufficiently emphasised the genuine ambivalence of the experience, and so have missed or underplayed what seems to me the most remarkable feature of seeing or reading the

---

[15] Eliseo Vivas, 'Kafka's Distorted Mask' repr. in *Kafka: A Collection of Critical Essays* (Englewood Cliffs, N.J., 1962), ed. Ronald Gray, p. 144.

play: that state of suspended response—delight, excitement, horror vying with a marked and sustained sense of the preposterous—that stems from, and ratifies, the basic crisis of feeling and conviction. Ionesco tells us, as quoted above, that 'laughter' and 'sympathy' 'co-exist' throughout the tragicomic play: 'one constantly repels the other, they show each other up, criticize and deny one another'. Such oscillations of feeling are everywhere in *The White Devil*. In another context I have shown how 'an elusive but unmistakable current of humour is made to play about almost every scene and incident'; here we might simply enumerate some specific occasions on which Webster sets side by side irreconcilable attitudes to the same occurrence, for these show more clearly than others how fully Webster's tragicomic techniques are in line with those Ionesco suggests. We have mentioned already the crisis of feeling over Vittoria; we might point now to the more obviously managed doubleness of our knowledge of Isabella. With a deliberateness that seems almost crude, and which on any naturalistic reading must appear impertinent and unconvincing, Isabella in Act II, scene i is made to reverse, totally, within little more than a hundred lines, her attitude to her husband Brachiano. Our knowledge that her first attitude is 'sincere', while her second is 'acted', merely intensifies and does not cancel the ambivalence of our response. What is at stake here is not the true nature of Isabella's feelings for Brachiano—Webster troubles very little in this play with relationships at this level—but the switchback of attitudes, underlined by virtual word-for-word repetition, which the audience sees enacted before them. An audience's response is caught between sympathy and laughter in what amounts to a quite explicit lesson in the aesthetics of tragicomedy. Equally explicit, and perhaps even more interesting, is Webster's handling of the dumb-shows, for here the audience's natural response (or sympathy) is filtered through, and interrupted by, a stage audience whose irreverence supplies the laughter term of the tragicomic duality. While the deaths of Isabella and Camillo are, by any standard, sufficiently bizarre, they do represent the emotional basis upon which the whole revenge narrative is built. Yet the levity of Brachiano's commentary, to say nothing of the Conjurer's absurdly zestful presentation, must ensure in any audience the characteristic division of feeling. The two ghost scenes, again, exercise a parallel contradictoriness of response, with Francisco and Flamineo providing the qualifying commentary on their own experience. Again we halt, puzzled and frustrated, between sympathy and laughter. A similar crisis of feeling, but far more emotionally strenuous, comes with the death of Brachiano. Here the strangling of the already demented Duke produces in us a deep sense of horror and revulsion; but equally powerful is our sense of the high comedy of the occasion and our relish of the witty deceits of Lodovico and the rest. The emotional incongruity is strengthened by incongruities of setting and language, the Capuchin disguises, the church furniture, and the Latin phrases playing against the vicious glee of the murderers. Such jesting with death explores a vein of tragicomic feeling not unlike the attitude of mind underlying certain medieval accounts of death, in the visual as well as the verbal arts. An even more exact parallel is also Webster's most inventive, most startling model of the play's contrarieties of response. Flamineo's two versions of dying, the burlesque and the real, concentrate and give extreme relevance to all the other ambivalences of feeling. The death of a man whose only values are intrigue and self-seeking is, on one view, preposterous; if, as the tragicomic writer claims, the only ultimate is mortality, then living and dying can only be absurd. And so Webster, in Flamineo's grotesque invention, makes us feel them. On another view, such dying is deeply pathetic, the lonely and bewildered man asserting to the last his independence of any system of values that would ease the pain or diminish the bewilderment. Just such pathos, too restless and energetic to be sentimental, Webster makes us feel at Flamineo's 'real' dying. Sympathy and laughter coexist, repel, criticise, and deny each other. The central feature of the play-experience, in my view, has, then, to do with what J. L. Styan has called the 'effort of consent and adaptation'[16] such incongruities of response force upon an audience. Such a strenuously-maintained, difficult, and sometimes (to use Ionesco's word) anguished state of mind as this is the true effective equivalent to the philosophical uncertainties of tragicomedy.

A continuing emphasis in recent 'absurdist' or 'dark comedy' writing, especially in the work of Beckett, Genet, and Ionesco, but also most recently in Weiss and Stoppard, has been the attention given to the conscious theatricality of the play-situation. Characters frequently call attention to, and overtly exploit, the dramatic framework in which they themselves exist. This, though not uncommon in other theatre, is a perfectly natural development of the tragicomic stance. For

[16] Styan, op. cit., p. 266.

tragicomedy, having given over absolutes, and seeing action and belief
scaled down to the limits of mortality, finds the provisional situation of
the actor peculiarly appropriate. In an absurdist world, action has lost
significance except as a way of asserting the basic fact of consciousness;
just as an actor finds meaning through the role he adopts. So, for
example, with the time-using fictions of Beckett's tramps. Webster's
writing, though nothing so stark in this respect as Beckett's, instinct-
ively recognises the aptness of the play-assumption to its own moral
position. In a general way, the play earns its title by exploiting the
ironies, of attachment and distance, sympathy and laughter, 'realism'
and 'convention', implicit in the term 'hypocrite' (Greek *hypocrites*, an
actor) to which it makes reference. Acting becomes the very idiom of
the piece, every attitude becoming a pose 'acted up', even the most
sincere of them appearing to be adopted like an actor's role. We find
ourselves accepting that the only criterion of excellence or value is
the distinction with which the actor plays his part: the lawyer we
dismiss, for example, because he miscalls the dramatic situation and
fluffs his lines. The whole play moves towards the condition of charade, most amply when the fifth act replaces verbal camouflage and
simple effrontery with the more theatrical hypocrisy of disguise. But
Webster's instinctive acceptance of this dramatic mode also makes
itself felt in more particular ways. At certain moments the play's theatricality is quite overtly recognised: scenes and occasions that remain
within the stage-illusion are interrupted by others that deliberately and
quite explicitly rupture it. Among these would come that extraordinary
acting-contract drawn up between Flamineo and Lodovico, with Marcello for audience, in Act III, scene iii. (Their 'melancholy' exchange is
astonishingly like certain 'runs' or 'tirades' in Beckett or Pinter; under-
taken merely as what we might call 'experiments in consciousness'.)
When Marcello advertises the theatricality of the moment:

Mark this strange encounter

we are nudged out of any simple and comfortable relationship to the
stage-fiction, and forced temporarily to adjust our attitude to the play's
events and characters. Similarly, in a less remarkable way, we revise
our sense of Flamineo's fictional status, though not at all our estimate
of his character, when at the end of Act IV, scene ii he explicitly draws
our attention to his tactics as actor:

> It may appear to some ridiculous
> Thus to talk knave and madman; and sometimes
> Come in with a dried sentence, stuff'd with sage.
> But this allows my varying of shapes,—
> Knaves do grow great by being great men's apes. (IV.ii.243–7)

Again Webster upsets our sense of the play's integrity as fiction when he parodies, through Flamineo and Francisco, the venerable Elizabethan convention of the ghost; these moments serve more than their narrative function because they again make us conscious of our difficult, always vulnerable, relation with the stage. Most explicit of all these questionings of illusion is Flamineo's presentation of his mother's sorrow and that of her companions:

> I will see them.
> They are behind the traverse. I'll discover
> Their superstitious howling. (V.iv.63–5)

The technical terms of theatre ('discover', 'traverse') help to remind us of the nature and degree of the curiosity that we as audience share with Flamineo. Again the audience is cast for a slightly new role. On each of these occasions, and others, by emphasising the provisional nature of the fictional world, and by making us frequently adjust our relation to it, Webster prevents the establishment of any simple convention of feeling—as tragedy or comedy is in this sense simple—between audience and stage. We find the spectacle fascinating but laughably without direction, compelling but without a meaning to which we can easily or consistently relate. J. L. Styan, surveying the techniques of modern writers of dark comedy, tells us

> the good modern dramatist will insist, by refreshingly questioning illusion and convention in the theatre, that we remain aloof though implicated. There can be no comforting sense of 'belonging to a side' in the experience of his theatre. There can be no relaxation in a play that acquits us by laughter at one moment and then convicts us the next. To place us in this unhappy limbo, the playwright will be busy measuring, expanding and contracting that vital gap between the world of his actors and the world of his audience, between art and life . . . That is the uncomfortable state of mind the writer of

dark comedy aims to create ... The detachment of comedy is not allowed us, nor the sympathy of tragedy.[17]

There we have most of the salient features of Webster's dramatic stance in *The White Devil*: the 'questioning' of illusion and convention, the ambivalent allegiances, the laughter that derives as much from embarrassment as from superiority, the acute and discomforting sense of theatre as illusion. All of which add up to the classic experience of the tragicomic.

The major distinction, for present purposes, between Webster's theatre and more recent tragicomedy is that Webster supplies us with a representative within the dramatic action, a figure who, while we might not wish to identify with the less pleasant aspects of his personality, nevertheless stands in much the same relation to events on stage as we do. Flamineo I take to be a brilliant invention of Webster's for resolving his tragicomic vision, the character given the largest number of lines because he occupies a pivotal situation in the play's philosophy. Flamineo represents us in that he maintains like us a deeply ambivalent and uncommitted attitude to the life of the play, and because he exercises, more fully than any other character, the prevailing sense of life-as-theatre. His typical mode is of course that of mockery, but the mockery isn't simple, for it is qualified both by its own zest and gusto—it stands as far as may be from the dismissive or coldly contemptuous—and by a delight in the object of mockery that, if it could be anything so straightforward or mean, might almost be called envy. Flamineo enjoys, in other words, just such an attitude as ours to the play-world: delighting in it but not of it, delight and mockery annealed in a flame of sheer zest. Moreover, as Professor Leech's brilliant study reminds us, Flamineo's sharpest sensations are second-hand, voyeurishly based on the experience of others.[18] For him, feeling is not a simple matter of response, but a spuriously creative activity merely prompted by what he sees before him: Vittoria and Brachiano embracing, the appearance of the Conjurer or Zanche. Even in the absence of such stimulus, false make-believe is what he relishes most: the 'feigned madness' over Vittoria's disgrace, the charade of dying. He maintains therefore a relationship to reality (the fictional reality of the play-world) not at all unlike that which we ourselves, under Webster's

[17] Styan, op. cit., p. 257.
[18] Clifford Leech, *John Webster: A Critical Study* (1951), especially pp. 49–52.

prompting, come to experience. Flamineo is manipulator, presenter, the least deceived character in a world of false appearance, a sort of bitter Harlequin of tragicomedy, whom we recognise as nevertheless maintaining just such a perilous and constantly revised hold on the play-situation as ours, and one as undetermined by absolutes. Even his farewell to the play-world is as theatrically oriented as his life in it:

> I have caught
> An everlasting cold. I have lost my voice
> Most irrecoverably. (V.vi.270–72)

It is an apt leave-taking for one whose life was governed, as is ours for as long as we accept Webster's tragicomic stance, by a credo of histrionics not sustained by any more comforting absolute.

*   *   *

If *The White Devil* can plausibly be argued to observe a tragicomic convention that insists primarily on division of feeling and assent, *The Duchess of Malfi*, as I hope to show, explores an even richer vein of tragicomedy, one still more disturbing because discovered through the emotions (or the nerves) rather than, though the distinction is crude, through intellect and understanding. Again, I do not think to offer a new interpretation of the play, but rather to suggest, largely through analogy with recent plays, how skilfully Webster uses the opportunities of his chosen convention.

The Duchess of Malfi, like *The White Devil*, has attracted censure as well as praise. The attack on the play's dramatic structure and on its language is long-standing and consistent: Webster's writing both on the small scale and on the large is bedevilled by an inability to develop his ideas, with consistency and purpose, beyond the single unit, whether that unit is the image (or sentence) or the complete scene; the small-scale work is staccato and uneven, the larger discontinuous and mixed in style and idiom. William Archer made the larger point when he complained that 'even under Elizabethan conditions, there was nothing, except his singular inexpertness, to prevent Webster from telling his story well'.[19] Later writers have used more sophisticated terms, but have merely varied and extended Archer's attack by commenting unfavourably on the mixture of modes and conventions Webster

---

[19] William Archer, '*The Duchess of Malfi*', repr. in Rabkin, op. cit., p. 18.

uses, the puzzling and restless shifts of perspective, and the apparent lack of design in imagery, narrative, and overall structure. On the small scale Webster's language has received similar comment; his 'inability to write a sustained passage of verse' is traced by W. A. Edwards to his adoption of 'the style of the conceited character-writer', a style that 'tends towards epigram and maxim' and whose 'short-windedness' is 'too far from speech-idiom' to be successful on stage.[20] That these attacks are at once accurate in detail and yet wide of the mark in their general bearing and conclusions is splendidly if inadvertently illustrated in a brilliant essay by T. B. Tomlinson; an essay that shows to my mind beyond dispute the need for an understanding of tragicomic convention if we are to grasp Webster's purposes without strain and distortion.[21] For Tomlinson's essay represents an heroic attempt to rescue what he quite clearly feels to be a great and moving play against the pressure of what are for him deeply ingrained dramatic expectations and prejudices.

In Tomlinson's eyes, Webster's dramaturgy falls short precisely because of that discontinuity that others have also observed: 'the wreckage of Tourneur's cunning construction strews the pages of *The Duchess* and makes them annoyingly untidy'; as a result 'for all its brilliance, the play still notably lacks the kind of continuously developing intelligence and order which are the mark of a dramatist's having something vital to say'. The small-scale attack is also familiar. Mr Tomlinson writes with acute appreciation of the way in which the feeling of the early stages of the play is dominated by Bosola, yet with an undertow of anxiety about what this implies for the play's stature as a work of art: Bosola's 'sardonic homilies' are 'self-contained', reflecting the 'intermittent and carelessly rapid' action, even if they also convey 'a strong sense of life, of activity'. Bosola's dominating mannerisms, in which Webster so evidently delights, go near, for Tomlinson, to wrecking the play; it is just held back from the plunge into chaos by 'a sudden and comparatively crude moral awakening' associated with Webster's exploration of 'the more difficult and intangible world of naturalism or near-naturalism in feelings and emotion', a world depicted of course in relation especially to the Duchess herself. In Act IV, according to Tomlinson, Webster develops a '*collective* image' that

---

[20] W. A. Edwards, 'Revaluations (1): John Webster', *Scrutiny*, II (1933), p. 17.
[21] T. B. Tomlinson, 'Websterian Tragedy: *The Duchess of Malfi*' in *A Study of Elizabethan and Jacobean Tragedy*, pp. 132–57.

bears a certain resemblance to similar images in Racine, and that is composed largely of postures adopted in that act by the Duchess, with Bosola for comment and tension. This 'collective image' sufficiently steadies the play for Webster to write a concluding act that is still fragmentary and 'impressionistic', 'but now with more direction and purpose behind it'. The play is reclaimed, if only just.[22]

Tomlinson's essay repays lengthy summary because it identifies so neatly the prejudices which have, often unconsciously, determined other critics' censure of *The Duchess*: that order (of narrative and characterisation and dramatic style) stands for intelligence and insight, that naturalism is the supreme and perhaps the only true voice of drama, and that an effective verbal style depends on consistency of image and idiom and pace. In saying how profoundly I disagree with Tomlinson's strictures on *The Duchess*, while admiring his subtlety and detailed analysis, I realise I am fighting battles in some senses already won: long ago Una Ellis-Fermor, most perceptive of dramatic theorists, argued that in *The Duchess* Webster discovered 'such form as, without slavery to verisimilitude, could mirror immediately his thought';[23] more recently, J. R. Brown, in his singularly penetrating introduction to the play, showed how, despite the way in which 'contradictions span the whole play', Webster achieves unity both of 'atmosphere' and of outlook, 'a unity of empirical, responsible, sceptical, unsurprised and deeply perceptive concern'.[24] Yet even Brown's analysis may I think be given additional weight and naturalness by suggesting how *The Duchess* observes the requirements of a tragicomic convention, and by claiming that tragicomedy exactly identifies the play's underlying philosophy or attitude of mind.

In attempting to outline this attitude of mind as briefly as possible, and as accurately, I am again indebted to a critic who has written brilliantly on this play. M. C. Bradbrook has shown how Bosola's 'great speech on the vanity of life [IV.ii.124–33] . . . epitomizes what the play is really concerned with'.[25] The speech she refers to is one that ponders the frustrations of the soul in such a frail and contemptibly

[22] The quotations come from Tomlinson, op. cit., pp. 141, 136, 138, 137, 133, 139, 134, 152.
[23] Una Ellis-Fermor, *The Jacobean Drama; An Interpretation* (4th revised ed., 1958), p. 41.
[24] J. R. Brown, ed., *The Duchess of Malfi*, The Revels Plays (1964), p. xlix.
[25] M. C. Bradbrook, 'Fate and Chance in *The Duchess of Malfi*', repr. in Rabkin, op. cit., p. 40.

impermanent body as ours. On one side the speech serves as consolation for the dying Duchess; on another it invokes that whole area of profoundly contradictory thought and feeling that characterises its source in the Book of Job. For there, while Job's comforters are urging the full comprehensibility of God's justice—reward and punishment for righteousness and sin—Job himself, insisting on his faith in God, nevertheless broods on the mystery of God's judgements and their inscrutability to man. Just such obscurity, such agnosticism, pervades *The Duchess*. But where the Book of Job remains within a convention of feeling that may properly be called tragic—the inscrutability of God's judgements goes near the centre of much tragic thinking—*The Duchess of Malfi* appears to me to divert tragedy into tragicomedy, the cul-de-sac of Ionesco's definition. It is here that another of Professor Bradbrook's analyses becomes immediately pertinent. Studying the use of omens and predictions in *The Duchess* Professor Bradbrook concludes that 'the alternative views that Fate [the agent of Divine Purpose] or Chance [arbitrary Fortune] rule the world are never set in open opposition to each other. It is precisely this uncertainty at the heart of the play which is the heart of its darkness: either explanation if it could be accepted as explanation, would give some relief.'[26] The play's value-judgements are not merely inscrutable, there is a serious question-mark against their being purposive at all. Precisely such radical uncertainty characterises modern tragicomic plays and the philosophy they embrace. The form of *The Duchess*, I want to argue, faithfully reflects this philosophy and this kinship.

If we look at some recent experiments in tragicomedy, especially in the so-called 'Theatre of Cruelty', we shall find that emphasis often falls on the theatrical value of discontinuousness; for now even the fictional continuities of Beckett, Kafka, and Ionesco, however reduced, seem unapt to the crisis of experience these plays reflect. Certainly this is true of such plays as *US*, of Peter Weiss's *Marat/Sade*, and of Charles Marowitz's adaptation of *Hamlet*. Introducing the last of these, Marowitz is preoccupied with the way the 'pertinences' of Shakespeare's play are, as he puts it, 'imprisoned in its narrative'. 'Once the narrative sequence is broken,' he goes on, 'one has direct access to the play's ambiances.'[27] Certainly, in constructing a 'collage' of *Hamlet*,

[26] ibid., p. 38.
[27] Charles Marowitz, *The Marowitz Hamlet: A Collage Version of Shakespeare's Play* (1968), pp. 15–16.

Marowitz isn't writing an original play; but his discovery (or rediscovery) of the uses of juxtaposition and abrupt cross-cutting—a discovery shared with other playwrights of the fifties and sixties—does recall Webster's use of this technique. Incidents do not relate in a narrative way, but like neighbouring areas of colour or sound in a painting or a musical composition. Immediately relevant is Marowitz's account of the contemporary meaning of discontinuousness; an account we may think naïve and superficial, but which is accurate as far as it goes, and which does echo an important part of the meaning of *The Duchess*. The lives we lead, says Marowitz, do not unfold like the formalities of an Aristotelian narrative; instead 'their rhythms are erratic; their points of focus varied and unpredictable; their time-structure, if not actually broken, psychologically disjointed and confused'.[28] Moreover, the old confidence about our knowledge of people and the life around us is now severely qualified: 'disconnected bits is [*sic*] all we know of most people's story, with the possible exception of our own. We piece together information, hunches, guesses, lies and hearsay about everything we know. Our much-touted "understanding" of people is simply this eclectic, incomplete, second-hand hodge-podge of poorly-filtered data.'[29] Marowitz sees his discontinuous structure as reflecting, therefore, both social disorientation (lives do not develop in socially satisfying patterns) and a, perhaps consequent, erosion of personal awareness. Just so, Webster's Duchess inhabits a world that is socially disoriented, a 'wilderness' as she tells Cariola without path or landmark: her life lurches from one moment of experience to another, its time-scheme and that of the play 'disjointed and confused'; the little circle of awareness which she shares with Cariola and Antonio exists precariously in a climate of knowledge as worryingly 'eclectic', 'incomplete', and 'poorly-filtered' as anything of which Marowitz speaks. The first effect of discontinuousness, therefore, is to provide a dramatic equivalent for a life-experience dominated by a breakdown of social and personal liaisons; in reflecting such breakdown the narrative becomes an active part of the dramatic statement.

Marowitz provides a useful but rather limited parallel for Webster; discontinuousness reflects deeper levels in the philosophy these plays embrace than Marowitz seems to think. The really illuminating parallel here is with Peter Weiss's *Marat/Sade*, a play that deals, disturbingly, with a state of society and of personal life that finds many points of

[28] Marowitz, op. cit., pp. 45–6.   [29] ibid., p. 47.

contact with *The Duchess*. On the surface, the play brings together
Sade and Marat to explore, in Weiss's own words, 'the conflict between
an individualism carried to extreme lengths and the idea of political
and social upheaval'.[30] Such dialectic is a genuine and important part
of the play-experience, but the piece makes its most powerful impression at the level at which Marat and Sade share, rather than contest,
attitudes. Behind the surface disagreement lies a shared sense of what
both men call the 'indifference' of Nature, 'this passionless spectator'
who represents in the play's idiom that philosophical emptiness or
puzzlement or irresolution that is the basic premise of tragicomedy. In
this philosophic vacuum, actions are and mean themselves, so that
amoral energy, violence, becomes the single value. The immediate concern for us is the dramatic formula Weiss chooses to embody this
tragicomic world. Peter Brook, who as the play's producer is well
qualified to speak of its viability as theatre, tells us that Weiss's force
lies

> not only in the quantity of instruments he uses; it is above all in the
> jangle produced by the clash of styles. Everything is put in its place
> by its neighbour—the serious by the comic, the noble by the
> popular, the literary by the crude, the intellectual by the physical:
> the abstraction is vivified by the stage image, the violence illumin-
> ated by the cool flow of thought.[31]

The formula sounds not unlike that which produces the classic division
of feeling and assent of tragicomedy; except that here Weiss extends
and complicates the theatrical experience by creating an ever-shifting
imaginative contract between audience and stage. To experience the
play is to be required to participate in the performance by a continuous
act of imaginative adjustment and acceptance; so that when the actors
spill off the stage and into the audience at the play's end they merely
confirm, unnervingly, a situation that has obtained throughout. Such is
the formula Weiss uses to reflect the 'no way out' situation of tragicomedy; in place of the satisfactions of prejudice that comedy or tragedy
provide, Weiss prisons us in the lunatic asylum where the play is set
and forces us simply to experience, to *feel*, defencelessly, the raw,
'unrelated' emotion that is the single remaining value of this world

---

[30] Peter Weiss, *The Persecution and Assassination of Marat . . . under the
direction of the Marquis of Sade* (1965), p. 111.
[31] ibid., p. 6.

without absolutes. Neither detachment nor involvement is allowed us, for each would provide some kind of emotional shelter; instead we engage relentlessly in the effort of feeling and understanding demanded by ever-shifting ever-dissolving conventions.

The terms we use of Weiss require of course some adjustment before they are applicable to Webster; yet the points of contact between the two dramatic styles are numerous and remarkable. Webster notoriously employs just such a 'jangle of styles' as Brook discovers in Weiss; where Weiss ranges over every theatrical idiom from the historical-naturalistic through song and pantomime and tableau to moments of Brechtian dogma, so Webster places under contribution a range of effects which, while all may be paralleled elsewhere in Elizabethan drama, are in Webster 'thrown together in bold and fearless connection' (to adopt Ruskin's phrase for the grotesque) in a singular manner: moments of naturalism alternate with others of an unmistakably symbolic character, dance and dumb-show and song interrupt more familiar levels of action, and give on to the remarkable dramatic expressionism of the fifth act. The alternations of stance Brook describes are there also in Webster: serious and comic, noble and popular, literary and crude, intellectual and physical (to use Brook's terms), all contributing to the zestful and alarmed contemplation of an amazingly various and restless world. So too, in an emphatic way, we find what Brook calls 'the violence illuminated by the cool flow of thought'; even if Webster's thought is rarely 'cool', *The Duchess* is marked by just such a cross-flow of attitudes: the satirico-moral emphasis in conflict with the aggressive-libertine, the zest and energy of often extravagant word and action crossed by a nicety of rational analysis. The play's early scenes in particular exemplify, splendidly, Webster's dramatic adventurousness: where he cuts back and forth between the Duchess's circle and the affairs of Bosola, Ferdinand, and the Cardinal; where he endlessly varies perspective, shifts location, alters dramatic style, slows and accelerates tempo, transforms the mood through the whole range from tender and appealing to bitterly sardonic and coarse. The same adventurousness—though I admit to finding this the weakest part of the case—is there also in the discontinuities of the dialogue, where fluency is interrupted by the satiric commonplaces, the *sententiae*, the phrase-making, the moral anecdotes, the sometimes almost vulgarly emotive imagery; a mixture that recalls the shifts of idiom, shifts of pace, shifts of emotional tone in the unpredictable and unprogressive, but never ran-

dom, dialogue, not only of Weiss, but also on occasion of Pinter and Beckett. And all this effort of construction—or anti-construction—contributes, I would argue, to the dramatic statement Webster is making, a
statement that takes in Marowitz's sense of minimum-security, mini-
mum-awareness living, but goes beyond it to the deeply-divided,
philosophically perilous, outlook Professor Bradbrook describes,
an outlook that the twentieth century has rediscovered in the work
of the existentialists and in those dramatists who, often unconsciously,
share the emotional basis of existentialist thought. For again in
Webster, just as in Weiss, we find ourselves compelled to engage in a
relentless effort of imaginative adaptation that reflects and arises out of
the uncertainties of our philosophic position. In Webster, we might
say, the familiar 'greed' of the Elizabethan dramatist takes on active
force, in making an audience feel, discomfortingly, the emotional consequences of a value-less world. By the play's end we in the audience
have full knowledge of the incoherence, the madness, of that world; if
in Webster's play the deranged actors do not invade the auditorium,
the nervous assault his play makes on us is scarcely any less emphatic.

It will be felt, I am sure, that in claiming a tragicomic reading for
her play I have allowed too little for the role of the Duchess herself.
Does she not, it might be asked, provide a centre of assurance from
which we may experience the play, and hence shelter from the com-
pounded insecurities of tragicomedy? There is a sense in which the
answer must be yes; we explore the various madnesses of the play-
world largely through the mind of the Duchess. And yet I think a
straight yes is misleading, simplifies the emotional difficulty of the play,
throws the whole piece out of balance, and in so doing miscalls tragicomedy tragedy. Here again I have a divided attitude to Mr Tomlinson's
account. On one hand I find him, because of his preconceptions about
the nature of drama, concentrating so heavily on the Duchess's personal fortunes as to be obliged to dismiss or apologise for other and
brilliantly successful aspects of the play. On the other hand, even
though I should want to restate and restress some of his arguments, I
find him the most penetrating critic I have read on the point that is
here of crucial importance: the degree to which the Duchess is *of* her
world, as well as threatened by it—the chaos within reflecting, promot-
ing, and opening the way to the chaos without. Mr Tomlinson is surely
right, for example, when he insists that the Duchess's 'innocence' 'can
hardly stand alone—it must in some sense derive from the world it

lives in'; so that in Act IV he sees the Duchess 'imprisoned by, and taking part in, a world of precisely defined violence and horror'.[32] Going further, he tells us that 'the one thing Webster seems concerned to stress as far as the Duchess is concerned is the energetic violence of her behaviour at this particular stage [Act IV, scene ii]. She is infected, "possessed" (almost in the Racinian sense of the term) by the chaos which she, therefore, partly represents.'[33] Mr Tomlinson's analysis is acute and his conclusions inescapable; his work receives valuable confirmation in the writing of Clifford Leech and J. R. Brown. The Duchess, I want to insist, stands in no simple relation to the tragicomic world of her brothers; the bond that unites sister with brothers, so keenly felt at several points in the play, is not just a physical or a social relation, but a matter of 'blood', in all the Elizabethan senses of that term. So that the Cardinal's intrigues with Julia, and Ferdinand's obsessional sexuality—attitudes of mind generalised in the surrounding action—have a bearing upon our response to the Duchess's behaviour, and that not merely a negative one: we feel the differences but we experience also the analogies. The Duchess, by acts of choice and by eddies of temperament, is firmly knit to the world that destroys her. If at the end of the Duchess's life we find ourselves quite unambiguously pitying her—a relationship too simple and too stable for tragicomedy—it is because the immediate presence of death simplifies the issues, and makes time and passion and relationship (the areas in which we here experience tragicomic uncertainty) irrelevant. Much more central to our knowledge of the Duchess is her attitude of mind immediately prior to these last moments. Her ties with madness are equivocal, resisting and denying it, but also recognising in it an echo of her own living so faithful as to be almost consoling. In a plain and important sense the Duchess typifies for us, gives especial point and poignancy to, the tragicomic experience in which the whole play deals. To present the play as though it were her personal tragedy seems to me a romantic fallacy, and one that has led to accusations of imbalance in its structure. In particular Act V has seemed to some critics and producers an 'irrelevance'. On the contrary, this last act is brilliant in its 'expressionistic' statement of the tragicomic world to which the Duchess has contributed so important, but also so integral, a part.

I want in conclusion to describe a little more precisely the nature of

[32] Tomlinson, op. cit., pp. 142–3, 144.
[33] ibid., p. 148.

that tragicomic world, for in so doing we can, I think, come to see why this play so markedly predicts modern interests and modern literary forms. Its 'modernity' does not lie especially in its violence and sexual greed, although such feelings, strongly present, do at once and for obvious reasons attract contemporary notice. Sexual greed and violence are, rather, mere symptoms of the general conditions of experience, the dramatic ethos, of which the Duchess's experience also forms part. That ethos may best be described as having to do with inhibition, frustration, isolation—the condition of mind for which the most concrete image is the Duchess's prison. Here again Act IV is the focus, but only in the sense that in that act Webster more patiently explores states of mind that are apparent everywhere in the play. The idiom is all-pervasive: in the superb evocation of watchful stillness that surrounds the Duchess and Antonio; in the furtive, ghastly-flippant promiscuousness of the Cardinal and of Delio; in Ferdinand's suppressed and powerfully urgent incest-feelings; in the darkness which surrounds crucial action and emotion, especially in the early scenes; in the misunderstandings, crudely inappropriate emotions, and failures of knowledge that accompany the Revenge narrative; in Bosola, forever not quite able to break through to really satisfying knowledge and experience, ever a spy and informer, a paid hack who recognises but doesn't quite know in himself the natural instincts and feelings. Inhibition makes itself felt within the Duchess–Antonio relationship, in the rather coy and difficult way in which the liaison is initiated, in the continuing feeling of imbalance in the relation, eroded certainly by moments of playful fondness, but issuing in Antonio's rather weak defection. It is even present, we might argue, in the way the Duchess–Antonio scenes are managed: the almost uninterrupted presence of Cariola, sympathetic but flippant and marginally prurient, a figure alien to the relationship, who helps the audience to feel a sense of distance between the Duchess and her husband long before circumstances prise the two apart, and the Duchess has to undergo the cruel but not wholly inappropriate torture of seeing Antonio and the children modelled for dead in wax. The sense of isolation the Duchess feels—her most poignant question in affliction is 'Dost thou think we shall know one another, / In th'other world?'—her sense of isolation permeates and justifies the fifth act: the terrible mental isolation of Ferdinand, obsessed with shadows, the Echo scene that emphasises Antonio's aloneness, the haunted Cardinal dying by the knife of a madman while helpers stand by in ignorance, Antonio killed in error by Bosola. All these give culminating expression to an isolation, an inhibiting distance between person and person that makes offers of relationship cruelly irrelevant, that makes violence of feeling or action the only 'meaningful' gestures, and for which another name is madness. While it can never be accurate to generalise about a play, I would be prepared to argue that the major inspiration of *The Duchess of Malfi*, radiating into every aspect of the dramatic style, may be pertinently described as an intuition of the solitude of the individual—every man's consciousness his own prison.

To draw out the parallels here with contemporary literature would be little more than an exercise in the commonplace. If we had to specify a single theme that runs through modern drama—finding its origin perhaps in Strindberg, much extended by Pirandello, and central to the theatre of the Absurd—we might no doubt offer something rather like what we are claiming as the common theme of *The Duchess*. Professor Bradbrook, speaking of the fourth-act prison in this play, reminds us that 'the image of the prisoner is charged with particular poignancy for this age; the "absurd" incongruous conjunction of adverse circumstances in Webster could be paralleled in Sartre or Camus'.[34] We may go further and remember Ionesco:

> But does not the character of Hamlet express solitude and anguish? And is not Richard II's cell the prison-house of all our solitudes? It seems to me that solitude and anguish especially characterise the fundamental condition of man.[35]

I am arguing here that Webster is prompted by just such a sense of the 'fundamental condition of man', a sense reflected not only in one or two familiar quotations from the play, but by its whole structure. I want to say also that the play's stylistics faithfully and adequately express this 'modern' insight, through the tactics of tragicomedy.

[34] M. C. Bradbrook, *English Dramatic Form*, p. 103.
[35] Eugene Ionesco, op. cit., p. 80.

Webster's Realism, or, 'A Cunning Piece Wrought Perspective'

INGA-STINA EWBANK

Webster's Realism, or, 'A Cunning Piece Wrought Perspective'

WHAT I WANT to talk about in this paper is not how Webster copies life, but how he makes us accept as 'real' the life he creates. 'Realism' is a notoriously vague critical term, and Webster's art has often proved to be refractory to conventional critical vocabulary. More than that of any other Jacobean dramatist, his art seems to build on a continual shifting of perspective—a method that makes both the moral attitude and the artistic unity of his plays difficult to define. Sometimes he seems to regard his action and characters as pegs to hang language on; sometimes he seems to regard language as a tool for communicating the felt life of a character or a situation. The vicissitudes of Webster criticism are a measure of how difficult it is to find a way to describe the sense in which Webster's people and their context are alive, or 'real'. We have had the Tussaud Webster, the Elizabethan Webster whose dramatic world was 'intensely contemporary', the Jacobean Webster of the 'downward (realist) estimate' of humanity, and recently Webster Our Contemporary, to whom reality is absurd.[1] Each of these Websters has his own validity, and all I hope to do here is to discuss a notion which I have found helpful in trying to see Webster's peculiar virtues, and faults, for what they are. I should also say that, in approaching Webster, I make the assumption that, in his two tragedies at least, he is a serious drama-

[1] Travis Bogard, *The Tragic Satire of John Webster* (Berkeley and Los Angeles, 1955), p. 16 and *passim*, speaks of the kinship between Webster's dramatic world and the contemporary political and social English scene; and so, in various ways, do F. L. Lucas, *The Complete Works of John Webster*, 4 vols (1927), and John Russell Brown, from whose Revels editions of *The White Devil* (1960) and *The Duchess of Malfi* (1964) my quotations in the text of this paper are taken. G. K. Hunter has an interesting discussion of the Jacobean 'realism' of Webster's attitude in 'English Folly and Italian Vice', in *Stratford-upon-Avon Studies 1: Jacobean Theatre* (1960), esp. p. 87. For Webster Our Contemporary, see Norman Rabkin's introduction to *Twentieth Century Interpretations of 'The Duchess of Malfi'* (Englewood Cliffs, N.J., 1968), esp. p. 8.

tist: which means, first, that the subject of his plays is human beings and their relationships and, second, that he is not playing tricks on us with a rag-bag of devices and a notebook of quotations but is dramatising a genuine vision of life—that is, that his dramatic method is identical with his way of seeing his subject.

One of the most effective instances I know of one critic spiking the guns of all the others is in Ben Jonson's sonnet 'In Authorem' prefixed to Nicholas Breton's *Melancholike Humours* (1600):

> Looke here on *Bretons* worke, the master print:
> Where, such perfections to the life doe rise.
> If they seeme wry, to such as looke asquint,
> The fault's not in the object, but their eyes.
>
> For, as one comming with a laterall viewe,
> Unto a cunning piece wrought perspective,
> Wants facultie to make a censure true:
> So with this Authors Readers will it thrive:
>
> Which being eyed directly, I divine,
> His proofe their praise, will meete, as in this line.[2]

In the comfortable finality of Jonson's verdict, 'a laterall viewe' will produce an incoherent jumble, whereas, if the work is viewed from the appropriate angle, there is 'perfection to the life'—which I take to be the Elizabethan-Jacobean version of that unsatisfactory nineteenth-century term 'realism'.[3] Readers of the *Melancholike Humours* may not be so sure that 'the fault's not in the object, but their eyes'; but readers of Webster (and producers and audiences) may find some illumination in the image that underlies Jonson's critical vocabulary here.

The connotations of Jonson's adjective 'perspective' are best explained by the *O.E.D.* definition of the related noun ('perspective', sb. 4b):

> A picture or figure constructed so as to produce some fantastic effect;
> e.g. appearing distorted or confused except from one particular point
> of view, or presenting totally different aspects from different points.

We know that such pictures or figures were popular in the Elizabethan-

---

[2] ed. G. B. Harrison (1929), p. 7.

[3] The earliest *O.E.D.* entry for 'realism' in its modern literary sense is 1856.—Cf. Webster's discussion of 'the true imitation of life' in the postscript to *The White Devil* and 'An Excellent Actor', ed. Lucas, iv, 42–3.

Jacobean age.[4] Although they are more of a freak than a phenomenon to be taken seriously in the history of art, the ideas behind them seem to have appealed to writers. The young William Drummond of Hawthornden, visiting the Fair of St Germains in 1607, was particularly impressed by the display of perspectives, which he calls 'double Pictures', for their image of the moral doubleness of life, such as

A Lady weeping over her dead Husband, accompanied with many Mourners, the First View; the second representing her Second Nuptials, Nymphs and Gallants revelling naked, and going to Bed.[5]

Shakespeare, too, was interested in the properties of perspectives and in their application to human experience: he seems to have found in them a metaphor for the unreality of reality.[6] Thus Richard II's Queen is told that

---

[4] The best known examples of perspectives in this country are Holbein's painting 'The Ambassadors' in the National Gallery and the puzzle-portrait of Edward VI in the National Portrait Gallery. Both are early (1533 and 1546, respectively), but the taste for this kind of art seems to have lingered on well through the seventeenth century. On this, see Rosemary Freeman, *English Emblem Books* (1948), who also draws attention to Drummond's account. A brief but clear account of the technique, as well as popularity, of the perspective is in James Byam Shaw, 'The Perspective Picture: A Freak of German Sixteenth-Century Art', in *Apollo*, VI (1927), 208–14 (reprinted in *J.B.S. Selected Writings*, 1968). See also Jurgis Baltrusaitis, *Anamorphoses ou Perspectives curieuses* (Paris, 1955) and review article on this book in *Sele Arte*, IV.20 (September–October 1955), 7–17; and Arpad Weixlgärtner, 'Perspektivische Spielereien bei Renaissance Künstlern', in *Festschrift der Nationalbibliothek in Wien* (Vienna, 1926), pp. 849–60.—I am much indebted to Mr J. B. Trapp of the Warburg Institute for help in the matter of perspectives.

[5] *The Works of William Drummond of Hawthornden* (Edinburgh, 1711), p. 141.

[6] It is not always easy to see just how Shakespeare envisaged the perspective. Only in Sonnet XXIV could he possibly be using the word 'perspective' in the modern, technical sense, and even this instance is ambiguous. Cf. Dover Wilson's edition of *The Sonnets* (Cambridge, 1966), pp. 123–4; J. W. Lever, *The Elizabethan Love Sonnet* (1956), p. 203; and the extended discussion of Shakespeare and perspectives in A. H. R. Fairchild, 'Shakespeare and the Arts of Design', *University of Missouri Studies*, XII, I (1937), 125–30. In the instance which I quote from *Richard II*, as well as in *H.V.*, V.ii.315, *All's Well*, V.iii.48–52, and *Twelfth Night*, V.i.208–9, he has in mind various forms of distortions of vision. Shakespeare's interest in 'cozening pictures' was shared by, e.g., Drayton: see *Mortimeriados*, 2332–8, and Kathleen Tillotson's helpful note on these lines (*The Works of Michael Drayton*, V, 1941, 43). More important it was shared by other dramatists whom Webster admired: see *The Alchemist*, III.iv.88–100; and many instances in Chapman (*Hero and Leander*, III.125–6; *Ovids Banquet of Sence*, st.3; *Eugenia*, 173–80; *All Fools*, I.i.47–8; *Chabot*, I.i.68–72).

Each substance of a grief has twenty shadows,
Which shows like grief itself, but is not so;
For sorrow's eye, glazed with blinding tears,
Divides one thing entire to many objects,
Like perspectives which, rightly gaz'd upon,
Show nothing but confusion—ey'd awry,
Distinguish form. (*R.II*, II.ii.14–20)

The idea behind the perspective must have been an attempt to over-
come the static quality of pictorial art. Perspectives (in the ordinary
sense) are distorted in the whole or part of the picture; several images
are superimposed one upon another; and the very point is that, for the
viewer, there should be a confusion of impressions until he finds the
right viewpoint, when one image clicks into focus. This asks for a
peculiar kind of collaboration from the viewer, and his experience of
the work will have a kind of dynamism: through confusion to clarity.
Furthermore, the aim of the perspective must have been to fix in
images the transient quality of reality: the way one impression will,
with a change of viewpoint, change into its opposite.[7]

It is my contention that the method of Webster's art in his tragedies
is much akin to that of the perspective, and that in *The Duchess of
Malfi* in particular he uses the perspective method to achieve a unique
kind of 'realism'—a realism at the heart of which lies, not a certainty,
but a question about what is the real nature, the real estimate, of man.
But before we look at what this means, we should, I think, look at what
it does *not* mean.

[7] This, at least, is the aim which struck the poets who used the perspective
analogy. Thus Chapman describes 'Religion': 'Her lookes were like the pictures
that are made, / To th'optike reason; one way like a shade, / Another monster
like, and euery way / To passers by, and such as made no stay, / To view her in
a right line, face to face, / She seem'd a serious trifle; all her grace, / Show'd in
her fixt inspection; and then / She was the onely grace of dames and men'
(*Eugenia*, 173–80; cf. Phyllis Brooks Bartlett's note on these lines in her edition
of *The Poems of George Chapman*, N.Y., 1962, p. 456).—Though I do not wish
to embark on a rigid *ut pictura poesis* analysis of Webster, it is worth noting how
often his characters see themselves, each other, and even their own deeds (cf.
Lodovico's 'night-piece') in terms of a painting, and also that to Webster 'an
excellent actor' is 'an exquisite painter' (Lucas, op. cit., 43). Wylie Sypher's
comment on mannerist art as an 'experiment with many techniques of dispro-
portion and disturbed balance' (*Four Stages of Renaissance Style*, Garden
City, N.Y., 1956, p. 116) is also relevant. It is also noteworthy that the new
appreciation of Webster in recent decades coincides with an interest in *trompe
l'oeil* phenomena, and paintings requiring visual readjustment, such as the
Ferdinand-like mental landscape of Salvador Dali's 'The Great Paranoiac' (Fig. 7).

Drummond was also much excited by another kind of picture at the Fair of St Germains, one in which the artist had turned Venus into a *memento mori* by representing her

> lying on a Bed with stretched out Arms, in her Hand she presented to a young Man (who was adoring her, and at whom little Love was directing a Dart) a fair Face, which with much Ceremony he was receiving, but on the other side, which should have been the hinder part of that Head, was the Image of Death; by which *Mortality* [the painter] surpassed the others [who had also depicted Venus], more than they did him by *Art*.[8]

Obviously this kind of picture is like a paradigm of the art—the vision and technique—of, say, Tourneur: the skull under the milk-bathed skin and the yellow labours of the silk-worm. The *raison d'être* of the picture, its structure and its meaning, is in the static visual (and implicitly moral) contrast between Venus and Death. Similar is the local effect of the 'pot of lily-flowers with a skull in it' which the ghost of Brachiano carries,[9] and of many other verbal and physical emblems scattered throughout Webster's tragedies—not least the famous 'apricocks' ripened in horse-dung. But this doubleness is not the art of the perspective, for the perspective cannot be simply allegorised: it is, rather, an image of the flux of the human mind, of the relativity of truth depending on viewpoint, and of the confusion and uncertainty when we grope for what is real. Something of this is contained in that complex moment of discovery in *Twelfth Night* when Orsino sees

> One face, one voice, one habit, and two persons!
> A natural perspective, that is and is not. (*T.N.*, V.i.208-9)

Similarly, moving from *The White Devil* to *The Duchess of Malfi* is often a question of moving from a world of emblems to one of natural perspectives, that are and are not. To take just one example, Flamineo's analysis of 'the maze of conscience' in his breast produces Brachiano's ghost, so conveniently equipped with his flowerpot. The situation is tangible enough: this ghost is clearly meant to be more objective than

---

[8] op. cit., p. 140. For this kind of double picture, see the Dürer engraving in Fig. 3, and for the obvious use of such doubleness in satire, see the double heads in Fig. 4.

[9] See J. R. Brown's note at *The White Devil*, V.iv.123, and R. W. Dent, *John Webster's Borrowing* (Berkeley and Los Angeles, 1960), pp. 161-2.

the ghost of Isabella which Francisco almost at will conjures up from his 'melancholic thought'; and Flamineo is made to tell us that it represents a mode of reality which is 'beyond melancholy'. It is a static and self-explanatory comment—it is noteworthy that Flamineo, who is otherwise only too keen to turn situations into verbal emblems, does not expound on it—and represents the ultimate in direct experience:

> I do dare my fate
> To do its worst. (*W.D.*, V.iv.144-5)

Now, when the Cardinal in *The Duchess of Malfi* looks into *his* 'tedious' conscience, the effect is not an emblem. Instead, as in a perspective from a certain viewpoint, his view of ordinary reality is jolted into a fearsome image:

> When I look into the fish-ponds, in my garden,
> Methinks I see a thing, arm'd with a rake
> That seems to strike at me:—(*D.M.*, V.v.5-7)

And when Bosola, over the dead body of the Duchess, speaks of 'a guilty conscience' as

> a black register, wherein is writ
> All our good deeds and bad, a perspective
> That shows us hell! (*D.M.*, IV.ii.357-9)

then his conscience has, as it were, become an optical instrument for producing a 'perspective' picture (*O.E.D.*, sb. 2). In effect Bosola is describing the 'perspective' nature of a human consciousness: good and bad deeds superimposed upon each other in a confusion which at this particular moment, under this angle of vision, crystallises into a vision of hell. (One might compare this to Vittoria's outcry, upon the death of Brachiano, 'O me! this place is hell.') In each of these last two cases it is a character within the play who is transcribing his experience of a world where things are and are not, but both seem to me to be performing within a small compass what Webster was doing in the play as a whole.

This, of course, is not the same as transcribing a world where things simply are not what they seem. That is the doubleness of the Venus–Death picture which Drummond saw. Needless to say, there is that direction in Webster's art, too: the satiric impulse to strip appearances down to reality. Assuming that Webster saw eye to eye with Dekker in the *Ho!* plays, he must have started his dramatic career from a vision of life as a comic panorama with satirical potentialities. The 'realism' of these city-comedies is a matter of looking so closely at the surface of ordinary life that the stuff hidden under the surface also becomes apparent. Again a speech by a single character may epitomise the view of the plays as wholes; thus Bellamont, in *Northward Ho!*, describes Sturbridge Fair:

> I tel you Gentlemen I haue obseru'd very much with being at *Sturbridge*; it hath afforded me mirth beyond the length of fiue lattin Comedies; here should you meete a *Nor-folk* yeoman ful-but; with his head able to ouer-turne you; and his pretty wife that followed him, ready to excuse the ignorant hardnesse of her husbands forhead; in the goose market number of freshmen, stuck here and there, with a graduate: like cloues with great heads in a gammon of bacon: here two gentlemen making a mariage betweene their heires ouer a wool-pack; there a Ministers wife that could speake false lattine very lispingly; here two in one corner of a shop: Londoners selling their wares, and other Gentlemen courting their wiues; where they take vp petticoates you should finde schollers and towns-mens wiues crouding togither while their husbands weare in another market busie amongst the Oxen; twas like a campe for in other Countries so many Punks do not follow an army. I could make an excellent discription of it in a Comedy. . . . (*N.H.*, I.i.39–54)[10]

In the comedies, as in this example (though one cannot help feeling that Bellamont's 'excellent description' might have made a better play than either of the two), the verbal pleasure lies as much in the transcription of the surface as in the analysis of what is found underneath it. In the tragedies, the satirist characters find their pleasure, and expend their verbal energy, in elaborating on the falseness of appearances, as in Bosola's

> There's no more credit to be given to th' face
> Than to a sick man's urine, which some call
> The physician's whore, because she cozens him:—
>
> (*D.M.*, I.i.236–8)

Flamineo and Bosola are, or course, the great 'strippers'; they think of

10 *The Dramatic Works of Thomas Dekker*, ed. Fredson Bowers, ii, 412.

themselves as (in Bosola's phrase) 'Men that paint weeds to the life'; whether those 'weeds' are Vittoria in her love, or her grief; or the Old Lady with her revolting cosmetics cupboard; or the Duchess herself as 'a box of worm-seed'. In *The Duchess of Malfi* such stripping some-times pushes the play towards psychological drama where the charac-ters have what we like to think of as a 'modern' insight into each other's motives; thus the Cardinal's reply to Julia's 'I would not now / Find you inconstant':

> Do not put thyself
> To such a voluntary torture, which proceeds
> Out of your own guilt. (*D.M.*, II.iv.7–10)[11]

Both plays, then, are full of 'realists' with a clear view of life as corrup-tion under a splendid surface. But in *The Duchess of Malfi* at least, this is not the ultimate viewpoint, or stance, of the play. In *The White Devil* the final stance does not seem to get us much beyond the simply double picture, not even in Flamineo's

> While we look up to heaven we confound
> Knowledge with knowledge. O I am in a mist;
>
> (*W.D.*, V.vi.259–60)

nor in his last *sententia*,

> This busy trade of life appears most vain,
> Since rest breeds rest, where all seek pain by pain;
>
> (V.vi.273–4)

and least of all in Giovanni's concluding couplet:

> Let guilty men remember their black deeds
> Do lean on crutches, made of slender reeds.
>
> (V.vi.300–1)

Yet I think most of us feel that that last moment forms too small an exit from the total experience of the play. The White Devil herself, in

---

[11] Norman Rabkin, op cit., p. 6, thinks that this insight of the Cardinal's 'would do credit to any psychoanalyst'. Related to this interest in the play is, no doubt, the tendency of its characters to deal with each other in terms of shock-therapy: Ferdinand's masque of madmen being, of course, the most notable example; but cf., e.g., Antonio's intention to surprise the Cardinal, as 'the sudden apprehension / Of danger . . . May draw the poison out of him' (V.i.68–71).

the energy with which she lives and dies, can hardly be reduced to such a satirical-moralistic double picture: she both is and is not both white and devil. In relation to her, Webster's creation of character is much more that of the perspective painter; we have to see her rather like Cleopatra sees Antony, when he has betrayed her by marrying Octavia, 'painted one way like a Gorgon, / The other way's a Mars'.[12] The perspective principle applies too, if not to other characters in *The White Devil*, to character relationships within the play: to the way Vittoria's and Brachiano's visions of each other tumultuously sway during the quarrel scene in IV.ii; and to the way the very identity of Isabella seems to have changed for Brachiano, so that her lips, for which—as she tells him—he has often 'neglected cassia or the natural sweets of the spring violet', now reek of 'sweet meats, and continued physic'. Within that scene (II.i) of marital confrontation, so heavily stylised by its two divorce-rites, there is also communicated the fearsome reality of a relationship that has turned so poisonous that the actual poisoning of Isabella's lips later almost appears a natural step; the reality of aversion described by Bertram in the last scene of *All's Well that Ends Well*:

> Contempt his scornful perspective did lend me,
> Which warp'd the line of every other favour,
> Scorn'd a fair colour or express'd it stol'n,
> Extended or contracted all proportions
> To a most hideous object. (*A.W.*, V.iii.48–52)

And Isabella is given the chance to make us see the perspective from a viewpoint of plain human sorrow. She *knows* what her lips are really like: 'they are not yet much withered'. On that half-line the perspective focuses, as so often in *The Duchess of Malfi*, on a strongly felt human actuality.

The plot structure, too, of *The White Devil* makes us feel that we are watching a perspective painting where, because of the sudden reversals

---

[12] In *Chabot* (c. 1621) one character gives a thumbnail sketch of another by means of this technique (see I.i.65 ff.: 'As of a picture wrought to optic reason, / That to all passers-by seems, as they move, / Now woman, now a monster, now a devil, / . . . So men, that view him but in vulgar passes, / Casting but lateral, or partial glances / At what he is, suppose him weak, unjust, / Bloody and monstrous; but . . .'); and Burton, in *The Anatomy of Melancholy*, similarly draws on the analogy with 'these double or turning pictures' to describe characters who, like Hannibal or Cosimo, 'had two distinct persons' in them ('Democritus Junior to the Reader'; see Shilleto, ed., N.Y., 1893, I, 132).

in the action and changes of viewpoint, now one configuration now another is brought into focus. Act V is, of course, particularly dependent on such jerks, but perhaps the most sudden adjustment of all is asked for near the end of the dumb-show scene (II.ii), when the hitherto carefully, even semi-comically, distanced action of the murders threatens to move into the room from which Brachiano is watching it in his 'charm'd' night-cap:

> And now they are come with purpose to apprehend
> Your mistress, fair Vittoria; we are now
> Beneath her roof: 'twere fit we instantly
> Make out by some back postern:— (*W.D.*, II.ii.49-52)

As a *coup de théâtre* this is effective (as when in a request programme on TV the cameras suddenly move into the house of the person making the request), but, as often in *The White Devil*, the change in the angle of vision fails to lead anywhere. Too many different modes have been superimposed upon one another, each for its own sake, rather like those nineteenth-century perspective inn-signs which show Lord Beaconsfield from one side, Mr Gladstone from the other, and a basket of flowers from the front.[13] Often, in *The White Devil*, viewpoints are moved around so schematically that there is no chance to focus on, or feel about, any one of them. The love scene between Vittoria and Brachiano in I.ii, commented on realistically or cynically by Flamineo, from one direction, and moralistically by Cornelia, from another, seems to me one such example; we can admire the visual grouping, the symmetry of the scheme, but it is difficult to perceive any 'perfection to the life'. And this, of course, is the great danger of the perspective method: that there will be nothing but 'laterall views' presented to us, that nothing will emerge from the confusion, leaving us all in a mist. Here, I think, lies the main reason for the precariousness of Webster's art, as for the collapse in *The Devil's Law-Case*.[14]

In *The Duchess of Malfi*, however, by a more assured use of the same

---

[13] See notes on *Antony and Cleopatra*, II.v.116-17, in the Old Arden ed.

[14] As the illustrations to this paper show, one condition of 'perspective' art seems to be that one image never *quite* incorporates or excludes another. One is always conscious of elements waiting to become part of an image other than that on which one is focusing—thus concentration is undermined and confusion is always around the corner. In this connection, it is worth remembering that— with the single exception of Holbein's 'Ambassadors'—none of the great Renaissance artists made serious use of the 'perspective' technique, any more than Shakespeare relied on the method of varied but unresolved perspectives.

method, Webster manages to render a world which is not just confused but unfathomable. The plot jerks are here truly productive of adjustments in the angle of vision. The Duchess, in the bed chamber scene, turns around, expecting to see Antonio and Cariola, and instead sees Ferdinand; Bosola thinks he has killed the Cardinal and finds it is Antonio—at each point a whole world-view is suddenly changed. The wooing scene, where structure and language insistently remind us that the Duchess woos herself and Antonio to death as well as to marriage, and the Duchess's death scene, with its parody of the marriage masque, are only the most sustained examples of 'cunning pieces wrought perspective'. But within other scenes this method of organising reality— cutting across spatial and temporal determinations and superimposing two images in a new kind of present[15]—is even clearer. In defiance of all logic of verisimilitude, and in a superb twist of the conventional echo-device, the Duchess becomes, as it were, psychologically present when Antonio sees her:

> ... on the sudden, a clear light
> Presented me a face folded in sorrow. (V.iii.44–5)[16]

The antithesis to this 'real' presence is that other superimposition of her image, in Ferdinand's rage in II.v:

> Methinks I see her laughing—
> Excellent hyena!—talk to me somewhat, quickly,
> Or my imagination will carry me
> To see her, in the shameful act of sin. (II.v.38–41)

The intensity of Ferdinand's involvement is suggested by the very confusion of sense impressions here: 'I *see* her laughing—/ Excellent hyena!' Instead of being stopped, Ferdinand is egged on by the Cardinal's 'With whom?' to imagine the over-sexed objects of the Duchess's desire, until, as James L. Calderwood puts it, Ferdinand 'directly addresses his sister from his imaginative station as voyeur':[17]

---

[15] I am borrowing my descriptive vocabulary here from Dorothy van Ghent, whose analysis of the way Estella's image and Miss Havisham's merge in the mind of Pip in *Great Expectations* has helped me to come to terms with Webster's technique. See 'The Dickens World: A View from Todgers's', *The Sewanee Review*, LVIII (1950), 419–38, esp. 430–31.

[16] Cf. J. R. Brown, ed., *The Duchess of Malfi*, p. xxxv, on the probable stage-effect here.

[17] *The Duchess of Malfi*: 'Styles of Ceremony', *Essays in Criticism*, XII (1962), 141.

> Go to, mistress!
> 'Tis not your whore's milk that shall quench my wild-fire,
> But your whore's blood. (II.v.46–8)

And so the actual scene on stage is overlaid with one, in Ferdin-
and's mind, beyond any censor's imagination. We know that the
Duchess is not a 'whore', just as we know that she is not really there in
the Echo scene, but the vigour of Ferdinand's evocation provides a
viewpoint from which, albeit momentarily and with a near-certainty
that it is with 'a laterall view', we see the goings-on at Malfi. When we
move from the romantic-idealistic wooing at the end of Act I—

> *Antonio*: And may our sweet affections, like the spheres,
>   Be still in motion.
> *Duchess*:   Quickening, and make
>   The like soft music— (I.i.482–4)

to the physical realities of the Duchess's pregnancy at the beginning of
Act II, then we are particularly conscious of one image of the Duchess
being overlaid by another.[18]

It is, of course, in the hallucinations of madness that the human
mind behaves most like a perspective picture—despite Francisco's
somewhat self-conscious comment that

> Statesmen think often they see stranger sights
> Than madmen. (*W.D.*, IV.i.117–18)

And the character of Ferdinand, in which image and actuality fuse, so
that he *becomes* the tempest, the wild-fire, even the devil, and finally
the wolf, of his own verbal imagery, is, of course, the most notable
projection of Webster's perspective vision. Here we are no longer in
the emblematic world of satire where, for example, animal imagery is
used to show people as they 'really' are. But Ferdinand's madness is
only a concentration of the relationship which, largely through the
imagery,[19] is established between people and animals, people and
devils, people and things, in this play. Bosola starts out comparing the
two brothers to 'plum-trees, that grow crooked over standing pools' in

---

[18] Bosola's scene with the Old Lady forms, as it were, the landscape out of
which this image of the Duchess emerges. Cf. Erhard Schön's perspective
woodcut representing lovers (Fig. 5(*a*)).

[19] See Hereward T. Price, 'The Function of Imagery in Webster', *PMLA*,
LXX (1955), 717–39; and, on Ferdinand in particular, my article in *Orpheus*,
III (1956), 126–33.

an elaborate simile, of a set-piece nature, but before he reaches the end of it, the 'they' and the 'their' of his discourse refer indiscriminately and interchangeably to the trees and the brothers; and before the act is over, their corruption has been demonstrated in word and deed. The persecutors of the Duchess, in the course of the action, *become* beasts of prey, so that, only once she is dead, 'they then may feed in quiet'. We may feel, in the antagonists of the Duchess, a lack not only of logical motivation but also of an inner life; but this is substituted for by the overall creation of a demonic world in which people and animals have exchanged attributes, and in which—as Dorothy van Ghent says about Dickens's imaginative world[20]—'living creatures [are manipulated] as if they were not human but things'. Part of that gruesome confusion against which the humanity of the Duchess is defined is a grotesque dismemberment of the human body itself. The 'leg of a man' which Ferdinand carries over his shoulder in his madness, and his vision of the other characters as reduced to nothing but 'tongue and belly', may come straight out of Webster's commonplace book,[21] but they are integral with the vision of a world in which a doctor may have his skin flayed off to cover one of his 'anatomies' and in which 'a lady in France, . . . having had the smallpox, flayed the skin off her face to make it more level' (II.i.26–8). We accept as 'real', in terms of this vision, the dead hand that the Duchess is given, much as we accept as real the way Mr Vholes in *Bleak House* 'takes off his close black gloves as if he were skinning his hands, lifts off his tight hat, as if he were scalping himself, and sits down at his desk', or the way the Coketown capitalists wish that Providence had seen fit to make the factory hands 'only hands, or, like the lower creatures of the sea-shore, only hands and stomachs'. In each case the grotesquery of the image is not an end in itself but a viewpoint from which we can feel about the inhumanity of man. The reason why this kind of dismemberment is so 'real' in *The Duchess of Malfi*—whereas we hardly remember Francisco's intention of playing football with the head of Brachiano, except as a piece of gratuitous horror—is, at least partly, that in the later play there is also so much assertion of the opposite possibility and the opposite viewpoint: of ordinary, wholesome, and fruitful humanity. There is not only a thematic contrast between the sterile and perverted sexuality of the brothers and the philoprogenitiveness of the Duchess and Antonio,

[20] op. cit., 422.
[21] See Dent, op. cit., pp. 246–8.

but also, in the handling of the latter couple, a genuine evocation of
normal, domestic, love—so that the Duchess's dying words,

> I pray thee, look thou giv'st my little boy
> Some syrup for his cold, and let the girl
> Say her prayers, ere she sleep, (*D.M.*, IV.ii.203–5)

are part of a *felt* context and not just an incidental piece of sentimentality.

Both Webster's Italianate tragedies contain elements of domestic
drama. The quarrel between Brachiano, on the one hand, and Monticelso and Francisco, on the other, in II.i, begins in the triple-pillar
idiom of *Antony and Cleopatra*:

> It is a wonder to your noble friends
> That you that have as 'twere ent'red the world
> With a free sceptre in your able hand,
>
> . . . .
>
> . . . should in your prime age
> Neglect your awful throne, for the soft down
> Of an insatiate bed. (*W.D.*, II.i.26–32)

But, as the quarrel develops, the tone becomes definitely bourgeois:

> *Francisco*: You shift your shirt there
>   When you retire from tennis.
> *Brachiano*:   Happily.
> *Francisco*: Her husband is lord of a poor fortune,
>   Yet she wears cloth of tissue. (II.i.52–5)

But in *The White Devil* this tone is not sustained in any important
fashion; it remains part of the sociological documentation of the play,
as when at the end of Act I Flamineo explains how he came to be what
he is. Webster is very good at this kind of realistic documentation:

> You brought me up
> At Padua I confess, where I protest
> For want of means,—the university judge me,—
> I have been fain to heel my tutor's stockings
> At least seven years, (*W.D.*, I.ii.319–23)

and, it seems to me, some of the strongest moments in *The Devil's
Law-Case* are those in which the documentary plainness of the verse
has all the nostalgia of felt life about it. Thus Leonora, talking to her

maid, in a speech which might almost have come out of *The Family Reunion*:

> Thou hast lived with me
> These fortie yeares; we have growne old together,
> As many Ladies and their women doe,
> With talking nothing, and with doing lesse:
> We have spent our life in that which least concernes life,
> Only in putting on our clothes. (ed. Lucas, III.iii.418–23)

In *The Duchess of Malfi*, the relationship of Antonio and the Duchess (whatever we think of the remarriage of widows) comes to form a strain of simplicity, of almost bourgeois sentiment, which establishes a viewpoint and a value.

When the Duchess woos Antonio, his initial vision of marriage is altogether domestic (I.i.398–403); and so is his response, in III.i, to Delio's inquiry about 'your noble duchess':

> Right fortunately well: she's an excellent
> Feeder of pedigrees; since you last saw her,
> She hath had two children more, a son and daughter.
>   (III.i.5–7)

This attitude is reflected in the couple's understanding of larger issues, too: to the persecuted Duchess, God's dealings with her make sense in terms of her little boy and his 'scourge-stick' (III.v.78–81), and the dying Antonio uses the conventional, but here strangely apt, image of boys chasing soap-bubbles to express his sense of the vanity of human wishes (V.iv.64–6). The greater wholeness of *The Duchess* compared with *The White Devil* means, among other things, that, where in the earlier play we are made to explore single and separate attitudes, in the later we are made to focus on man as an integral being. Instead of a single abortive flash of 'compassion' in Flamineo, we have the whole of Act V devoted to the effect of the Duchess's death on her brothers and their tool; instead of a couple of speeches, the Duchess has two whole long scenes in which to face death and define who she is. Thus the viewpoint of innocence and simple love, which in *The White Devil* is represented by some rather mawkish set-pieces from Giovanni and a glimpse of Isabella, is brought into full action in *The Duchess of Malfi* through the Duchess and her children (who fortunately do not speak). Family relationships are very important in *The White Devil*, but they are, it seems to me, mainly used as pointers to the theme of social disintegration rather than being explored *as* relationships—so that, for example, the brother-brother killing moves away from human reality towards symbolism. Cornelia's motherly grief goes some way towards being an exception from this rule, and no doubt Webster is here feeling his way to a realised situation; but it is significant that he has to do it through such particularly wholesale borrowings from Shakespeare. In *The Duchess of Malfi*, on the other hand, family relationships are the very stuff on which the play is made. Robert Ornstein, in his sensitive treatment of the play, points out that

> The Duchess' strength is not a lonely existential awareness of self but a remembrance of love, expressed in her parting words to Cariola and in her answers to Bosola.[22]

As a sister, the Duchess is defeated by a confused and demonic world; but as a wife and mother she gains a kind of victory. The peculiar effect of her death scene is, at least partly, achieved by the superimposition upon each other of these two images of her; and this perspective effect is concentrated in the famous moment when Ferdinand, looking at her dead body, suddenly sees her from a human viewpoint— that is, sees what he has done to his twin sister. Truly may his eyes 'dazzle' when he sees her face. That moment is perhaps the clearest indicator of where the peculiar 'realism' of *The Duchess of Malfi* lies: in doing what E. M. Forster calls 'bouncing' us into accepting as real a world where verisimilitude and fantasy, actuality and metaphor, have merged. They have merged into a 'perspective' which, 'eyed directly', gives an insight into human suffering: into what man may do to man.

It goes without saying, and is in any case implicit in what I have said already, that Webster's language is very largely instrumental in this 'bouncing' process. Yet I shall have to say something about the language in particular, for I believe that in Webster's linguistic patterns we see the same kind of 'perspective' technique: through confusion (here expressed as verbal profusion, intricate analogies, and extended similes) to a kind of simple literalness—yet one which is meaningful only in relation to the confusion from which it has emerged. Here again we have to make a distinction between the two tragedies. Needless to say, there are many similarities: both plays have the same tendency

---

[22] *The Moral Vision of Jacobean Tragedy* (paperback ed., Madison and Milwaukee, 1965), p. 148.

towards generalising experience into axioms or *sententiae*, the same ability to embody emotion in a flash of striking imagery or a plain statement, the same tortuous and often apparently contrived looking for analogies, and the same emergence of a kind of clarity, often literalness, in characters' speeches as they face death. But there is also a different kind of concern about language in the two plays, respectively.

In *The White Devil* the importance of language as a self-conscious device is constantly kept before us. Language in the *realpolitik* world of the court is part of the power-struggle, as Flamineo well knows—the dialogue between him and Marcello in III.i, where Marcello pointedly interrupts a particularly florid simile which Flamineo is about to develop (III.i.56–7), is a good example of this—and it is, above all, a way of hiding the truth. See, for example, Francisco's grossly exaggerated lament for his sister (III.iii.341–3) and his eulogy of Lodovico, the assassin:

> If thou dost perish in this glorious act,
> I'll rear unto thy memory that fame
> Shall in the ashes keep alive thy name. (V.v.9–11)

The curious dialogue between Flamineo and Lodovico after Vittoria's trial is a very blatant demonstration of language as attitudinising—one which in itself undercuts the verbal activity of the malcontent critic, for the proper activity in the world as seen by them would be to

> [*Lodovico*:] Sit some three days together, and discourse.
> [*Flamineo*:] Only with making faces. (III.iii.77–8)

It is not for nothing that, in his ravings, Brachiano sees the Devil as 'a rare linguist'!

Related to this is Webster's interest in playing off, within a dialogue, one idiom against another, from the opening scene in which the social and moral clichés of the Antonelli–Gasparo chorus are punctured by Lodovico's cynical brutality. His 'Leave your painted comforts!' rejects both the attitude and the verbal style of his interlocutors. The sense of life in *The White Devil*, the cut and thrust of mind against mind, is very much based on this sort of contrast. There is action in the very pattern of the dialogue when Cornelia's intendedly rhetorical question to Flamineo,

> What? because we are poor,
> Shall we be vicious? (I.ii.314–15)

does not receive the obvious answer,[23] but instead provokes Flamineo's vigorously realistic analysis of how, in this society, poverty is bound to mean viciousness; or when a clichéd exclamation from Cornelia, 'O that I ne'er had borne thee', meets with the blunt retort: 'So would I'. The trial scene, which has tremendous linguistic vitality, is in a sense also a scene about the uses and possibilities of language. The apparently irrelevant dialogue between Vittoria and the Latinate lawyer introduces the whole question of language as obscuring the truth, and Vittoria and Monticelso then develop this, each as an expert at the emotional control of response through language, and Vittoria scoring in so far as she is able to pick up Monticelso's metaphors and redirect them. Ultimately, therefore, it also becomes a scene in which Webster questions the very style that most of his characters use most of the time, and particularly their ways of trying to get at meaning through metaphor.

The Cardinal's 'whore' speech has recently been criticised by David Frost as an example of how 'Webster has sometimes to force excuse for an extended simile'; but this seems to me to overlook the fact that Webster himself has built such a criticism into the dialogue and so achieved a much more complex effect than Mr Frost would allow.[24] The Cardinal's laborious searching for definitions, much like the way other Webster characters tend to explore a single idea by the use of one image after another, adds up to a near self-defeat of language. And the defeat is completed by Vittoria's deflating interjections: 'This character scapes me'; and, as Monticelso tries to get new wind, 'Well what then?' J. R. Mulryne, in his illuminating essay on Webster's style, has spoken, particularly in reference to *The Duchess of Malfi*, of 'a self-critical intelligence behind the words on the page, checking any tendency to false rhetoric, deflating over-emphatic statement or posturing'.[25] I would agree with this but go still further and say that, in many of these instances of deflation, Webster is concerned with the ultimate inability of language, even when metaphorical, to reach and convey some kinds of experience. One remembers Bosola's description of the suffering Duchess: 'her silence, / Methinks expresseth, more than if she spake' (IV.i.9–10). At key-points in *The Duchess of Malfi* the characters, like

---

[23] Dent, op. cit., p. 89, points out that Cornelia's question is 'a stoical (and Christian) commonplace [which] includes the obvious answer'.

[24] David L. Frost, *The School of Shakespeare* (Cambridge, 1968), pp. 155–6.

[25] '*The White Devil* and *The Duchess of Malfi*', in *Stratford-upon-Avon Studies 1: Jacobean Theatre* (1960), p. 216.

Edgar at the end of *King Lear*, speak what they feel, not what they ought to say; and the reality of what they feel is as much in what they do *not* speak as in their spoken words. Not only that, but the moments of rejecting elaborate language tend also to be moments at which we are made to view the perspective from a new viewpoint—notably, of course, in the dialogue between the Duchess and Bosola in IV.ii. The language of *The Duchess of Malfi* as a whole tends to serve less of a social-political function than that in *The White Devil*. Webster is less concerned with defining the nature of the court as such and more with defining the nature of the whole world in which the Duchess in particular and man in general live. The language, as has often been pointed out, is subservient to the vision of the play as a whole. So, when the Duchess asks Bosola 'Who am I?', his answer,

Thou art a box of worm-seed, at best, but a salvatory of green mummy:—what's this flesh? a little crudded milk, fantastical puff-paste; our bodies are weaker than those paper prisons boys use to keep flies in; more contemptible, since ours is to preserve earth-worms. Didst thou ever see a lark in a cage? such is the soul in the body: this world is like her little turf of grass, and the heaven o'er our heads, like her looking-glass, only gives us a miserable knowledge of the small compass of our prison, (IV.ii.124–33)

is an epitome of one of the ways in which the play's language tries to define man: through the realistic, 'stripping', imagery of moral satire, and through a series of associatively linked metaphors which turn the question over and over, worrying away at it, like a dog with a bone. The Duchess's plain retort, 'Am not I thy duchess?', turns Bosola towards another kind of realism, and he tries to look at her from the outside, as she really is, but again his vision is distracted into metaphors, and again the Duchess punctures his flow:

I am Duchess of Malfi still.

And when Bosola counters this assertion with a *sententia* which, like so many of the Webster characters' *sententiae*, appears to try to get away from the human situation at issue,

Glories, like glow-worms, afar off shine bright,
But look'd to near, have neither heat, nor light,

then it is met by her calmly deflating irony: 'Thou art very plain'. But

7—JW • •

the effect of this is not simply to discredit Bosola's language (as was the case with Lodovico's rejection of 'painted comforts'). The simplicity of the Duchess's replies must be understood in terms of Bosola's contortions, not as simple contrast, but rather as end-product. In the structure of this dialogue we are, I think, witnessing a movement rather like that of Herbert's 'Prayer':

> Prayer; the Churches banquet, Angels age,
> Gods breath in man returning to his birth,
> The soul in paraphrase, heart in pilgrimage,
> The Christian plummet sounding heav'n and earth;
> Engine against th'Almightie, sinners towre,
> Reversed thunder, Christ-side-piercing spear,
> The six-daies world transposing in an houre,
> A kinde of tune, which all things heare and fear;
> Softnesse, and peace, and joy, and love, and blisse,
> Exalted Manna, gladnesse of the best,
> Heaven in ordinarie, man well drest,
> The milkie way, the bird of Paradise,
> Church-bels beyond the starres heard, the souls bloud,
> The land of spices; something understood.

The poem works through an *accelerando* of elaborate attempts at analogy to rest in a resolution which, in pointed contrast, is plain and literal: 'something understood'. Yet the simplicity is meaningful only in relation to the complexity of what has gone before: both are necessary stages in the process, enacted by the poem, of finding a truth, defining an experience which, we feel, in the end exists beyond words altogether. Similarly, it is Bosola's speeches which fill the Duchess's plain replies with meaning: she is both 'a box of worm-seed' and 'thy duchess', both a grey-haired woman who cannot sleep and 'Duchess of Malfi still'. Each of them may see only, or mainly, one side of the dialectic, but we see the whole dramatic image. And that image, in which Bosola's view of the Duchess and her own view are superimposed upon one another, is very much 'a cunning piece wrought perspective'. Nor is it cunningness for its own sake, but a view into particular human situation as well as an intuition of a whole human condition. In so far as this is 'perfection to the life', Webster is a realist.

The Duchess of Malfi: *a Theological Approach*

D. C. GUNBY

The Duchess of Malfi: *a Theological Approach*

UNTIL COMPARATIVELY RECENTLY the standard view of *The Duchess of Malfi* was of a melodrama distinguished by its poetry. Today the tendency is to see the play in more or less existentialist terms. To John Russell Brown, for instance, the play is 'a unity of empirical, responsible, sceptical, unsurprised, and deeply perceptive concern for the characters and society portrayed'.[1] Similarly J. R. Mulryne speaks of the dramatist's 'restless, mocking intelligence',[2] while Robert Ornstein believes that Webster

> presents in art the skeptical, pragmatic nominalism of the late Renaissance; the weariness with meaningless abstraction and endless debates over words.[3]

To my mind the more recent view is as far from the truth as the older one. Although they contain characters like Flamineo, Bosola, and Romelio, Webster's plays reveal, I would argue, an outlook not pragmatic but dogmatic, not wearily nominalist but vigorously didactic, not sceptical but fideistic. And the faith upon which Webster's world-view rests is, it seems to me, that of Jacobean Anglicanism. By discussing *The Duchess of Malfi* in the light of the views of the Jacobean Church of England, particularly on providence and free will, grace, security, and despair, the limitations of evil and the sovereignty of God, I hope to demonstrate what seems to me basic to an understanding of the play—that it is essentially a work of theodicy.

An examination of the character and motives of Ferdinand might

---

[1] John Russell Brown, ed., *The Duchess of Malfi*, The Revels Plays (1964), p. xlix.

[2] 'The White Devil and The Duchess of Malfi', in *Stratford-upon-Avon Studies 1: Jacobean Theatre*, ed. John Russell Brown and Bernard Harris (1960), pp. 200–25.

[3] *The Moral Vision of Jacobean Tragedy* (Madison, Wisc., 1960), p. 134.

seem an unpromising first step towards justifying this assertion. The Duke's behaviour is so irrational, his reaction to his sister's marriage so disproportionately violent, that it seems inexplicable except as insanity. The problem is aggravated by Ferdinand's reluctance to explain his actions (see, for instance, I.i.275–6 and III.ii.127 ff.), and by his one muddled and unconvincing attempt to 'examine well the cause' of his behaviour. His admission of avarice, of hopes—'(Had she continu'd widow) to have gain'd / An infinite masse of Treasure by her death,' (IV.ii.303–4),[4] reads like evasion, or an attempt to rationalise motives too terrible to face.

What these motives are Webster reveals obliquely, through images of fire, storm, darkness, hell, and animal savagery.[5] Closely patterning these images, Webster establishes, within the framework of theme and character, three interrelated levels of motivation, all of them contributing to an understanding of the suffering and death of the Duchess, and of the remorse and retribution attending her murderers.

At the simplest level, it is clear that with Ferdinand Webster started from the traditional concept of the choleric man, just as he based the Cardinal on the phlegmatic, the Duchess on the sanguine, and Bosola on the melancholic. The images of fire which characterise the Duke's speech thus aptly mirror his fierce energy and ungovernable temper. From the touchy rebuke of I.i.124–6 to his final admission that he is consumed by 'a fire, as great as my revenge, / Which nev'r will slacke, till it have spent his fuell' (IV.i.168–9), we see the accuracy of Pescara's comment:

> Marke Prince *Ferdinand*,
> A very *Salamander* lives in's eye,
> To mocke the eager violence of fire. (III.iii.58–60)

In revealing what Antonio rightly calls a 'perverse, and turbulent Nature', the storm imagery is equally appropriate. The Duchess is optimistic that 'time will easily / Scatter the tempest' (I.i.539–40), but in II.v Ferdinand loses control of himself so completely that his brother has to rebuke him for making himself 'So wild a Tempest' (II.v.24). The Duke himself seizes on the metaphor:

---

[4] My quotations are from Lucas's edition of *The Duchess of Malfi* (1927).

[5] The importance of some, at least, of these groups of images is discussed by Moody E. Prior in *The Language of Tragedy* (New York, 1947), pp. 121–32. Prior concentrates, however, more on their atmospheric than their architectural value.

Would I could be one,
That I might tosse her pallace 'bout her eares,
Roote up her goodly forrests, blast her meades,
And lay her generall territory as wast,
As she hath done her honors. (II.v.25–9)

The fire and storm images symbolise more than choler, however. In II.v a second level of motive emerges with Ferdinand's obsessive linking of fire with his sister, the Duchess. When the Cardinal says, 'Shall our blood / (The royall blood of *Arragon*, and *Castile*) / Be thus attaincted?' (II.v.30–2), Ferdinand cries,

Apply desperate physicke—
We must not now use Balsamum, but fire,
The smarting cupping-glasse, for that's the meane
To purge infected blood, (such blood as hers:)
(II.v.33–6)

A little later he implies that the fire is burning within himself:

Goe to (Mistris.)
'Tis not your whores milke, that shall quench my wild-fire,
But your whores blood. (II.v.62–4)

It is not only the link between fire and blood which is significant, but also the different meanings which blood has for the brothers. To the Cardinal it is synonymous with rank or lineage; but to Ferdinand it is, as Inga-Stina Ekeblad first pointed out, literally his sister's blood.[6] This distinction is part of the evidence adduced by critics in favour of incestuous jealousy as Ferdinand's motive for persecuting his sister. Since the play has been thoroughly combed for signs of this unnatural (and perhaps unconscious) passion, the matter need not be gone over in detail.[7] All that needs saying here is that the fires and storms which rage inside Ferdinand are those of lust as well as of choler.

Alongside this complex pattern of motives and emotions, resting on the twin connotations of storm and fire as metaphors for anger and lust, Webster develops a third level, more important than either:

---

[6] 'A Webster Villain', *Orpheus*, III (1956), 131.
[7] For reliable summaries, see McD. Emslie, 'Motives in Malfi', *Essays in Criticism*, IX (1959), 391–405; and J. R. Brown's introduction to the Revels Plays *Duchess*, pp. lii–liv.

> I would have their bodies
> Burn't in a coale-pit, with the ventage stop'd,
> That their curs'd smoake might not ascend to Heaven:
> Or dippe the sheetes they lie in, in pitch or sulphure,
> Wrap them in't, and then light them like a match: (II.v.87–91)

Webster draws on the traditional association of fire and wind with hell to reinforce the frequent images of devils and witchcraft, and to establish them in the pattern of meaning and motive. The relationship is brought out explicitly in V.iv, when the courtiers comment on the storm which had raged earlier:

> *Grisolan*: 'Twas a foule storme to-night.
> *Roderigo*: The Lord *Ferdinand's* chamber shooke like an Ozier.
> *Malateste*: 'Twas nothing but pure kindnesse in the Divell,
>   To rocke his owne child. (V.iv.23–6)

One might not, perhaps, take seriously this hint at a direct relationship between Ferdinand's violence and that of the elements, and of demonic origins for both, were it not part of an elaborate and carefully articulated pattern. Through this pattern is revealed the fundamental reason for the brothers' persecution of their sister.

A second storm image involves witchcraft in the pattern. When Ferdinand loses control of himself in II.v, his brother reproves him in these terms:

> How idlely shewes this rage!—which carries you,
> As men convai'd by witches, through the ayre,
> On violent whirle-windes—(II.v.65–7)

The remark is apt, for Ferdinand early reveals his obsession with witchcraft, particularly in relation to his sister. In I.i he warns her that

> ... they whose faces doe belye their hearts,
> Are Witches, ere they arrive at twenty yeeres,
> I: and give the divell sucke. (I.i.343–5)

This tells us more about Ferdinand than about the Duchess. So too does his involuntary cry, 'The witch-craft lies in her rancke b[l]ood' (III.i.94), which follows a casual reference to witches in another context. The principal significance of the repeated references to witchcraft, however, lies in the Jacobean belief that witches were demonically possessed. It is no coincidence that the offering of the severed hand and the use of the wax effigies are related to the rites of witchcraft (see IV.i.65–6 and 73–6), for as will become clear, Ferdinand is himself possessed by the Devil, and his torment of his sister is explicitly anti-religious.

Moving from the storm images to those of fire, we find the same relationship with the idea of hell and devils. The comment of the Second Madman tells us that

Hell is a meere glasse-house, where the divells are continually blowing up womens soules, on hollow yrons, and the fire never goes out. (IV.ii.81–3)

Behind this, as behind the ravings of the other madmen, lies an important statement. For along with a topical reference to the glass factory and a stock comment on feminine vanity, we are offered a mirror to Ferdinand's actions. In seeking to destroy his sister's soul, Ferdinand is creating a hell on earth, a hell whose fires burn within himself. In this connection it is important to note Webster's borrowing from Deuteronomy to describe the Duchess's plight:[8]

Th'heaven ore my head, seems made of molten brasse, the earth of flaming sulphure, yet I am not mad: (IV.ii.27–8)

Here, then, is the deepest motive underlying the actions of Ferdinand and his brother. For even if incestuous feelings are admitted as implicit in the Duke's conduct, and if the choleric element in his nature is acknowledged; and, equally, if pride of lineage and a cold selfishness born of his phlegmatic temperament are put forward to explain the Cardinal's behaviour, it is nonetheless clear that Webster's fundamental concern is with a conflict between good and evil, in which the brothers are demonically impelled to destroy good, in the person of the Duchess, through an unwilling Bosola. The metaphoric and dramatic means by which Webster makes this clear must now be considered.

First Webster constantly and directly associates both Ferdinand and the Cardinal with the Devil. Bosola says of the Cardinal:

Some fellowes (they say) are possessed with the divell, but this great

---

[8] See M. C. Bradbrook, 'Two Notes Upon Webster', *MLR*, XLII (1947), 281–94.

fellow, were able to possesse the greatest Divell, and make him worse. (I.i.45–8)

The malcontent's bitter jibe is quickly reinforced by Antonio's estimate:

> Last: for his brother, there, (the Cardinall)
> They that doe flatter him most, say Oracles
> Hang at his lippes: and verely I beleeve them:
> For the Divell speakes in them. (I.i.187–90)

During Bosola's interview with Ferdinand later in the scene, frequent reference is made to hell and devils. Bosola accuses the Duke of making him 'a very quaint invisible Divell, in flesh: / An intelligencer', and at first refuses payment, saying

> Take your Divels
> Which Hell calls Angels: these curs'd gifts would make
> You a corrupter, me an impudent traitor,
> And should I take these, they'll'd take me [to] Hell. (I.i.285–8)

But driven to accepting a post which will enable him to spy on the Duchess, and make him in his own eyes 'the divells quilted anvell', he comments bitterly:

> ... Thus the Divell
> Candies all sinnes [o'er]: and what Heaven termes vild,
> That names he complementall. (I.i.299–301)

However, the most illuminating comment in the earlier part of the play, because of the light it sheds on the relationship of Ferdinand to Bosola, is made by Antonio:

> You would looke up to Heaven, but I thinke
> The Divell, that rules i'th'aire, stands in your light. (II.i.97–8)

Having thus established Ferdinand and the Cardinal on the side of hell in this conflict, Webster sets up in opposition to them the positive goodness of the Duchess and Antonio. Virtue and serenity are keynotes in Antonio's praise of his mistress in I.i:

> Her dayes are practis'd in such noble vertue,
> That sure her nights (nay more her very Sleepes)
> Are more in Heaven, then other Ladies Shrifts. (I.i.205–7)

This impression is strengthened by subsequent images, by Antonio's

vow that he 'will remaine the constant Sanctuary' of the Duchess's good
name, and the Duchess's plea that Ferdinand explain

> Why should onely I,
> Of all the other Princes of the World
> Be cas'de-up, like a holy Relique? (III.ii.160–62)

Later, when the Duchess confesses to Bosola her secret marriage, she
receives even from him an apparently sincere tribute:

> Fortunate Lady,
> For you have made your private nuptiall bed
> The humble, and faire Seminary of peace, (III.ii.323–5)

The irony is bitter, since this peace is already threatened.

Webster develops this contrast between the order of the Duchess's
life and the disorder of her persecutors', between peace and conflict,
religion and anti-religion, by employing in imagery and action the
archetypal symbols of good and evil—light and darkness. It is significant how much of the action of *The Duchess of Malfi* takes place either
at night (five scenes: II.iii, II.v, III.ii, V.iv, and V.v) or in the gloom
of prison (two scenes: IV.i and IV.ii). It is significant, too, that in at
least two of these scenes (II.iii and V.iv) there are storms in progress.
It is against this background that the gentle and luminous figure of the
Duchess, who in Antonio's loving words, 'staines the time past: lights
the time to come' (I.i.214), faces the persecution of the brothers who
threaten to 'fix her in a generall ecclipse' (II.v.102).

In IV.i this threat comes closer when Ferdinand visits his sister
under cover of darkness. His ostensible reason for doing this is
announced by Bosola:

> Your elder brother the Lord *Ferdinand*
> Is come to visite you: and sends you word,
> 'Cause once he rashly made a solemne vowe
> Never to see you more; he comes i'th' night:
> And prayes you (gently) neither Torch, nor Taper
> Shine in your Chamber: he will kisse your hand:
> And reconcile himselfe: but, for his vowe,
> He dares not see you: (IV.i.25–32)

The Duchess agrees, the lights are removed, and Ferdinand enters. His
first words, 'This darkenes suites you well', reveal his perverted values:

it is he whom the darkness suits; it was he who requested it, unable to face his sister without its protection. He is closer to the truth when he says:

> It had bin well,
> Could you have liv'd thus alwayes: for indeed
> You were too much i'th' light: (IV.i.48–50)

For behind the pun lies the irony of an attitude akin to that of Iago's resentment of Cassio: 'He hath a daily beauty in his life / That makes me ugly.' It is significant, too, that Ferdinand needs darkness for his diabolical trick of giving his sister the dead hand. As she calls distractedly for lights and he rushes from the room, we feel the devilishness of behaviour which seems surely inspired by more than mere anger or unnatural lust.

I have suggested that 'Th' Arragonian brethren' are diabolically driven in persecuting their sister. The time has now come to elaborate on this motivation. Ferdinand, it has been said, is usually reluctant to explain his actions. But on one occasion, in IV.i, he makes an explicit, if gnomic, confession:

> Bosola: Why doe you doe this?
> Ferdinand: To bring her to despaire. (IV.i.139–40)

That this statement is to be interpreted in a specifically religious sense can be inferred from Bosola's earlier reproof of the hysterical Duchess:

> O fye: despaire? remember
> You are a Christian. (IV.i.87–8)

The importance of Ferdinand's admission lies in the fact that bringing man to despair was considered one of the Devil's chief aims, since in despairing of God's mercy, his love, or even his very existence, man lost all hope of salvation.[9] For parallels in the drama we have Marlowe's *Faustus* or Massinger's *A New Way to Pay Old Debts*, where Sir Giles Overreach, the incarnation of anti-religion, bids his servant Marrall go to the scapegrace hero, Wellborn, and 'do anything to work him to despair' (II.i.66).[10] When Marrall tries to carry out his master's

---

[9] For a valuable discussion of the significance of despair, see Arieh Sachs, 'The Religious Despair of Doctor Faustus', *JEGP*, LXIII (1964), 625–47.

[10] References to *A New Way* are cited from the Falcon Press Edition, ed. M. St Clare Byrne (1949).

commission, Wellborn rejects his advice as 'the Devil's creed', commenting:

> 'Twill not do; dear tempter,
> With all the rhetoric the fiend hath taught you.
> I am as far as thou art from despair. (II.i.120–22)

Ferdinand's intentions are, I suggest, the same as Overreach's. Certainly the Duke is contemptuous in speaking to Bosola of 'that which thou wouldst comfort, (call'd a soule)' (IV.i.148).

To find the positive values which the play offers, we must first consider the character of the Duchess and then her relationship with Bosola. I do not intend to discuss the already exhaustively treated— and it seems to me, peripheral—questions of the Duchess's guilt, or the propriety of the remarriage of widows.[11] It is obvious, after all, where our sympathies are meant to lie: the moral issues are never in doubt. For present purposes the Duchess's remarriage is important only in that it highlights three important traits of character: her courage, pride, and wilfulness. We see these traits equally displayed in her refusal to be swayed by her brothers' threats, her determination that 'if all my royall kindred / Lay in my way unto this marriage: / I'll'd make them my low foote-steps' (I.i.382–4). There is evidence of her pride in her wooing, too. For although she claims to 'put of[f] all vaine ceremony, / And onely ... appeare ... a yong widow', she nonetheless raises the kneeling Antonio with

> Sir,
> This goodly roofe of yours, is too low built,
> I cannot stand upright in't, nor discourse,
> Without I raise it higher: raise your selfe,
> Or if you please, my hand to helpe you: so. (I.i.478–82)

It is no accident that we are never told the Duchess's name, for here she is very much the great lady, acutely conscious of her status, even in love, while later, isolated and facing death, she reaches a state of humility such that she wants nothing more than anonymity, and, reversing her earlier gesture, kneels to enter heaven. We can chart the full

---

[11] On these issues, see Emslie, op. cit.; Clifford Leech, *Webster: The Duchess of Malfi* (1963), pp. 51–7; and F. W. Wadsworth, 'Webster's *Duchess of Malfi* in the Light of Some Contemporary Ideas on Marriage and Remarriage', *PQ*, XXXV (1956), 394–407.

distance of the spiritual pilgrimage revealed by these two acts, by considering her relationship with Bosola, particularly in III.v, IV.i, and IV.ii.

Bosola is generally recognised as a man divided against himself. Forced by penury to serve a cause he knows to be wrong, he mitigates when he can the effects of the evil he is doing. Webster uses this conflict to demonstrate that a man can be at once an agent of God and of the Devil. Bosola torments the Duchess yet comforts her, destroys yet saves her. In a conflict like this the Jacobeans firmly believed that God could always nullify the intrigues of the Devil. As Calvin put it:

> Now when we say that Satan resisteth God, that the works of Satan disagree with the works of God, we doe therewithall affirme that this disagreement and strife hangeth vpon the sufferance of God.[12]

Through Bosola this is demonstrated, not crudely, as in the homilectic tales of Thomas Beard or in a play like Massinger and Dekker's *The Virgin Martyr*, but subtly, presenting divine providence in its continuity rather than as random miraculous intervention.

We find clear indications of this continuity in III.v. First Antonio and the Duchess acknowledge the existence of divine order in their lives. Antonio says:

> Best of my life, farewell: Since we must part,
> Heaven hath a hand in't: but no otherwise,
> Then as some curious Artist takes in sunder
> A Clocke, or Watch, when it is out of frame
> To bring't in better order. (III.v.74–8)

The Duchess is similarly convinced that her suffering is not without purpose:

> Must I like to a slave-borne Russian,
> Account it praise to suffer tyranny?
> And yet (O Heaven) thy heavy hand is in't.
> I have seene my litle boy oft scourge his top,
> And compar'd my selfe to't: naught made me ere
> Go right, but Heavens scourge-sticke. (III.v.90–95)

Here too we see Bosola for the first time as agent of providence. For

---

[12] John Calvin, *The Institution of Christian Religion*, tr. Thomas Norton (1611), p. 70.

when the Duchess breaks down he arrests her hysteria through her pride:

> *Bosola*: Fye (Madam)
> Forget this base, low-fellow.
> *Duchess:* Were I a man:
> I'll'd beat that counterfeit face, into thy other—(III.v.139–42)

The crisis passes, and the scene ends with one of the tales to which so many critics have taken exception. As a recent editor of the play has noted, however, this is more than the 'apparently simple fable':

> the Fisher is God; the gathering in of the fishes is a harvest at which not wheat and tares, but good and bad fish are to be judged; the Market is the Judgement; the Cook is another symbol for God; the fire represents hell-fire: at the Judgement one is as close to hell as to the joys of heaven.[13]

In the remaining acts this separation and judgement of the good and the bad is demonstrated. But before the Duchess can enter heaven she must pass through severe trial; since

> when God will send his own servants to heaven, he sends them a contrary way, even by the gates of hell.[14]

In IV.i the gates of hell gape wide, for through his elaborate torments Ferdinand almost succeeds in breaking the Duchess's spirit. She wishes only for death:

> That's the greatest torture soules feele in hell,
> In hell: that they must live, and cannot die:
> *Portia*, I'll new kindle thy Coales againe,
> And revive the rare, and almost dead example
> Of a loving wife. (IV.i.82–6)

At this point Bosola steps in, reproving her for giving way to despair, and offering what comfort he can to divert her from thoughts of suicide. The Duchess, however, lapses into hysteria and self-pity, wishing on the world the chaos which seems to fill her own life:

> *Duchess*: I could curse the Starres.

[13] Elizabeth M. Brennan, ed., *The Duchess of Malfi*, The New Mermaids (1964), p. xxi.
[14] William Perkins, *Works*, 3 vols. (1616–18), i, 492.

Bosola: Oh fearefull!

Duchess: And those three smyling seasons of the yeere
    Into a Russian winter: nay the world
    To its first Chaos. (IV.i.115–19)

Bosola's reply, 'Looke you, the Starres shine still', has often been taken, as by F. L. Lucas, to express 'the insignificance of human agony before the impassive universe'.[15] But it is also a further attempt to strengthen the Duchess in her suffering; an affirmation of faith in the divine order which still exists, undisturbed by the chaos around her. In this one great line Bosola's double role is epitomised.

Towards the end of the scene we are given a clear indication that in future Bosola's help to the Duchess will be more direct. Revolted by what is happening, he protests to Ferdinand, and when his protests are dismissed, bluntly declares the terms on which he will continue to carry out the Duke's orders:

Bosola: Must I see her againe?

Ferdinand: Yes.

Bosola: Never.

Ferdinand: You must.

Bosola: Never in mine owne shape,
    That's forfeited, by my intelligence,
    And this last cruell lie: when you send me next,
    The businesse shalbe comfort. (IV.i.158–64)

Thus, in a manner wholly characteristic, Webster provides a naturalistic explanation of the disguises which Bosola will adopt—disguises whose purpose is not only to make him unrecognisable, but also to symbolise his role in the Duchess's purification and preparation for death.

For the Duchess, IV.i is a spiritual nadir; thereafter, as Bosola predicted, 'Things being at the worst, begin to mend' (IV.i.92). Hence when IV.ii opens we find her in a more composed state of mind, self-pity and hysteria replaced by quiet resignation:

    I am acquainted with sad misery,
    As the tan'd galley-slave is with his Oare,
    Necessity makes me suffer constantly,
    And custome makes it easie—(IV.ii.29–32)

[15] *The Complete Works of John Webster*, 4 vols. (1927), ii, 179.

Not even the madmen, symbols of a world disordered and depraved, can shake her composure. In one sense, therefore, she is prepared for death. In another she is not. Bosola still has to free her from pride. In III.v consciousness of rank had helped to keep her from despair and suicide. Now it is a hindrance, an impediment to be set aside if she is to enter heaven. Now, therefore, Bosola directs all his efforts towards instilling in the Duchess an awareness of the insignificance of rank by comparison with the lasting reality of death. First he must convince her that she is 'sick':

> *Bosola*: I am come to make thy tombe.
> *Duchess*: Hah, my tombe?
> Thou speak'st, as if I lay upon my death bed,
> Gasping for breath: do'st thou perceive me sicke?
> *Bosola*: Yes, and the more dangerously, since thy
> sicknesse is insensible. (IV.ii.115–20)

As yet the Duchess is unwilling—and unable—to understand. It is important, however, that we should appreciate his diagnosis. We can do so by glossing his statement with this passage from an anonymous devotional work, *The House of Mourning*:

> Consider the evil of this security you are in, of this disposition of heart, when you cry, peace, peace, to your selves in the midst of God's displeasure. It is an evil disease, a spiritual Lethargy. That disease we know in the body, it takes a man with sleep, and so he dieth. . . . It is more dangerous, because it is a senseless disease, a disease that takes away the senses from the soul: and diseases (we know) that take away the senses, are dangerous: for it is not only a sign that nature is overcome by the disease, but besides, it draweth men from seeking for cure. Thus it is with the spiritual Lethargy; it shews not only that sin hath prevailed in the heart . . . , but it hindreth you from seeking the means to escape out of it.[16]

Clearly the Duchess's sickness is security or spiritual lethargy, scarcely less dangerous to the soul than despair. As Lancelot Andrewes remarks in one of his sermons:

---

[16] ΘΡΗΝΟΙΚΟΣ, *The House of Mourning* (1672), p. 155.

Now perseverance we shall attain, if we can possess our souls with the due care, and rid them of security. . . . And, to avoid security, and to breed in us due care, St. Bernard saith, 'Fear will do it.' Vis in timore securus esse? securitatem time; 'the only way to be secure in fear, is to fear security.'[17]

Bosola's task is to make the Duchess recognise her peril. So when she asks the question, 'Who am I?', he replies:

Thou art a box of worme-seede, at best, but a salvatory of greene mummey: what's this flesh? a little cruded milke, phantasticall puffe-paste: our bodies are weaker then those paper prisons boyes use to keepe flies in: more contemptible: since ours is to preserve earth-wormes: (IV.ii.123-7)

This stark vision is, however, offset by what follows:

didst thou ever see a Larke in a cage? such is the soule in the body: this world is like her little turfe of grasse, and the Heaven ore our heades, like her looking glasse, onely gives us a miserable knowledge of the small compasse of our prison. (IV.ii.127-31)

Here Bosola is speaking wholly in the *contemptu mundi* tradition, placing, as Donne often does in his sermons, human existence in an eternal perspective.

The Duchess, however, still seeks to assert herself: 'Am not I, thy Duchesse?' Bosola again refutes her claim:

Thou art some great woman sure, for riot begins to sit on thy fore-head (clad in gray haires) twenty yeares sooner, then on a merry milkmaydes. Thou sleep'st worse, then if a mouse should be forc'd to take up her lodging in a cats eare: a little infant, that breedes it's teeth, should it lie with thee, would crie out, as if thou wert the more unquiet bed-fellow. (IV.ii.133-8)

Once more the Duchess tries, crying 'I am Duchesse of *Malfy* still', and once more Bosola replies, more bluntly than before:

That makes thy sleepes so broken:
'Glories (like glowe-wormes) afarre off, shine bright,
But look'd to neere, have neither heate, nor light.' (IV.ii.139-42)

[17] *Ninety Six Sermons*, ed. J. P. Wilson and James Bliss, 5 vols. (Oxford, 1841-3), ii, 72.

This time he is successful, and the Duchess answers quietly, 'Thou art very plaine'. Bosola drives home his point by introducing what might seem gratuitous satire:

> Duchess: Do we affect fashion in the grave?
> Bosola: Most ambitiously: Princes images on their tombes
>   Do not lie, as they were wont, seeming to pray
>   Up to heaven: but with their hands under their cheekes,
>   (As if they died of the tooth-ache)—they are not carved
>   With their eies fix'd upon the starres; but as
>   Their mindes were wholy bent upon the world,
>   The selfe-same way they seeme to turne their faces.
>
>   (IV.ii.152–9)

The Duchess recognises a little, at least, of the deeper significance of this passage, for she says quietly:

> Let me know fully therefore the effect
> Of this thy dismall preparation,
> This talke, fit for a charnell? (IV.ii.160–62)

This long exchange has indeed been a preparation. Its success we may judge from the Duchess's reception of the 'present' her brothers have sent: the coffin, cords, and bell:

> Let me see it—
> I have so much obedience, in my blood,
> I wish it in ther veines, to do them good. (IV.ii.167–9)

The Duchess has attained humility. Consequently Bosola can drop the role of tomb-maker, and take up his second disguise:

> Bosola: I am the common Bell-man,
>   That usually is sent to condemn'd persons
>   The night before they suffer:
> Duchess: Even now thou said'st,
>   Thou wast a tombe-maker?
> Bosola: 'Twas to bring you
>   By degrees to mortification: (IV.ii.173–9)

Having been brought 'by degrees to mortification', the Duchess must now have her thoughts directed towards eternity—the purpose of the bellman in Jacobean England.[18] In the famous dirge, intoned to the tolling of the bell, Bosola calls on the Duchess to 'don her shrowd', contrasting the turmoil of this life with the serenity to come:

> *A long war disturb'd your minde,*
> *Here your perfect peace is sign'd—* (IV.ii.186–7)

Then he re-emphasises the vanity of earthly concerns:

> *Of what is't fooles make such vaine keeping?*
> *Sin their conception, their birth, weeping:*
> *Their life, a generall mist of error,*
> *Their death, a hideous storme of terror—*(IV.ii.188–91)

and ends with a renewed call to purification before the journey to eternity.

Bosola's preparation of the Duchess is complete. Although Webster never explicitly states that she has attained a state of grace, we can infer this from her composure in the face of death, composure which enables her to counter Bosola's question, 'Doth not death fright you?' with the calm assurance of

> Who would be afraid on't?
> Knowing to meete such excellent company
> In th'other world. (IV.ii.216–18)

A more specific indication, however, is the degree to which she is now free from earthly concerns, and able to focus her thoughts upon heaven. For as Richard Baxter says in his treatise upon 'that Excellent unknown Duty of *Heavenly Meditation*', *The Saints Everlasting Rest*:

Consider, A heart set upon heaven, will be one of the most unques-

---

[18] It is worth noting that when, in 1605, a certain Robert Dove, Merchant Taylor, made a deed of gift providing that a bellman should visit condemned felons in Newgate Prison on the eve and morning of their execution, one of the witnesses to the charity was a 'John Webster'. (See F. P. Wilson, *Elizabethan and Jacobean* (Oxford, 1945), p. 106.) And though, as Wilson points out, 'the name is too common for us to be sure that he is the dramatist', this could well be, since Webster tells us, in the dedication to his mayoral pageant, *Monuments of Honor* (1624), that he was 'borne free' of that guild (see *Works*, iii, 315). What makes Dove's bequest so pertinent, however, is the requirement that the bellman put the condemned 'in minde of their mortalitie', and so 'awake their sleepie senses from securitie, to saue their soules from perishing'. (See *London's Dove*, 1612, C4v.).

tionable evidences of thy sincerity, and a clear discovery of a true
work of saving grace upon thy soul.[19]

Or again:

How shall I know that I am truly sanctified? Why, here is a mark
that will not deceive you, if you can truly say that you are possessed
of it; Even, a heart set upon Heaven.[20]

Unlike Cariola, therefore, who clings to life, lying, begging, and fighting for a moment's respite, the Duchess faces her executioners with no
more than a momentary tremor, revealed in a longing to be 'out of your
whispering', and kneels to accept the gift of death:

> Pull, and pull strongly, for your able strength,
> Must pull downe heaven upon me:
> Yet stay, heaven gates are not so highly arch'd
> As Princes pallaces—they that enter there
> Must go upon their knees: (IV.ii.237–41)

The Duchess's pilgrimage is over. What is left of the lives of Bosola
and his masters illustrates that in the Duchess's death evil did not
vanquish good, but was itself defeated.

Had I time, I would now seek to demonstrate this view, showing
how justice is done—and seen to be done—according to a pattern of
retribution as apt as it is all-embracing. I would try to show that in
every respect the fate which befalls Ferdinand and the Cardinal can be
related to what has happened earlier. I would show (as critics have in
part done)[21] that Ferdinand's 'cruell sore eyes' and fear of the light
were directly related to his need for darkness in IV.i, and to the famous
'Cover her face: Mine Eyes Dazell'. I would emphasise the significance of the Duke's Lycanthropia—its connection with wolves and
witchcraft, with his incestuous passion for his sister, and through the
traditional beliefs that wolves disclose murders by digging up the victims and that those suffering from Lycanthropia have wolf's hair under
the skin like the hair shirts of penitents, with the twin emotions of guilt
and remorse. I would emphasise, too, that the diabolic impulses underlying the actions of Ferdinand and the Cardinal lead them, as the two
men clearly see, into the mouth of hell. I would dwell particularly, in
this connection, on the fact that the brothers suffer finally from the

---

[19] 4th ed. (1653), pt. 3, p. 207.   [20] Pt. 3, p. 207.
[21] See, for instance, Prior, op. cit., pp. 124–6.

despair which they had tried to induce in their sister, and that the
Cardinal finds himself, like Marlowe's Faustus or Shakespeare's
Claudius, unable to pray for mercy:

> ... O, my Conscience!
> I would pray now: but the Divell takes away my heart
> For having any confidence in Praier. (V.iv.30–32)

Since, however, I have space to develop none of these points, I will
conclude my commentary with a discussion of one aspect of the last
act: the roles of Antonio and Bosola. In doing so, I will try to refute
the view, persuasively argued by Gunnar Boklund, that Bosola's sense
that 'We are meerely the Starres tennys-balls (strooke, and banded /
Which way please them)', represents the play's final message. Boklund
writes:

> The theme of retribution that occupies Webster throughout the act
> is simple only if superficially considered. No religious significance
> can be extracted from it, for the perversity of superhuman inter-
> vention is demonstrated as thoroughly as is the bankruptcy of human
> intelligence. The Aragonian brothers are killed, but so is Antonio. Not
> only does providence lack a tool in *The Duchess of Malfi*, it does not
> even operate, even in the form of nemesis. What governs the events
> is nothing but chance.[22]

On the contrary, it is perfectly possible to reconcile the confusion and
futility of the last act with a providential order.

I described Bosola earlier as a man divided against himself. He has
'loath'd the evill' he has had to commit, yet carried out his orders,
partly in hopes of reward, and partly, as he tells Ferdinand, because he
'rather sought / To appeare a true servant, then an honest man'
(IV.ii.358–9). When the Duke proves ungrateful, Bosola no longer has
an anodyne for his conscience, and is stricken with remorse:

> What would I doe, we[r]e this to doe againe?
> I would not change my peace of conscience
> For all the wealth of Europe: (IV.ii.365–7)

Since he is obviously penitent, and since, too, his role has been that of
an agent of God as well as of the Devil, we may wonder whether he

[22] *The Duchess of Malfi: Sources, Themes, Characters* (Cambridge, Mass.,
1962), pp. 129–30.

will escape damnation. When the Duchess stirs, it seems briefly as though he will, and all his long-frozen humanity breaks forth in joy and hope:

> ... She stirres; here's life:
> Returne (faire soule) from darkenes, and lead mine
> Out of this sencible Hell: She's warme, she breathes:
> Upon thy pale lips I will melt my heart
> To store them with fresh colour: who's there?
> Some cordiall drinke! Alas! I dare not call:
> So, pitty would destroy pitty: her Eye opes,
> And heaven in it seemes to ope, (that late was shut)
> To take me up to mercy. (IV.ii.367–75)

Yet heaven only 'seemes to ope.' The Duchess's recovery is only momentary, and her death confirms Bosola in despair and remorse:

> Oh, she's gone againe: there the cords of life broake:
> Oh sacred Innocence, that sweetely sleepes
> On Turtles feathers: whil'st a guilty conscience
> Is a blacke Register, wherein is writ
> All our good deedes, and bad: a Perspective
> That showes us hell; that we cannot be suffer'd
> To doe good when we have a mind to it! (IV.ii.382–8)

His chance of salvation has gone, his change of heart comes too late. He is damned.

Yet even with his 'estate . . . . suncke below / The degree of feare', Bosola tries to warn Antonio of the plot against him, and to join him in 'a most just revenge'. His motives are mixed: he wishes to destroy the brothers, but he also wants to atone for what he has done, and hopes, however faintly, that atonement will bring the fruits of penitence:

> The weakest Arme is strong enough, that strikes
> With the sword of Justice: Still me thinkes the Dutchesse
> Haunts me: there, there! . . . 'tis nothing but my mellancholy.
> O Penitence, let me truely tast thy Cup,
> That throwes men downe, only to raise them up. (V.ii.379–83)

Only when his plans miscarry, and by a stroke of bitter irony he slays 'the man I would have sav'de 'bove mine owne life!' (V.iv.62), does he recognise the futility of his efforts, and abandon hope.

Bosola's part in the death of Antonio, an 'accident' if one may call it that, proves conclusively both to him and to us, that the time is past when atonement is possible. To understand why Antonio should be the victim we must consider his character.

The Duchess's husband is an honest man, a loving husband and father, and a faithful friend, but he is also hesitant and ineffectual in a crisis, and unimpressive beside his more vigorous wife. As Boklund's study of the source-material shows, the original Antonio was a glowingly cavalier figure; at Webster's hands he is transformed into a character of thoroughgoing ordinariness.[23] In part, no doubt, Webster's motives for this are dramatic. The Duchess must stand alone. Yet one may also suspect didactic considerations, since there are hints that Antonio is intended to illustrate the limitations of neo-stoic philosophy. The more oblique of these, the stress placed on Antonio's lack of ambition, and his bloodless and hesitant approach to life, both of which might be related to the neo-stoic belief in the contentment that retirement brings, and to the ideal of the golden mean, or *mediocritas*, can be quickly passed over, since to linger would be to exaggerate the strength of the argument. Rather more attention is due, however, to what Antonio says on matters religious and philosophical. At one point the Cardinal remarks that Antonio accounts 'religion / But a Schoolename' (V.ii.136–7). This is patently untrue, yet it may not be oversubtlety to detect in Antonio's utterances on religion a generality which makes them as likely to be the product of a stoic as of a Christian outlook. There may be nothing more than orthodox piety in his view of the enforced parting as a move by heaven to bring himself and the Duchess 'in better order', or in his conviction that 'Heaven fashion'd us of nothing: and we strive, / To bring ourselves to nothing:' (III.v.97–8). But alongside these remarks stands another with a distinctly stoic air:

> Make Patience a noble fortitude:
> And thinke not how unkindly we are us'de:
> 'Man (like to *Cassia*) is prov'd best, being bruiz'd. (III.v.87–9)

Later in the play the stoic element becomes more explicit, with Antonio talking in terms of 'Necessitie' (V.iii.41–4), and seeing his predicament less in terms of submission to heaven than in relation to the stoic doctrine of will:

[23] op. cit., pp. 92–6.

Though in our miseries, Fortune have a part,
Yet, in our noble suffrings, she hath none—
Contempt of paine, that we may call our owne. (V.iii.70–72)

Pain, Antonio seems to assert, is pain only if the sufferer chooses to acknowledge it. The distinction is the traditional stoic one between external circumstances and the individual's response to them.

For all his philosophising, however, Antonio cuts an increasingly sorry figure as the play progresses, and by the last act he is drifting aimlessly in the vague hope of reconciliation with his persecutors. Nor do his dying moments raise his stature, particularly when they are compared with those of his wife. For where in her last minutes we can discover a deep sense of the value of death in relation to the life to come, Antonio's last speech is essentially negative:

> . . . I would not now
> Wish my wounds balm'de, nor heal'd: for I have no use
> To put my life to: In all our Quest of Greatnes . . .
> (Like wanton Boyes, whose pastime is their care)
> We follow after bubbles, blowne in th'ayre.
> Pleasure of life, what is't? onely the good houres
> Of an Ague: meerely a preparative to rest,
> To endure vexation: I doe not aske
> The processe of my death: onely commend me
> To *Delio*. (V.iv.73–82)

To him death seems not a prelude to something highly prized, but an end to what he no longer cares about. Like the Cardinal, he wishes to 'be layd by, and never thought of' (V.v.113). Here, I suggest, is the core of Webster's criticism of the amalgam of Christian and stoic beliefs upon which Antonio seems to base his attitudes. The Jacobeans believed, traditionally, that the chief end of philosophy was to teach men how to die. Measured by this yardstick, Antonio's beliefs are unimpressive.

It is now clear why Antonio dies as he does. Without the Duchess he is aimless and apathetic, only half-alive. Yet his death needs to be a fitting one, and in the apparently casual irony of an 'accident' we can find a reflection of the aimlessness which has preceded it.

With this in mind, we see the fifth act not as Gunnar Boklund's game of blind chance, but as a carefully organised sequence of events demonstrating at all points the guiding hand of providence. To say this, of course, is to raise a crucial issue, that of responsibility. As the agent of providence, Bosola has acted (like Hamlet and Vindice) as both a minister and scourge, one through whom God works both to save and to destroy.[24] Like Vindice (if not like Hamlet), he ends his life in the jaws of hell. Is this just? Logic says that it is not, if Bosola has not been a free agent, but acting under divine compulsion. Theologically, however, this view of Bosola's role is untenable. It is true that the Church of England believed quite literally that there was 'a special providence in the fall of a sparrow,' and that it exhorted the faithful to eschew belief in chance and see God's hand in all things:

> Thus must we in all things that be done, whether they be good or evil (except sin, which God hates and causes not,) not only look at the second causes, which be but God's means and instruments whereby he works, but have a further eye, and look up to God.[25]

It is also true, however, that Anglicans believed in man's freedom of will. As Thomas Rogers puts it in *The Catholic Doctrine of the Church of England*:

> We deny not, that man, not regenerate, hath free will to do the works of nature, for the preservation of the body, and bodily estate; which things had and have the brute beast, and profane gentile.[26]

How these two beliefs were reconciled is explained by Peter Baro, Lady Margaret Professor of Divinity at Cambridge from 1574 to 1596, in the course of a disputation on the theme 'God's purpose and decree taketh not away the liberty of man's corrupt will':

> God the creator and governor of all things is not the destroyer of the order by him appointed, but the preserver. For he would that in the nature of things that there should be divers and sundry causes, namely some necessary and othersome also free and contingent: which according to their several natures, might work freely and contingently, or not work. Whereupon we conclude, that secondary

---

[24] For an excellent discussion of this subject, see F. T. Bowers, 'Hamlet as Minister and Scourge', *PMLA*, LXX (1955), 740–49.

[25] James Pilkington, *Works*, ed. J. Scholefield (Cambridge, 1853), p. 227.

[26] ed. J. J. S. Perowne (Cambridge, 1854), p. 104.

causes are not enforced by God's purpose and decree, but carried willingly and after their own nature.[27]

Bosola, it is clear, is one of these 'secondary causes'. God has worked through him, taking advantage of his divided nature, his desire to serve Ferdinand yet comfort the Duchess. Yet Bosola has never been under compulsion: he has not been 'enforced by God's purpose and decree, but carried willingly and after his own nature'. His free moral choices have come first, and God's use of them second. He must therefore bear the responsibility for what he has done.

Were this not so, of course, we would find Bosola far less interesting than we do. As it is we can respond simultaneously to his agony of soul and to the reassurances that our understanding of the action gives us, and in our recognition of the latter discover an added poignancy in his ignorance of the extent to which he has really served the cause of good. There is a similar complexity in our response to his final attempt to make sense of his life, with all its confusion, horror, and lost chances:

> *Malateste*: Thou wretched thing of blood,
> How came *Antonio* by his death?
> *Bosola*: In a mist: I know not how,
> Such a mistake, as I have often seene
> In a play: Oh, I am gone—
> We are only like dead wals, or vaulted graves,
> That ruin'd, yeildes no eccho: Fare you well—
> It may be paine: but no harme to me to die,
> In so good a quarrell: Oh this gloomy world,
> In what a shadow, or deepe pit of darknesse,
> Doth (womanish, and fearefull) mankind live!
> Let worthy mindes nere stagger in distrust
> To suffer death, or shame, for what is just—
> Mine is another voyage. (V.v.116–29)

For we know, as Bosola does not, that Antonio's death was meaningful, just as we also know that he has been the unwitting instrument in assuring the triumph of that cause which part of him always longed to serve. His may be 'another voyage' from that of 'worthy mindes', but it has not been made entirely in vain.

[27] Quoted by H. C. Porter in *Reformation and Reaction in Tudor Cambridge* (Cambridge, 1958), p. 377.

Bosola dies confused and lost. But we are able to respond fully to the note of optimism upon which *The Duchess of Malfi* ends. Firstly there is the presentation of the surviving child of the Duchess and Antonio; a symbol, like Giovanni in *The White Devil*, of hope, innocence, and renewal. Then follows what can be read simply as moral comment:

> ... These wretched eminent things
> Leave no more fame behind 'em, then should one
> Fall in a frost, and leaves his print in snow—
> As soone as the sun shines, it ever melts,
> Both forme, and matter: I have ever thought
> Nature doth nothing so great, for great men,
> As when she's pleas'd to make them Lords of truth:
> *'Integrity of life, is fames best friend,*
> *Which noblely (beyond Death) shall crowne the end.*
>
> (V.v.138–46)

There is also, however, a deeper and more specifically religious level of meaning in this last, choric utterance. Through what is, significantly, the only sun image in a dark play, Webster offers a confident assertion of the power of God to counter and destroy evil. That this confidence is not wrongly or lightly placed, the play as a whole has testified.

Religion and John Webster

DOMINIC BAKER-SMITH

Religion and John Webster

D R A W I N G T O T H E end of the *Advancement of Learning* Francis
Bacon turns his hostile attention on those who try to attain com-
pleteness in divinity, to make it round and uniform. True, Bacon was
following a humanistic precedent, for many writers since Petrarch had
expressed distrust of the all-embracing system, but we can probably
relate Bacon's distrust to Calvinism in particular. Calvin had reduced
to clear and reasoned formulae Luther's great insights concerning
God's transcendence. In their anxiety to preserve the incomprehensi-
bility of God the reformers eyed man's natural faculties with suspicion,
yet the very humanism that promoted scriptural study and contributed
so much to the impetus of the Reformation was primarily a study of
the secular classics. The salvation of the good pagan had been a live
issue in medieval theological debate but to the sixteenth century it
became an explosive issue. No longer did the debate deal simply with
the post mortem fate of some remote sages, instead the validity of
man's natural judgement was in question. Once Petrarch expressed
confidence in the moral relevance of classical literature a crisis on some
scale was inevitable. One answer was to evolve like Ficino a *prisca
theologia* by which divine wisdom filtered down devious channels from
Adam; another was to allow with Erasmus that the Spirit had guided
the ancients, providing as it were an unofficial and subordinate revelation. Or one could simply rule out antiquity as a spiritual vehicle
altogether and limit its value to philology and natural learning. In the
latter case reason and divinity are likely to be as sympathetic as oil and
water.

It was against this tendency that Hooker wrote in his *Ecclesiastical
Polity*:

> But so it is, the name of the light of nature is made hateful with
> men; the 'star of reason and learning', and all other such helps,
> beginneth no otherwise to be thought of than if it were an unlucky

comet; or as if God had so accursed it, that it should never shine or give light in things concerning our duty any way towards him, but be esteemed as that star in the Revelation called Wormwood, which being fallen from heaven, maketh rivers and waters in which it falleth so bitter, that men tasting them die thereof. A number there are, who think they cannot admire as they ought the power and authority of the word of God, if in things divine they should attribute any force to man's reason. For which cause they never use reason so willingly as to disgrace reason.[1]

But Hooker did not fully represent the spirit of his time, his conservative values were undermined by the Calvinists on the one hand and by the 'devout sceptics' on the other. Puritan fundamentalism and the sophisticated reserve of fideism, expressed so powerfully in Donne's *Anniversaries*, combined to sap confidence in the reason. This in its turn served to displace Hooker's vision of law stretching in a continuous series from the divine throne to the lowest forms of nature. While Hooker saw God's will acting through law, his opponents released God from these apparently anthropomorphic constrictions and expressed Him as absolute will. Calvin's theology centres on this fearful vision of arbitrary will,

> While the reprobate are the vessels of the just wrath of God, and the elect vessels of his compassion, the ground of the distinction is to be sought in the pure will of God alone, which is the supreme rule of justice.

> This plan [election] was founded upon his freely given mercy, without regard to human worth, but by his just and irreprehensible but incomprehensive judgement he has barred the door of life to those whom he has given over to damnation.[2]

The late Middle Ages had been dominated by the vision of hell. Something morbid enters Latin spirituality side by side with Franciscan lyricism: the sense of community, the emphasis on the positive aspects of Redemption, which are characteristic of liturgical poetry from Notker Balbulus to Thomas Aquinas are replaced by the desper-

---

[1] Bk. III, viii, 4.
[2] *Theological Treatises*, tr. J. K. S. Reid (1954), p. 179; *Institutes*, tr. F. L. Battles (1961), II, 931.

ate egocentrism of the *Dies Irae*. The preachers and the flagellants have gone but the art remains. The scope of Christianity has been confined to a personal quest for salvation and the idea of mercy clouded in deep pessimism. Death has been invested with horror, it cannot be seen as a release or as the consummation of a good life. To late medieval spirituality it comes as a final and almost arbitrary test, when man finds his true likeness in utter isolation. The very posture suggests masochistic impulses and most medieval representations of the Last Judgement or of Hell support this. Rogier van der Weyden's *Last Judgement* altarpiece in the Hôtel-Dieu at Beaune is supremely refined by average standards. No devils are included, the faces of the damned tell their own story and the solitary tongue of flame in the background is superfluous. The concentration on the pale flesh tints and the natural forms is a disturbing reminder of human vulnerability; the frenzied efforts to escape, men and women clawing at each other in their struggle, show the havoc of selfishness as vividly as Sartre's *Huis Clos*. In contrast the ideal figures of Mantegna convey, even in the Crucifixion, a confidence appropriate to statues; but van der Weyden's medieval people are more immediately identifiable, the bodies are our own, the emotions all too familiar. They convey a terrifying insecurity, still evident in the mannerist contortions of *The Judgement* sketched by Hermann Tom Ring in 1555.

As Erich Fromm has suggested it is this insecurity that the reformers attempted to remedy.[3] Luther's personal problems, his desperate craving for assurance of salvation, are clearly problems of security. Fromm relates this insecurity to social changes brought about by economic development and the rise of the middle classes. Certainly it is true that the note of insecurity that first appears in devotional writing in the late thirteenth century coincides with changes in Italian social patterns. One reaction to this concern with personal salvation was an exaggerated theology of works in which the theory of indulgences assailed by Luther played a central part. A Franciscan preacher at Tournai in 1482 asserted that the Pope had absolute jurisdiction over the souls in Purgatory and could empty it at will.[4] Clearly this sort of anthropomorphic caricature could not provide security to a searching intelligence. Luther and Calvin swept aside all the works of man to find a more lasting security in divine election. Purgatory was an early casualty. Of course

[3] *The Fear of Freedom* (1960), p. 74.
[4] A. Renaudet, *Préréforme et humanisme à Paris* (Paris, 1916), p. 21.

they did not deny good works; the godly man performed godly deeds but these were a consequence rather than a cause of his election. Now this situation did raise problems for the sensitive Protestant: Purgatory was gone, Heaven or Hell remained the only possibilities. If a loved relative died, whose life might not suggest the highest flights of godliness, what was his destination? A very intense crisis must inevitably follow in the mind of the bereaved, a horror that is not discussed in the literature of the time but which must have been felt by many. It was not discussed because concern for the dead questioned God's will and imposed a human pattern of perception on the unknowable. To satisfy natural instincts might have been acceptable to Hooker's thomism ('God being the author of Nature, her voice is but his instrument')[5] but Calvin would prefer Bosola's observation.

Security some men call the suburbs of hell (*D.M.*, V.ii.332).[6]

This is not to claim any clear theological commitment in Webster's work but a playwright has a particular end in view, to arouse the feelings of his audience and to order these feelings according to a pattern. To work on an audience in this way it is essential that the playwright touch on sensitive areas; he must know the raw nerves of his audience, even if only by instinct. Some playwrights, and Webster is among them, are seriously concerned with the issues of the day but there is an ambiguity in any playwright's reference to these issues—how far is he stirring discussion, how far using a pre-existent tension for his own purposes.

R. M. Frye has indicated in his *Shakespeare and Christian Doctrine* the danger of allowing too literal interpretation of religious references in Shakespeare's drama. Often Shakespeare will utilise a religious reference—to the parable of the prodigal son in *As You Like It* or to Christ's passion in *Richard II*—for a purely dramatic purpose. The associative energy of the reference is used to enrich a dramatic situation or to suggest an archetypal sequence of events. While Shakespeare's use of religious references seems chiefly concerned with the delineation of structural patterns Webster appears more concerned with touching

[5] *Laws*, I, viii, 3.

[6] My quotations from *The Duchess of Malfi* and *The White Devil* are taken from Elizabeth M. Brennan's editions in The New Mermaids (2nd impression 1967 and 2nd impression 1969 respectively). For *The Devil's Law-Case* I have quoted from Lucas's edition (1927).

the raw nerve and playing up the pessimism generated by a Calvinistic view of man. Calvin did not intend to devise a view of man, it is merely a corollary to his view of God. But the cultural effects of theology are rarely pure. Certain effects of the rise of Puritanism suggest clearly enough where the raw nerves could be found. It has been suggested already that predestination was one. The most bitter internal debates of Calvinism took place during the first decade of the seventeenth century and were initiated by Arminius' revolt against the absolute determinism of Calvin. Arminius placed the divine act of election after the Fall and allowed that the Atonement opened salvation to all men. Grace could be rejected by man's free choice. On the other hand the *supralapsarians* led by the theologian Gomarus, who had studied at Oxford and Cambridge, argued that God willed the fate of each man before the creation of the world. Every man was therefore absolutely determined in his course to Heaven or Hell and had been before time began. The two parties fought out their views before the Dutch States-General in 1608 and 1609, and for a time the supralapsarians were triumphant.

There are some grounds for seeing the early years of the seventeenth century as a climax in the growth of religious pessimism and in stress on the arbitrary will of God. The Lambeth Articles of 1595 are a clear indication of the ascendancy of Calvinism during this period, and though the number of convinced Calvinists may not have been great their influence on the climate of mind was considerable.[7] Nothing is more infectious than a bad conscience.

One of the most obvious consequences of predestination, especially in its supralapsarian formulation, is determinism. Man is a puppet worked by the inscrutable will of God. The Renaissance assessment of man as a metaphysical chameleon, his destiny in his own hands, is quite shattered. Hooker's position is fundamentally this, but more representative of his time is William Perkins who resolutely upheld the supralapsarian position in late Elizabethan Cambridge.[8] Revolt against

---

[7] This is borne out by Wilbur Sanders's observations in *The Dramatist and the Received Idea* (Cambridge, 1968), chapter 12.

[8] 'He would pronounce the word *Damne* with such an emphasis as left a dolefull Echo in his auditors ears a good while after. And when catechist of Christ Colledge, in expounding the Commandments, applied them so home, able almost to make his hearers hearts fall down, and hairs to stand upright.' Thomas Fuller, *The Holy State* (Cambridge, 1648), p. 82.

parental example is now a familiar behaviour pattern: Perkins's successor in 1602 as vicar of St Andrew's Church, Cambridge was his collab-
orator in divinity, one Rafe Cudworth. His son, Ralph, the most
distinguished of the Cambridge Platonists, adopted the stance of the
so-called latitude men in reaction against the severity of his father's
teaching. Looking back at the Calvinism of his youth Cudworth traces
the debauchery, scepticism, and infidelity of his own day to 'the Doctrine of the Fatal Necessity of all Actions and Events, as from its
proper root'. Three sorts of Fatality are subjected to hostile scrutiny:
Atheistic Fate or 'Atomick material necessity', Stoical Fate which
places all things in dependence on a chain of necessary causes, and
thirdly 'Theologick Fate'. Under this third heading Cudworth criticises
those who present the divine will as source of all values,

> In consequence whereof, God's will is not regulated by his essential
> and immutable Goodness and Justice: God is meer arbitrary will
> omnipotent: and in respect to us, moral good and evil are positive
> things, and not so in their own nature . . .[9]

Echoing Renaissance optimism, Cudworth again upholds what he calls
man's 'potential omniformity'. This generous language is notably lacking in discussion of man's destiny during the early decades of the century: in its place stood 'arbitrary rule omnipotent'.

Now that very issue that stirred Cudworth's outburst was the disintegration of moral life—debauchery, scepticism, and infidelity—under
the threat of eternal reprobation. The germ of Calvin's theology, security in God alone, easily it seems became alienation. The irrelevance of
moral achievement or the disturbing failure to generate signs of election could create grave tensions. Paralysing fear could be one consequence or worldly distraction another: the reprobate 'labours to relieve
his heavy heart, by a strong and serious casting his mind, and nestling
his conceit upon his riches, gold, greatnesse, great friends, credit
amongst Men . . .'[10] But the bubble of this conceit burst against the
terrible fact of divine retribution, the reality of hell.

Hell is, of course, the sharpest nerve for the dramatist to vibrate. The
realm of torment of fiery floods and thick ribb'd ice, had always been
real enough to the Christian imagination. But if Dante holds us in

---

[9] *A Treatise of Eternal and Immutable Morality* (1731), pp. iv–vi.
[10] Robert Bolton, *Instructions for a Right Comforting Afflicted Consciences*
(1635), p. 271. Cited in Sanders, op. cit., p. 249.

check by his intellectual order, the Renaissance inherited an image of hell that defied conscious control. It is impossible to define the complex reactions stimulated by this late-medieval vision but it is clear that a pornographic element is present and in part accounts for the energy and tension lacking in pictures of the elect. Ford's purely medieval hell, described by the Friar in *'Tis Pity She's a Whore* (III.iv), relates all the specific torments lovingly reproduced in numerous fourteenth-century murals. The ambivalence of these meditations is clear enough in the painting attributed to René of Anjou from the monastery of the Celestines at Avignon described by Huizinga. It showed 'the body of a dead woman, standing in a shroud, with her head dressed and worms gnawing her bowels', the inscription read 'Once I was beautiful above all women But by death I became like this, My flesh was very beautiful, fresh and soft, Now it is altogether turned to ashes', and so on.[11] This visual emphasis, allied with the imaginary places of the art of memory, underlies the *Exercises* of St Ignatius: the exercitant places himself in a context defined by the senses,

> The first point will be to see with the eyes of the imagination those great fires, and the soules as it were in bodies of fire. The second, to hear with the ears the wailings, the groans, the cries, and blasphemies against Christ our Lord, and against all his saints.
> The third to smell with the sense of smell the smoke, the brimestone, the filth and the corruption.[12]

The exercitant can also add his own amplifications, the career of a soul from innocence through temptation, fall, and death to its damnation, or again (and here Ford's Friar comes to mind) the mode and intensity of punishment awarded to various kinds of sinner.

This drive to present post-mortem experience in sensuous terms ensured a lowest common denominator for all treatment of the afterlife, thus the line of demarcation between temporal suffering and eternal pain becomes increasingly vague. If this means a crude depiction of the after-life it equally means that the temporal sufferings of men can take on a spiritual dimension, as it were. The sufferings of the reprobate, pursued by divine justice in this life, can anticipate the torments of hell. Set against the background of divine election and judgement

---

[11] *The Waning of the Middle Ages* (1955), p. 143. Cf. also the 'perspectives' seen by Drummond of Hawthornden described by Mrs Ewbank, above, pp. 161–3.
[12] *Spiritual Exercises*, tr. W. H. Longridge (1919), pp. 66ff.

revenge can only be complete if it causes damnation, if present violence
can serve as the threshold to hell. By the end of *The Unfortunate
Traveller* very little is left that could stir numbed responses but Cutwolf's account of his revenge on Esdras of Granado. Esdras is allowed
an extremely pious and conventional plea for life only to prepare himself to die, 'Wounds I contemne, life I prize light, it is another worlds
tranquilitie which makes me so timerous: everlasting damnation, everlasting houling and lamentation. It is not from death I request thee to
deliver me, but from this terror of torments eternitie.'[13] But Cutwolf's
sole interest is the damnation of Esdras: at his death his body turns
black, 'the devill presently branded it for his own'. Similarly in the
stifling world of *The Revenger's Tragedy* the duke's death scene
(III.v) brings together lechery, cuckoldry, and the agony of death in a
relentless stirring of religious associations. As the Duke dies, the victim
of just retribution, his adulterous Duchess cries 'Why there's no pleasure sweet, but it is sinful' (l. 203) some twenty lines after the Duke's
agonised 'Is there a hell besides this, villains?' Of course there is, and
the audience would not fail to place the Duke in his correct stratum.
By touching religious responses Tourneur can escape from the stub-
born limits of mundane suffering to unlimited horrors of the imagination. The Duchess's association of pleasure and sin, grotesque distortion though it be, still has enough theological content to stimulate a
sense of helpless determinism and inescapable corruption heightening
the implications of the Duke's question. There is another hell, but it is
already latent in this world, a consequence of God's eternal judgement
on each soul. There is something feverish and salacious in the
responses indicated by this writing and nowhere is this clearer than in
'Lechery's tragedy: Or the life and death of Veneria the lustful' from
The History of Morindos. The deceived King of Bohemia places the
murdered body of the queen's scullion lover in a coffin 'then to the
same dead body, beginning now to putrify and stink, he tied the live
body of his queen, and so in the coffin closed them up both together,
that as she enjoyed his fellowship in life, so might she consume with
him being dead, by which means the very worms that bred upon the
dead carcass in a manner devoured up her live body. And thus were
the sins of lust and adultery scourged with a plague but seldom heard

---

[13] P. Henderson, ed., *Shorter Elizabethan Novels* (Everyman Library), pp.
353f.

of.'[14] The conclusion is revealing, it is the fossilised remnant of a religious tradition: the substance of the meditation has been allowed to obscure its proper end. Indeed it could be argued that the revenge convention reverses the meditative pattern; death is not a gateway into the next world, but rather a gateway by which the sanctions of the next world enter mundane experience. 'O me! this place is hell', Vittoria cries (*W.D.*, V.iii.177), and that is exactly what it was to Calvin's reprobate. This is not to argue for conscious theological precision in the drama but rather to accept Professor Bradbrook's observation that 'to a suggestible and superstitious people vague implications are more terrifying than straightforward assertions'.[15] The bulk of religious references in the drama of the period appear to be consumer-orientated.

At the opening of *The White Devil* Ludovico appeals to Democritus. He is laughing, which is only proper when calling on the laughing philosopher whom tradition placed beside the weeping Heraclitus to comment on human folly.[16] But this is not the only suggestion in Ludovico's speech, it is possible that he is also appealing to Democritus as the notorious exponent of 'atomick material necessity' and his speech opens the play on a deterministic note. Man has, in fact, no final control over events, 'policy' may ameliorate his circumstances but this can only be temporary,

> Fate's a spaniel,
> We cannot beat it from us. What remains now?
> Let all that do ill take this president:
> *Man may his fate foresee, but not prevent.*
> And of all axioms this shall win the prize,
>
> (*W.D.*, V.vi.174–9)

Essentially the world of Webster's two tragedies is a fallen world in which grief is the eldest child of sin and heavenly retribution is an instinctive explanation of disaster:

[14] 1609; reprinted in C. C. Mish, *Short Fiction of the Seventeenth Century* (New York, 1963). Cf. *The White Devil*, II.i.394 ('Let him cleave to her and both rot together') and *The Duchess of Malfi*, IV.i.68–9.

[15] *Themes and Conventions of Elizabethan Tragedy* (repr. Cambridge, 1966), p. 196.

[16] '[. .] tot enim undique Stultitiae formis abundat, tot in dies novas comminiscitur, ut nec mille Democriti ad tantos risus suffecerint: quamquam illis ipsis Democritis rursum alio Democrito foret opus'; Erasmus, *Stultitiae Laus* in *Opera Omnia* (Leyden, 1705), IV, 455A. For other associations see R. W. Wallace in *Art Bulletin*, L (1968), 21–31.

There are some sins which heaven doth duly punish
In a whole family. (*W.D.*, V.ii.20–21)

     ... for I do think
It is some sin in us, Heaven doth revenge
By her. (*D.M.*, II.v.65–7)

In this world the extent of moral responsibility is never clear. Vittoria blames her guilt on her blood, Flamineo claims that men suck in their deceit 'from women's breasts, in our first infancy'; the effect of human action is to add misery to misery, 'All things do help th' unhappy man to fall'.[17] Human activity is either guilty or fateful, only passive acceptance escapes divine retribution. In *The White Devil* Webster depicts the consequences of action, giving us a play that is dominated by the destructiveness of sin. The ambivalent character of Vittoria lacks the moral weight to restrain this destructive force. In *The Duchess of Malfi* he turns instead to the constructive possibilities in this dark world of human corruption, but here virtue is confined to the role of suffering, action compromises its purity. The goal of virtue is the acceptance of preordained events which emerge from the tangles of policy.

It is a commonplace of criticism to distinguish between Shakespeare's interest in the development of character and Webster's static champions of defiance.[18] There is indeed a gulf between the exponents of 'policy' and those who attain selfless detachment which seems unbridgeable. Isabella, in her pretence to refuse Brachiano the rights of marriage, Antonio and the Duchess of Malfi in their parting, achieve a conquest of the ego which is impossible in the shifting world of policy. There is no need to argue for Shakespeare's familiarity with exponents of natural law, his sympathy with a tradition that stressed the common springs of all human acts is obvious. This is why his villains share a common humanity with the children of light, no character escapes our act of identification. But in Webster we are aware of a distinction analogous to Calvin's division of mankind into sheep and goats. We may take it that he did not write with the *Institutes* open before him but determinism is in the air.

The world of 'policy' is the world of the ego, a desperate struggle for 'security' and security is seen by Webster as something unwholesome:

[17] *White Devil*, IV.ii.178–80; V.vi.237; *Duchess of Malfi*, III.iv.43.
[18] e.g. D. L. Frost, *The School of Shakespeare* (Cambridge, 1968), p. 135.

Small mischiefs are by greater made secure. (*W.D.*, II.i.316)

Security some men call the suburbs of hell (*D.M.*, V.ii.332)
>   your soule
> Being heretofore drown'd in securitie,
> You know not how to live, nor how to dye (*Devil's Law Case*,
> V.iv.123–5)

Security is created by those defences which the ego constructs around itself; with the mental props of wealth, influence, and power man can blind himself to the nature of reality. Such an artificial state can only be attained by manipulation of the wills of others. The world of policy is a confused tangle of misinterpreted motives, an unending cycle of deceit in which the blind lead the blind. It violates the fundamental canons of Calvinist theology, the knowledge of self and the knowledge of God,

> Nearly all the wisdom we possess, that is to say, true and sound wisdom consists of two parts: the knowledge of God and of ourselves. (*Institutes*, I.i.i)

> Thus from the feeling of our own ignorance, vanity, poverty, infirmity and—what is more—depravity and corruption, we recognise that the true light of wisdom, sound virtue, full abundance of every good and purity of righteousness rest in the Lord alone. (ibid.)

Accurate self-knowledge is a fearful thing, inevitably it will lead to despair if we do not turn to God to support us in our frailty. The first requirement, then, is emancipation from false values, the lumber of security—

> For if in broad daylight we either look down upon the ground or survey whatever meets our view round about, we seem to ourselves endowed with the strongest and keenest sight; yet when we look up to the sun and gaze straight at it, that power of sight which was particularly strong on earth is at once blunted and confused by a great brilliance. As long as we do not look beyond the earth, being quite content with our own righteousness, wisdom and virtue, we flatter ourselves most sweetly and fancy ourselves all but demigods. (ibid, I.i.2)

The image of the true eagle which can gaze upon the sun and casts degenerates out of the nest if they blink is used in spiritual works throughout the Middle Ages. Francisco in *The White Devil* uses this image to sting Brachiano,

> Some eagles that should gaze upon the sun
> Seldom soar high, but take their lustful ease
> Since they from dunghill birds their prey can seize. (II.i.49–51)

and in *The Duchess of Malfi* mad Ferdinand distinguishes eagles that fly alone from crows, daws, and starlings that flock together (V.ii.30–31). Only in 'solitariness' can man escape from the self-regarding world of policy in which he seems all but a demigod.

The violent division made by Calvin between those content with their own nature and the disabused few who accept 'imputed justice' stimulates irony, as Milton fully appreciated. Ignorance of others, culminating in pain and fearful realisation, has a certain attraction for us, perhaps because of the sense of power it provides. This sadistic irony played an important—if unacknowledged—part in the pleasures that the blessed enjoyed since these included knowledge of the sufferings of the damned.[19] It certainly plays its part in the Jacobean drama. The medieval irony of the *de casibus* tradition and Fortune's wheel found a natural echo here, sharpened by the humanistic satire of Erasmus and More.[20] But the cruellest turn is the final dehumanisation of the reprobates by predestination. In the world of politic fools, where men 'come to preferment . . . as gallowses are raised i'th' Low countries': one upon another's shoulders' (II.i.318–19), manipulation is all. Here 'popery' is the natural religion, subordinating God to the convenience of man.

This world of human activity is a community of guilt: 'He's a base thief that a thief lets in.' (*W.D.*, IV.ii.134) Man is influenced and

---

[19] This idea is found in Augustine and dies hard in the eighteenth century when William Baker wrote: 'The goodness as well as the happiness of the blessed will be confirmed and advanced by reflections naturally arising from their view of the misery which some shall undergo: (which seems to be a very good reason for the creation of those beings who shall be finally miserable, and for the continuation of them in their miserable existence).' *An Essay on the Origin of Evil* (1702). I owe this passage to D. P. Walker, *The Decline of Hell* (1964), p. 31

[20] In Francis Meres's *Palladis Tamia* (1598) More is rated as the only post-classical epigrammist worthy of imitation.

influences others in turn; the element of unpredictability in events inevitably overwhelms the politician in time. But once involved in the cycle escape is almost impossible: 'We are engag'd to mischief and must on' (*W.D.*, I.ii.335). The linking cause of this world is dependence, summarised in Bosola's image of Ferdinand and the Cardinal as 'plum trees that grow crooked over standing pools, they are rich and o'erladen with fruit, but none but crows, pies, and caterpillars feed on them' (*D.M.*, I.i.49–52)

Policy is closely related to the diabolic. There are perhaps two reasons for this: frequent reference to devils and diabolic influence adds force to the drama, tautens the nerves of the audience; it also suggests the ubiquity of the prince of this world under the disguise of human endeavour. The devil is in Vittoria's dream (*W.D.*,I.ii.239) which suggests the murder of her husband and her rival Isabella. Her brother sees her as an 'Excellent devil'. To Monticelso she seems goodly fruit, like the ash-filled apples of Sodom and Gomorrah; she is the devil pictured in good shape (III.ii.64–5; 214–15). In the Cardinal's black-book lurk 'the names of many devils': the human agents are identified with the evil forces that promote their work (IV.i.36). Despite Francisco's trick there is justice in Lodovico's exclamation 'There's but three Furies found in spacious Hell; / But in a great man's breast three thousand dwell'. When Flamineo interrupts Vittoria's devotions with worldly business she labels him 'ruffin' or devil. It is especially in Brachiano's death scene, which like all such scenes in the Renaissance drama is dominated by the inexpressible possibilities beyond the grave, that the diabolic seems a part of life, the transition from palace to hell so slight. When Brachiano sees the devil in his delirium it is as the presiding spirit in this terrible revenge. The seal is set on this impression by Vittoria's despair: 'O me! this place is hell'. But there is also the Duke's vision of Flamineo:

> See, see, Flamineo that kill'd his brother
> Is dancing on the ropes there and he carries
> A money-bag in each hand, to keep him even,
> For fear of breaking's neck. (V.iii.109–12)

There is no clearer statement of fallen man's enslavement in his quest for an illusory security.

Working against security is the rhythm of retribution. There is no need for Webster to depict direct intervention by heaven, the very workings of policy bring their dubious reward as certainly as Fortune's wheel. *The White Devil* is, it has been suggested, dominated by destruction; it is a negative play in the sense that no serious alternative is offered to the way of the world. With remorseless irony all the characters are exposed to the bitter fruits of their self-seeking. The high incidence of references to venereal disease offers examples of this;[21] they provide apt comment on the destructive effects of lust.

> Earthquakes leave behind,
> Where they have tyrannised, iron or lead, or stone,
> But, woe to ruin! violent lust leaves none. (I.ii.208–10)

Monticelso's definition of a whore, 'the true material fire of hell' (III.ii.85), reinforces this theme. Vittoria, the 'white devil', described as a providential instrument in Brachiano's downfall, is a 'devil in crystal' (IV.ii.85).[22] It is above all in Brachiano's death that the theme of retribution is laid bare, drawing in all the fearful associations of hell and eternal pain that I have already discussed. As in *The Revenger's Tragedy* sexual indulgence and damnation are counterposed to arouse violent response. When the conspirators meet to review alternative plans their rival motives are to ensure his damnation (the unexpected death is fearsome, the incongruity of death at play has morbid fascination) or to expose the 'rankness of his lust', in sadistic humiliation (V.i.84ff.). Their actual performance (V.iii) is really quite successful and no opportunity is lost to evoke the horrors of hell. Brachiano is unfit to die: his heart has a covenant with the world, the peace of a natural death is described in contrast to his agony ' 'Mongst women howling', and his panic, 'let no man name death to me/It is a word infinitely terrible'. Moreover, there are greater sins on his conscience than we have guessed,

He was a kind of statesman, that would sooner have reckon'd how

---

[21] II.i.76; ibid., 90 and 92; III.iii.9; IV.ii.45; ibid., 51; V.i.164; also by insinuation III.ii.80.

[22] This despairing accusation by Brachiano deserves comparison with Vittoria's estimate of her role, 'So may you blame some fair and crystal river / For that some melancholic distracted man, / Hath drown'd himself in't.' (III.ii.202ff.)

many cannon-bullets he had discharged against a town, to count his expense that way, than how many of his valiant and deserving subjects he lost before it. (V.iii.60–63)[23]

The rites of the bogus Capuchins bring his torment to its conclusion. Flamineo and Vittoria see his reaction to the crucifix favourably. Perhaps this is wishful thinking, certainly the dramatic purpose of their words is to heighten the irony of the conspirators' disguise. Is Brachiano conscious of their catalogue of his sins, their bitter counsels to despair? Again this sort of naturalistic approach is out of place. The tirades are really directed at the religious consciousness of the audience in order to elicit from darker pockets of the imagination the horror that the resources of the theatre could not hope to convey. The tension created by this juxtaposing of illicit pleasure and nameless horror gives force to Ludovico's trite moralising,

> Such a fearful end
> May teach some men that bear too lofty crest,
> Though they live happiest, yet they die not best. (V.iii.74–6)

The same preoccupations mark *The Duchess of Malfi*. The Cardinal and Ferdinand are linked with the devil (I.i.47; I.ii.108; III.i.23; III.v.39); when Bosola relays their commands he is a devil that counterfeits heaven's thunder (III.v.95).

Now many of these uses can be taken as straightforward abuse, yet the overall impression they create is inescapable. Bosola's exchange with the two brothers (I.ii.179–212) lends support to a literal reading. Bosola sees the Cardinal's proposal as an invitation to be one of his familiars, 'a very quaint invisible devil in flesh', a 'kind of thriving thing' which can hope to arrive at a higher place. Bosola's reaction to the brothers' proposals offers a critique of their world: where coins termed 'angels' do the work of devils and lead men to hell, language is inverted:

> Thus the devil
> Candies all sins o'er: and what Heaven terms vild,
> That names he complemental.

---

[23] Cf. IV.i.8ff.: 'for all the murders, rapes, and thefts, / Committed in the horrid lust of war, / He that unjustly caus'd it first proceed, / Shall find it in his grave and in his seed.'

The apricots that the Duchess greedily devours are ripened in horse-dung: this juxtaposition of sweets and corruption is anticipated in Bosola's appointment to the provisorship of the Duchess's horse which seals him as Ferdinand's 'creature',

> say then my corruption
> Grew out of horse-dung.

The devil controls the world of appearance and false show,

> For they whose faces do belie their hearts
> Are witches, ere they arrive at twenty years,
> Ay: and give the devil suck.

Bosola concludes, 'A politician is the devil's quilted anvil' (III.ii.321).

Obviously true self-knowledge is intolerable in such a context, as it dissolves the candy which gratifies man's ego. Instead 'religion' in Webster's drama is Roman Catholicism as the average Jacobean Englishman saw it, the bogey of the reformers' caricatures. It represents the dilution of Christian truth with human institutionalism. Its standards are exterior, its concern external works rather than inner change of heart. It is the Church of bland security, encouraging superstition and reducing the operations of grace to magic.

The presentation of religion in *The White Devil* is singularly negative. Hypocrisy, such a constant theme in Webster's drama, is summarised in Cornelia's curse,

> Be thy act Judas-like, betray in kissing (I.ii.287)

Monticelso's 'rape' of justice at Vittoria's trial is typical of such ecclesiastical politicking. On his election to the tiara his first action is to excommunicate Brachiano and Vittoria in the confidence that 'We cannot better please the divine power'. These attacks on institutional religion reach a climax in Flamineo's reflections in Act III, scene iii:

> A cardinal . . . there's nothing so holy but money will corrupt and putrify it, like victual under the line.

> Religion; oh how it is commeddled with policy. The first bloodshed in the world happened about religion.

The refrain is soon taken up by Francisco as he meditates on the abuse of books,

> Divinity, wrestled by some factious blood,
> Draws swords, swells battles, and o'erthrows all good
>
> (IV.i.95–6).

If one reflects on the religious history of the sixteenth century there is a world of weariness in these complaints. The spiritual disease of this Roman religion is manifested in the Erasmian echoes of 'mariners' prayers uttered in extremity' (V.i.173) and the bogus rites of Brachiano's last agony (V.iii.130ff.)[24]. In this spirit—so far removed from Calvin's sense of the numinous—the conspirators take the sacrament together to cement their murderous intentions. Equally crude is Zanche's conception of repentance, little more subtle than changing sides,

> urg'd with contrition, I intend
> This night to rob Vittoria (V.iii.249–50).

Throughout *The White Devil* the audience is faced with a corrupt religion dedicated to external and therefore irrelevant concerns; the only hint of an alternative, apart from Flamineo's nihilism, is offered by the ambiguous figure of Vittoria herself:

> It shall not be a house of convertites.
> My mind shall make it honester to me
> Than the Pope's palace, and more peaceable
> Than thy soul, though thou art a cardinal . . . (III.ii.287ff.)

Though Vittoria's true character teases our final estimate this defiance of Monticelso's 'painted devil' points the direction that Webster follows in *The Duchess of Malfi*. The familiar world of Italianate religion is depicted but in more sinister light: *The White Devil* contains much ecclesiastical abuse but it is not far removed from the farcical spirit of *The Devil's Law-Case*. The Duchess's cardinal brother, however, is a darker figure than Monticelso: behind his worldly front—' / he / will play his five thousand at tennis, dance, court ladies'—hides the soul of a melancholy churchman. He is unable to feel confidence in prayer (V.iv.25ff.), a fatal sign of reprobation; behind his authority and his devious scheming lies despair. In tune with this is his use of 'divinity', irrelevant exercises of the schools. With all his divinity he cannot direct Bosola the way to greater honesty (I.i.40ff.) and he opens the final scene with speculation on hell.

[24] Brachiano's rites are derived from Erasmus' colloquy and the mariners' prayers may well echo the famous colloquy which was adapted by Rabelais.

I am puzzl'd in a question about hell:
He says, in hell there's one material fire,
And yet it shall not burn all men alike.
Lay him by. How tedious is a guilty conscience!
When I look into the fishponds, in my garden,
Methinks I see a thing arm'd with a rake
That seems to strike at me.

This passage conveniently summarises the two elements in Webster's use of 'Italian' church furnishings: the satirical treatment of Catholicism—here typified by a morally irrelevant scholasticism—and an evocation of the diabolic that spills over into irrational fear. The prejudices of a Protestant audience would also be well gratified by the Cardinal's treatment of Julia (who deceives her husband to visit an 'anchorite'); by making her kiss the poisoned Bible he echoes the theme of the Judas kiss. His greatness is only outward. Moreover, he is a microcosm of his world: the College of Cardinals lay the country waste with their feuds (III.iii.35ff.). The ecclesiastical trappings discarded at Loretto have no spiritual significance, indeed they allow man's carnal nature to pursue its appetites unhindered. When the Pope seizes Malfi from the Duchess's jurisdiction, 'forehearing of her looseness', the memory of Pius V's excommunication of Elizabeth must have stirred among Webster's audience.

It is important to recall these manifestations of 'religion' when considering the charges that the Duchess and Antonio are irreligious. The case against the lovers can be briefly stated. According to the Cardinal she makes 'religion her riding hood / To keep her from the sun and tempest', while Ferdinand questions whether her brats were christened (III.iv.59ff.). Similarly Antonio is accused that

he do account religion
But a school-name, for fashion of the world. (V.ii.130ff.)

When we consider the sources of these accusations our reaction must contain serious reserve. Here the accusations turn ironically on their projectors. In the first place the marriage is solemnised by the lovers themselves. Without delving into the gordian knots of Elizabethan matrimonial law there seems little here that is certainly wrong. As the two are united they show no hostility to the Church; the view that they contract themselves is sound theology, ' 'tis the Church / That must but echo this.' We do not see an ecclesiastical endorsement but there are many things we do not see in Webster's time-scheme. The Duchess's suggestion (I.ii.414) that they lay a naked sword between them may well imply that she looks to a regularisation of their status. If we take her warning to Ferdinand,

> You violate a sacrament o'th' Church
> Shall make you howl in hell for't. (IV.i.39–40)

as a reference to her marriage then this is no profligacy.[25] Ferdinand's sudden thought that her brats are unbaptised is perhaps no more than an expression of his resentment. Ferdinand himself is guilty of the most irreligious utterance in the play,

> Damn her! that body of hers,
> While that my blood ran pure in't, was more worth
> Than that which thou would'st comfort, call'd a soul
> $$\text{(IV.i.119–21)}$$

Faced by this we can perhaps give the Duchess the benefit of the doubt. As for her exchange with Cariola on pilgrimages, this seems no more than a tilt at Catholic superstition (III.ii.316).[26]

It would seem as Professor Bradbrook has asserted that 'Hers was original, not personal sin . . .'[27] If she is condemned by the perverted religion of the Cardinal she still appeals to the 'eternal Church' (the best that a Roman Catholic could do) and to reach it she must leave the world of policy and material pleasure,

> Since we must part
> Heaven hath a hand in't: but no otherwise
> Than as some curious artist takes in sunder
> A clock, or watch, when it is out of frame
> To bring't in better order. (III.v.59–63)

To describe the Duchess's acceptance of suffering as stoical is not strictly accurate. It is useful here to return to Calvin, who attacks Stoic apathy in Book III of the *Institutes*:

[25] As Ferdinand has just referred to the status of bastards and legitimate issue (l. 36) it seems hard to avoid this conclusion. Antonio shows a proper awe for marriage as the first good deed (I.ii.313).

[26] It is worth noting that the Duchess disapproves of Castruchio's fool (I.ii.52–5). This argues that her reaction to Cariola is not simply 'lightness'.

[27] op. cit., p. 209.

You see that patiently to bear the Cross is not to be utterly stupefied and to be deprived of all feeling of pain. It is not as the Stoics of old foolishly described 'the great-souled man': one who having cast off all human qualities, was affected equally by adversity and prosperity ... (III.viii.9)

The Christian admits his suffering as Christ admitted his, but he yokes it to a purpose: '[our Father] afflicts us not to ruin or destroy us but, rather, to free us from the condemnation of the world.'

> O Heaven, thy heavy hand is in't.
> I have seen my little boy oft scourge his top,
> And compar'd myself to't: nought made me e'er go right,
> But Heaven's scourge-stick.

Together the Duchess and Antonio stand outside the world of intrigue and selfishness, or rather they create an inner world of values to counter the political turmoil:

> All discord, without this circumference,
> Is only to be pitied, and not fear'd. (I.ii.384-5)

Indeed Webster creates a pastoral aspiration with his references to 'The Birds, that live i'th' field' which heightens this contrast. This circumference does not enclose a world of cosy domesticity as some critics have suggested but one of almost sacral relationships. The extreme formality of their wooing is significant. Antonio himself, far from being an inept prude, suggests something of the charismatic quality usually attributed to Cordelia. His virtue is a foil to those around him and on at least two occasions provides a striking contrast to Bosola.

> *Bosola*: Miserable age, where only the reward of doing well, is the doing of it. (I.i.32-3)

> *Antonio*: Were there nor heaven, nor hell,
> I should be honest: I have long serv'd virtue,
> And nev'r tane wages of her. (I.ii.354-6)[28]

> *Antonio*:   Could I take him
> At his prayers, there were hope of pardon.

[28] To take wages of virtue suggests a Romish theology of works.

Bosola: Fall right my sword: [*strikes Antonio down from behind*]
I'll not give thee so much leisure as to pray. (V.iv.42–5)

Antonio's brilliant horsemanship, fruit of his stay at the French court, is set against Bosola's insinuation into the office of provisor of the horse, corruption 'derived from dung'. Antonio has in fact a radiant quality which is the opposite pole to the brothers' egotism; he does not act because he represents an option. The Duchess must choose. Her one failing is the deceit she unwillingly practises to hide her marriage. Once the secret is out she accepts the dreadful consequences and can claim 'now I am well awake'. At her death this awakening is shared with Bosola: 'I am angry with myself now that I wake' and for a moment he hopes to escape this 'sensible hell'. But the intention is not enough, opportunity is outside our control. The accidental murder of Antonio is the final ironical fruit of Bosola's repentance. His pessimistic outburst,

> We are merely the stars' tennis balls, struck and banded
> Which way please them,

summarises the world of reprobation of human action but it misses the world of obedient suffering through which the Duchess has passed.

The Duchess of Malfi was written for the King's Men during Shakespeare's lifetime. From this it has been suggested that Webster's drama of resistance does contain the hint of character resistance shaped by initial faults. But there is no sign of those ethical decisions that contribute to Shakespeare's delineation of character. Instead the issue of integrity is presented as a choice between loyalties rather than actions, it is a drama of alignment. The characters are not allowed the sort of control over the consequences of their alignment that fits ethical drama; this is one reason why passivity seems more admirable in Webster than action. From one viewpoint the whole action is amoral. In the setting of determinism, whether it be 'Atomick material necessity' or 'Theologick Fate'—Theophrastan or Calvinistic—morals lose the central importance they possess for Shakespeare.[29] Webster's undercutting of every hope, every assumption that his characters betray,

[29] In Pelagianism or Synergism moral achievement assists an ontological transformation of the individual, but to Calvin imputed justice leaves him morally unchanged, indeed reprobate.

has its counterpart in Calvin's critique of false security and rationalised virtue

> For I am going into a wilderness,
> Where I shall find nor path, nor friendly clew
> To be my guide. (*D.M.*, I.ii.278–80)

The audience is in a rather similar position when evaluating these plays. Religion is a major theme in them. We have the satirical exposure of Roman malpractice; the violent use of morbid religious associations that expose human vanity and vulnerability. There is nothing new or distinctive about this, but there is marked consistency in the use of these religious materials to define a view of the human situation. Webster adopts the resources provided for him by the Christian social experience. It seems reasonable, also, to see in his disregard for moral choice, his obvious determinism, some response to the spiritual temper of his particular age.

In *The White Devil* the only counter-movement to destruction is Vittoria's assertion of her own will. This has been called brazen, it is certainly too involved in the ambiguities of the play to offer an adequate resistance to the negative pull. Vittoria has only her own strength. The Duchess of Malfi initiates and maintains a creative movement precisely because she can invoke all the weight of a Christian pattern. But this is not to make Christianity the *raison d'être* of the play. We may trace the success of *The Duchess* to this adoption of Christianity as a dramatic formula but this is not necessarily to call Webster's play a Christian drama. Webster's God, unlike his devil, is a hidden one. This does not mean that He is not there, but we are offered 'nor path nor friendly clew' to find Him.

Index

Titles are italicised. Characters in Webster's and other contemporary works are indexed individually.

Index

Printed in Great Britain by
The Garden City Press Limited
Letchworth, Hertfordshire